W9-AGL-655

THE
BEST OF
THE BEST
AMERICAN
POETRY
1988–1997

◇ ◇ ◇

Harold Bloom, Editor

David Lehman, Series Editor

SCRIBNER

SCRIBNER
1230 Avenue of the Americas
New York, NY 10020

Set in Bembo

Manufactured in the United States of America

1 3 5 7 9 10 8 6 4 2

ISBN 0-684-84279-3
ISSN 1040-5763

CONTENTS

David Lehman was born in New York City in 1948. He attended Cambridge University as a Kellett Fellow and went on to receive his doctorate in English at Columbia University, where he was Lionel Trilling's research assistant. He is the author of three books of poems, including *Valentine Place* (Scribner, 1996) and *Operation Memory* (Princeton, 1990). His prose books include *Signs of the Times: Deconstruction and the Fall of Paul de Man* and *The Big Question*. He is the general editor of the University of Michigan Press's Poets on Poetry series and is on the core faculty of the graduate writing programs at Bennington College and the New School for Social Research. He divides his time between Ithaca, New York, and New York City.

FOREWORD

by David Lehman

◊ ◊ ◊

When The Best American Poetry was conceived ten years ago, it seemed to me an idea so inevitable that I wondered that no one else had acted on it. I had the vision of an annual anthology that would chronicle the taste of our leading poets and would reflect the vigor and variety of an art that refuses to go quietly into that good night to which one or another commentator is forever consigning it. I had been reading literary magazines by the dozens and was impressed by the quality of the poetry that regularly appeared in print to little fanfare. Not only were Ashbery and Merrill and Ammons and other masters writing in peak form, but extraordinary specimens by poets I'd never heard of were turning up every day in remote periodicals, experimental journals, staid old quarterlies, flashy new ones, and desktop broadsides from Maine to Alaska. Wouldn't it make sense—and perhaps dollars, too—to cull the year's most compelling works and perpetuate them in a handsome volume? Done right, the anthology would transcend sectarian differences and tribal conflicts in a spirit of generosity and ecumenicism, but with the firm insistence that aesthetic excellence must be the paramount imperative. We would honor the notion that poems from rival traditions can consort together to their mutual advantage. Each year's book would represent the predilections of a different guest editor, himself or herself an eminent practitioner. We would ask the poets selected for inclusion to provide comments about the poems, how they had been written or what had occasioned them. The magazines in which the poems appeared would be listed, their editors named, their addresses given, to aid the potential subscribers and prospective contributors in our audience. We were bound to have one. Readers hungry for poetry would respond with ardor.

Or would they? Book publishers, with their customary air of noble irresolution, did their best to disabuse me. "You'll be lucky to sell two thousand copies," one executive said sympathetically. I could see her point. It was a truth universally acknowledged that the book trade now functioned within a vast literary-industrial complex whose corporate masters were ruled by an unforgiving bottom line. Would we please and excite readers in sufficient quantities to pay our own freight? I couldn't help recalling the analogy that Don Marquis, the creator of *archy and mehitabel,* had spun when the century was young. Publishing a book of verse, he observed, was like dropping a rose petal in the Grand Canyon and waiting for the echo. What made me think that the gesture would be less futile now? If someone had forecast that The Best American Poetry would still be going strong ten years later—with a readership that grows wider each year—even I, with my unreasonable attachment to the project, would have laughed. Yet that is what has happened.

The success of the series is due largely to the efforts of the ten poets who have served as guest editors: John Ashbery, Donald Hall, Jorie Graham, Mark Strand, Charles Simic, Louise Glück, A. R. Ammons, Richard Howard, Adrienne Rich, and James Tate. Each willingly took on the task of surveying the year's poetry, selecting seventy-five poems from a pool containing more than ten times as many candidates. Each contributed an introduction about his or her principles of selection, or about the state of American poetry, or about the process of writing a poem, or about the experience of reading for the anthology. (Excerpts from the introductions—themselves fascinating documents—are offered as an appendix in the present volume.) There was never any presumption that the guest editors would substantially agree with one another or that their taste would necessarily overlap. In retrospect it seems to me that one might peruse the ten volumes, forge some sort of consensus view, and arrive at tentative conclusions regarding not only literary reputations, who's in, who's out, but a host of critical questions having to do with the characteristic forms, styles, subject matter, and attitudes of poets in America today. But the purpose of this series is not to arrive at conclusions so much as to suggest a good starting point for readers preparing to embark on their own journey. The Best American Poetry does not set out each year to ratify a pantheon, and indeed the books in the series can be understood to be having a dialogue with one another—dialogue that sometimes turns into impassioned debate.

The debate is joined in *The Best of the Best American Poetry 1988–1997.* Now that ten years have gone by, it seems an opportune moment to return to the 750 poems that have been anthologized thus far and hazard an educated guess about which of them may endure into the next century. Since poets have done the selecting for the individual volumes, I thought to entrust this new task to a critic—preferably a fearless and influential one, with strong opinions, sophisticated taste, and a passion for poetry that matches any poet's. If the books in the series have lived up to their collective title, this anthology of anthologies might define a contemporary canon. Choosing the contents would therefore test any editor's nerve. Luckily, the one critic who has unabashedly and unapologetically committed himself to the idea of a literary canon, to the possibility of making one and to the necessity of having one, is a critic who long ago made a name for himself as a highly discriminating reader of the poetry of his time, whose provocative judgments have turned out often—remarkably often—to be right.

Harold Bloom has fascinated me since the September day in 1967 when I, a Columbia sophomore, drove up to Yale to visit a friend and sat in on Professor Bloom's modern poetry course. It was the first day of classes, and Bloom was going over his reading list, which consisted mainly if not exclusively of William Butler Yeats, Wallace Stevens, Hart Crane, and, I think, D. H. Lawrence. There was to be no Eliot, no Pound, no Auden, no William Carlos Williams. From memory Bloom recited Wordsworth and Emerson and Whitman and Stevens by the yard. He tossed off paradoxes worthy of Oscar Wilde and followed by quoting Wilde to the effect that all bad poetry was unfailingly sincere, a slogan that Bloom has since said he would like to see emblazoned on the gates of university campuses. I didn't know it then, but Bloom was still fighting Eliot's neoclassicism, royalism, and Anglo-Catholicism— still crusading for a "visionary company" of poets, such as Shelley, who had fallen into disfavor with the Eliot-inspired New Criticism—and he was not in the mood to give any quarter. Although the poets he excluded from his course were among those I loved the most, I was taken with his flamboyant manner and his idiosyncratic approach—not every professor was so candid or so sure of himself. And I found him to be wholly convincing when, in the early 1970s, he began to extend his "Romantic line" to the poets of the American present, championing Ammons and Ashbery and Merrill as our top bards.

This was the same time that Bloom propounded his theoretical model for the study of poetry. A quartet of studies, the first of which added a phrase to the lexicon ("the anxiety of influence"), made its author the most controversial critic of the period. The study of literary influence had once rested on naively benign premises; it was assumed that influence and inspiration were virtually indistinguishable, and literary history was seen as a series of successful baton exchanges in a

11

marathon relay race. This understanding of how influence works was complicated by Walter Jackson Bate, who argued that the "burden" of the past can inhibit the new poet struggling to establish an original poetic voice. Bloom went further, advancing the thesis that "strong" poets manage to overcome the anxiety aroused by inevitable self-comparisons with their father figures. Proposing parallels between rhetorical tropes and psychological defense mechanisms, Bloom argued that poems always refer to (and "misread") antecedent poems, that poets wage Oedipal battles with their precursors, and that in a sense "all literature is plagiaristic." Bloom's efforts to "de-idealize" the study of literary influence aroused an anxiety equal to the one he had analyzed. Angry poets, resentful that he has overlooked them, have vilified and lampooned him. "I am the pariah of the profession," he told me when I interviewed him for a *Newsweek* profile in 1986.

Bloom has made few pronouncements about contemporary poetry in the last ten years. He has been absorbed by other subjects: Freud, Shakespeare, Genesis, indigenous American religions, and the making of a Western canon. As I write this, he is completing a magnum opus entitled *Shakespeare: The Invention of the Human*. An anomaly in a conformist's academy, he has risen to the defense of literature against the plethora of new ideologically inflected approaches that would subdue it. "I am," he writes in *The Western Canon,* "your true Marxist critic, following Groucho rather than Karl, and take as my motto Groucho's grand admonition, 'whatever it is, I'm against it.' " Bloom is eloquent in his defense of literature as an aesthetic realm, autonomous and unsponsored. "Reading deeply in the Canon will not make one a better or a worse person," he writes. "All that the Western Canon can bring one is the proper use of one's own solitude, that solitude whose final form is one's confrontation with one's own mortality."

In *The Best of the Best American Poetry 1988–1997,* Bloom has relied on what he has called "the only pragmatic test for the canonical"—he has chosen seventy-five poems that he thinks worthy of rereading. They are not the only poems of excellence to have been published in the last ten years; 675 others have appeared in this series alone; but they have passed the test of rereading, they have given pleasure more than twice over, and they demonstrate in their differing ways that something very important is going on in American poetry today. "The first thing that strikes a reader about the best American poets is how utterly unlike each other they are," W. H. Auden once observed. That was true of the generation of Pound, Williams, Stevens, Frost, Marianne Moore,

e. e. cummings, and Laura Riding. It is equally true today, as readers of this anthology will see. The last ten years of American poetry have witnessed a continual widening of limits. Our poets have addressed themselves with unprecedented candor—and with wit and humor—to carnal knowledge and other taboo subjects. They have celebrated their freedom not only by their choice of subject matter but by relentless formal innovation. Our poems range from the tightly controlled (sonnets, sestinas, villanelles) to the wild and seemingly lawless (prose poems, spontaneous oratory), with plenty of room for ad hoc forms (a poem in the form of a codicil to a will, a poem that plays fast and loose with the period as a punctuation mark). The diversity on display has little in common with a sense of diversity based on demographic properties. It is rather a diversity of means, metaphors, visions, and voices, and it occurs in response to the common challenge facing the modern poet. "Originality no longer means a slight modification in the style of one's immediate predecessors; it means a capacity to find in any work of any date or place a clue to finding one's authentic voice," Auden wrote. "The burden of choice and selection is put squarely upon the shoulders of each individual poet and it is a heavy one." The writer's burden, transmuted by the imagination, becomes the reader's gift. It is the grace of art that it conceals the struggle that went into its making.

Harold Bloom was born in the Bronx in 1930. He is Sterling Professor of Humanities at Yale University and Berg Professor of English at New York University. In his first book, *Shelley's Mythmaking* (1959), Bloom made a spirited case for a poet then out of favor with the academic critical establishment. His subsequent books include *The Visionary Company* (1961), *The Anxiety of Influence* (1973), *A Map of Misreading* (1975), *Poetry and Repression* (1976), and *The Western Canon* (1994). He has edited numerous volumes, including several hundred critical studies of major authors that appear under the Chelsea House imprint. *Ruin the Sacred Truths* (1989) presents the lectures Bloom delivered as the Charles Eliot Norton Professor at Harvard. In *The Book of J* (1990), Bloom speculated that the author of the oldest portions of the Hebrew Bible may have been a woman in the court of King Solomon. He has also written on religion in two other books, *The American Religion* (1992) and *Omens of Millennium: The Gnosis of Angels, Dreams, and Resurrection* (1996). Bloom, who has held a MacArthur Fellowship, is currently finishing a study of Shakespeare under the title *Shakespeare: The Invention of the Human.*

INTRODUCTION

by Harold Bloom

◊ ◊ ◊

They have the numbers; we, the heights.

1

My epigraph is from Thucydides and is spoken by the Spartan commander at Thermopylae. Culturally, we are at Thermopylae: the multiculturalists, the hordes of camp-followers afflicted by the French diseases, the mock-feminists, the commissars, the gender-and-power freaks, the hosts of new historicists and old materialists—all stand below us. They will surge up and we may be overcome; our universities are already travesties, and our journalists parody our professors of "cultural studies." For just a little while longer, we hold the heights, the realm of the aesthetic. There are still authentic poems being written in the United States. Elizabeth Bishop, May Swenson, and James Merrill are gone, but two great poets remain in John Ashbery and A. R. Ammons, and there are a score of contemporaries almost of their eminence. This anthology cannot assert that it contains all of the best poets and poems of the last decade. My charge was to select 75 poems out of 750, and not to look outside the volumes of this series. There is thus nothing here by Edgar Bowers in an older generation or by Henri Cole in the middle one, to mention just two poets whom I greatly admire. Nor would I suggest that all seventy-five poems I have chosen are going to be permanent achievements; I have made a heap of all the best I could find, where I was instructed to search. Nevertheless, there are poems here that should be perpetuated for future generations. These pass my personal test for the canonical: I have reread them with pleasure and with profit.

One of the ten volumes is not represented at all; I failed to discover more than an authentic poem or two in it. The series editor, David Lehman, kindly suggested some possibilities, but the poets involved had done better work elsewhere in these volumes. That 1996 anthology is one of the provocations for this introduction, since it seems to me a monumental representation of the enemies of the aesthetic who are in the act of overwhelming us. It is of a badness not to be believed, because it follows the criteria now operative: what matters most are the race, gender, sexual orientation, ethnic origin, and political purpose of the would-be poet. I ardently wish that I were being hyperbolical, but in fact I am exercising restraint, very difficult for a lifelong aesthete at the age of sixty-seven. One cannot expect every attempt at poetry to rival Chaucer and Shakespeare, Milton and Wordsworth, Whitman and Dickinson, Wallace Stevens and Hart Crane. But those poets, and their peers, set the measure: any who aspire to poetry must keep such exemplars always in mind. Sincerity, as the divine Oscar Wilde assured us, is not nearly enough to generate a poem. Bursting with sincerity, the 1996 volume is a Stuffed Owl of bad verse, and of much badness that is neither verse nor prose.

How could this have happened? The last thirty years of intellectual decline provide the answer: cultural guilt. Enthusiastic young men and women (and some of their middle-aged gurus) rushed forth in a Great Awakening of Rock Religion in the closing years of the 1960s. Their immediate provocation was the obscene American slaughter of the Vietnamese, but the Saturnalia that reigned for a few years, from Tokyo to Paris, quickly transcended the occasion. The epiphenomenon of the Revival went by soon enough, but it was clear to discerning spirits in 1968–70 that the consequences, though minimal for our capitalist society's ruling powers, would be endless for any cognitive and aesthetic activities throughout the Western world. Robber barons, in all countries, were immune from the contamination of the New Enthusiasm. Nothing has changed, except perhaps for the worse, in our political and economic life. The true legatees of the mock-Revolution were Ronald Reagan and now his parody, Bill Clinton. The change, all but catastrophic, instead afflicted our intellectual, cultural, educational, and aesthetic spheres, in a kind of Creation-Fall. Robert Hughes has termed what was born "the Culture of Complaint," whose hucksters—academic, journalistic, pseudo-artistic—I've named "the School of Resentment," a rabblement of lemmings leaping off the cliffs into the waters of oblivion.

Perhaps none of this matters, since good poems continue to be written, printed, and sometimes even read (whether well or not, few seem to care). Yet it will matter to some young people, as once it did, when we went to the poets to make our souls, as Yeats said. My mind was formed by Blake and Hart Crane, and then by Wallace Stevens and Shelley. The uses of great poetry are manifold, provided that an educated readership survives. Criticism, both academic and journalistic (a distinction that now scarcely exists), is dying, mostly because the universities have replaced literary criticism by "cultural criticism," a would-be social science. To survive, criticism would have to move outside the academy, but it certainly can find no home in the media. If what Walter Pater called "Aesthetic criticism" dies, then what he termed "Aesthetic poetry" must in time die also, since we will cease to know good from bad poetry. By "Aesthetic" in regard both to poetry and to criticism, Pater simply meant "authentic" or "good," since he kept in mind always the Greek meaning of *aesthesis:* "perceptiveness." If we lost all sense of the aesthetic, then we scarcely will see the difference between Emily Dickinson and Ella Wheeler Wilcox, or between John Ashbery and his weaker imitators.

2

Scolding the universities, or the media, is useless: enormous social pressures—that do not affect the people in general, or the Republican Congress and not very Democratic president the people elected—have been loosed upon institutions hopelessly vulnerable to cultural guilt. Every variety of "studies" at last will be housed: if sexual orientation is to be placed with race, ethnic group, and gender as sources of aesthetic and cognitive values, then why should we not have "Sado-Masochistic Studies," in particular honor of the god of resentment, the late Michel Foucault? If there is a Homosexual Poetic, then why not a Poetics of Pain? If representation-by-category is to be the law of the universities, and of all those they influence, what "minority" is to be excluded? Shakespeare and Dante were European males; is that worth remarking? William Wordsworth invented modern poetry. I do not know whether the more than fifty poets I anthologize all have read Wordsworth, but if they haven't, they have anyway, since all but a few write Wordsworthian poetry, in the broad sense. Even where they have ostensible subjects, almost all of the poems in this volume manifest Hazlitt's characterization of Wordsworth's work:

> He takes a subject or a story merely as pegs or loops to hang thought
> and feeling on; the incidents are trifling, in proportion to his contempt

for imposing appearances; the reflections are profound, according to the gravity and aspiring pretensions of his mind.

Hazlitt's personal ambivalence toward Wordsworth is palpable, but so is the critic's realization that Wordsworth had reinvented poetry. Yet nearly all current published criticism of Wordsworth and almost any class taught on him at our universities and colleges now actively condemn this greatest of all modern poets *on political grounds,* because he "betrayed" his early allegiance to the French Revolution! By our means test, Wordsworth cannot pass. So absurd have the professors become that I can see no way to salvage literary study except to abolish tenure. Tenure is an archaic survival anyway, but it becomes pernicious when faculties are crowded by thousands of ideologues, who resent Wordsworth even as they resent Shakespeare. When I was a young teacher of poetry at Yale, the English Romantic poets were Wordsworth, Coleridge, Byron, and Keats, as well as Blake and Shelley, whose place in the canon I helped restore. On hundreds of campuses now, these poets have to share attention with the "women Romantic poets": Felicia Hemans, Laetitia Landon, Charlotte Smith, and Mary Tighe, among some others. These were, to understate, justly neglected verse writers, though superior to many in *The Best American Poetry 1996.* Anthologies of seventeenth-century English literature now give us, side by side with Donne, Ben Jonson, and Milton, a group including the Duchess of Newcastle, Lady Mary Chudleigh, Anne Killigrew, and the venerated Aphra Behn. I have seen my profession dying for over a quarter century now, and in another decade it may be dead. If its function is to appreciate and teach Laetitia Landon and Lady Mary Chudleigh, then the demise cannot come too soon.

One asks again: how could this have happened, and not just in the universities but in the publishing world and in the media? *The New York Times* essentially is now a countercultural newspaper. When Maya Angelou read a poem for Clinton's first inauguration, the *Times* printed the text, a monument of sincerity, and in an editorial praised this effusion for its "Whitmanian amplitudes." Recently, one of the *Times* rock critics proclaimed our contemporary Mozart to be the glyph formerly known as Prince. Literary satire is impossible when the *Times* exceeds Nathanael West and Terry Southern in outrageousness. If all aesthetic and cognitive standards are abandoned by professors and journalists alike, then the tradition of American poetry can survive only by a profound inward turning.

Walt Whitman was not only the strongest of our poets (together with the highly antithetical Emily Dickinson), but he is also now the most betrayed of all our poets, with so much of the ongoing ideological balderdash being preached in his name. Whitman's poetry generally does the opposite of what he proclaims its work to be: it is reclusive, evasive, hermetic, nuanced, and more onanistic even than homoerotic, which critics cannot accept, particularly these days when attempts are made to assimilate the Self-Reliant Whitman into what calls itself the Homosexual Poetic. If we are to have gay and lesbian studies, who will speak for Onan, whose bards include Whitman and the Goethe of *Faust, Part Two*? The most figurative of all our poets, Whitman will elude every effort to entrap him in an ideology. As elitist a democrat as his master Emerson, Whitman continues with his ideas of representation to outwit his historicizing and eroticizing critics. The crucial figure in Whitman is neither his self—Walt Whitman, one of the roughs, an American—nor his soul, but "the real me" or "me myself," a conceptual image that prophesies Wallace Stevens, T. S. Eliot, and particularly John Ashbery:

Apart from the pulling and hauling stands what I am,
Stands amused, complacent, compassionating, idle, unitary,
Looks down, is erect, bends an arm on an impalpable certain rest,
Looks with its sidecurved head curious what will come next,
Both in and out of the game, and watching and wondering at it.

That Whitmanian "what I am," his "real me" or "me myself," is both an inspiration to strong American poetry after him and a reproach to the cultural and erotic dogmas now circulated in his great name. It is no accident that the best American poets who have emerged from Whitman—sometimes insisting that they owed him nothing—are formalists, major artists of verse: Stevens, Eliot, Hart Crane, and even Ashbery when at his most gravely traditional. Cast out the aesthetic, and you cast away Whitman, who was a major poet and a poor prophet, and who was, above all else, a very difficult poet, whose synecdoches do not unravel without very frequent rereadings. Authentic American poetry is necessarily difficult; it is our elitist art, though that elite has nothing to do with social class, gender, erotic preference, ethnic strain, race, or sect. "We live in the mind," Stevens said, and our poetry always is either Emersonian or anti-Emersonian, but either way is informed by Emerson's dialectics of power:

> Life will be imaged, but cannot be divided nor doubled. Any invasion of its unity would be chaos. The soul is not twin-born, but the only begotten, and though revealing itself as child in time, child in appearance, is of a fatal and universal power, admitting no co-life. Every day, every act betrays the ill-concealed deity. We believe in ourselves, as we do not believe in others. We permit all things to ourselves, and that which we call sin in others, is experiment for us. It is an instance of our faith in ourselves, that men never speak of crime as lightly as they think: or, every man thinks a latitude safe for himself, which is nowise to be indulged to another. The act looks very differently on the inside, and on the outside; in its quality, and its consequences. Murder in the murderer is no such ruinous thought as poets and romancers will have it; it does not unsettle him, or fright him from his ordinary notice of trifles: it is an act quite easy to be contemplated, but in its sequel, it turns out to be a horrible jangle and confounding all relations. Especially the crimes that spring from love, seem right and fair from the actor's point of view, but, when acted, are found destructive of society. No man at last believes that he can be lost, nor that the crime in him is as black as in the felon. Because the intellect qualifies in our own case the moral judgments. For there is no crime to the intellect. That is antinomian or hypernomian, and judges law as well as fact.

That does not allow any room for the false generosity of any Affirmative Action in the judging of poetry. Printing, praising, and teaching bad poems for the sake of even the best causes is simply destructive for those causes. "We believe in ourselves, as we do not believe in others" is a truth that makes us wince, but no one ever can write a good poem without it. Tony Kushner, who could be a great playwright but for his obsession with the ideologies of political correctness, ought to ponder Emerson's "Experience," from which I have just quoted. Every attempt to socialize writing and reading fails; poetry is a solitary art, more now than ever, and its proper audience is the deeply educated, solitary reader, or that reader sitting within herself in a theater.

4

It was inevitable that the School of Resentment would do its most destructive damage to the reading, staging, and interpretation of

Shakespeare, whose eminence is the ultimate demonstration of the autonomy of the aesthetic. Cultural poeticians, ostensible feminists, sub-Marxists, and assorted would-be Parisians have given us French Shakespeare, who never wrote a line but instead sat in a tavern while all the "social energies" of early modern Europe pulsated into his quill and created Hamlet, Falstaff, Iago, and Cleopatra, with little aid from that mere funnel, the Man from Stratford. It has not been explained (at least to me) just why the social energies favored Shakespeare over Thomas Middleton or John Marston or George Chapman or whoever, but this remarkable notion totally dominates today's academic study of Shakespeare. First, Paris told us that language did the thinking and writing for us, but then Foucault emerged, and Shakespeare went from being language's serf to society's minion. No longer can we speak of the best writer—Auden's Top Bard—and if Shakespeare recedes, why call a volume *The Best American Poetry*? Certainly the 1996 volume should have been retitled *The Most Socially Energetic American Poetry,* and if I were not Bloom Brontosaurus, an amiable dinosaur, we could have called this book *The Most Socially Energetic of the Socially Energetic.* The madness that contaminates our once high culture cannot be cured unless and until we surrender our more than Kafkan sense that social guilt is not to be doubted. Nothing can be more malignant than a disease of the spirit that sincerely regards itself as virtue.

Shakespeare, precisely because he is the only authentic multicultural writer, demonstrated that our modish multiculturalism is a lie, a mask for mediocrity and for the thought-control academic police, the Gestapo of our campuses. Each time I make the mistake of glancing at the *Yale Weekly Bulletin,* I shudder to see that the dean of Yale College has appointed yet another subdean to minister to the supposed cultural interests of another identity club: ethnic, racial, linguistic, with gender and erotic subsets. Shakespeare, performed and read in every country (with the sporadic exception of France, most xenophobic of cultures), is judged by audiences of every race and language to have put them upon the stage. Shakespeare's power has nothing to do with Eurocentrism, maleness, Christianity, or Elizabethan-Jacobean social energies. No one else so combined cognitive strength, originality, dramatic guile, and linguistic florabundance as virtually to reinvent the human, and Shakespeare is therefore the best battlefield upon which to fight the rabblement of Resenters. Our multiculturalists are reductionists; the 1996 volume actually is asserting: "Our bad poets are just as good as your bad poets." Shakespeare, pragmatically the true multiculturalist, is the least reductive of all writers; his men and women never invite us to believe that when we know the worst about them, then we know exactly who they are. Emerson, in *Representative Men,* caught this best:

> Shakespeare is as much out of the category of eminent authors, as he is out of the crowd. He is inconceivably wise; the others, conceivably. A good reader can, in a sort, nestle into Plato's brain, and think from thence; but not into Shakespeare's. We are still out of doors. For executive faculty, for creation, Shakespeare is unique. No man can imagine it better. He was the farthest reach of subtlety compatible with an individual self,—the subtilest of authors, and only just within the possibility of authorship. With this wisdom of life, is the equal endowment of imaginative and of lyric power. He clothed the creatures of his legend with form and sentiments, as if they were people who had lived under his roof; and few real men have left such distinct characters as these fictions. And they spoke in language as sweet as it was fit. Yet his talents never seduced him into an ostentation, nor did he harp on one string. An omnipresent humanity coordinates all his faculties. Give a man of talents a story to tell, and his partiality will presently appear. He has certain observations, opinions, topics, which have some accidental prominence, and which he disposes all to exhibit. He crams this part, and starves that other part, consulting not the fitness of the thing, but his fitness and strength. But Shakespeare has no peculiarity, no importunate topic; but all is duly given; no veins, no curiosities: no cow-painter, no bird-fancier, no mannerist is he: he has no discoverable egotism: the great he tells greatly; the small, subordinately. He is wise without emphasis or assertion; he is strong, as nature is strong, who lifts the land into mountain slopes without effort, and by the same rule as she floats a bubble in the air, and likes as well to do the one as the other. This makes that equality of power in farce, tragedy, narrative, and love-songs; a merit so incessant, that each reader is incredulous of the perception of other readers.

If this be Bardolatry, then let us have more of it, for it may be the only medicine that can cure us of the French blight that afflicts our culture and our academies. It is no accident that poetry is the principal victim of the decline and fall of our literature faculties. Almost no one these days is taught how to read a poem; there are very few who know how to instruct in that difficult art of interpretation, and the going ideologies distrust poetry anyway. How do you politicize this?

All day within the dreamy house,
The doors upon their hinges creak'd;
The blue fly sung in the pane; the mouse
Behind the mouldering wainscot shriek'd,
Or from the crevice peer'd about.
Old faces glimmer'd thro' the doors,
Old footsteps trod the upper floors,
Old voices called her from without.
    She only said, "My life is dreary,
    He cometh not," she said;
    She wept, "I am aweary, aweary,
    I would that I were dead!"

The sparrow's chirrup on the roof,
The slow clock ticking, and the sound
Which to the wooing wind aloof
The poplar made, did all confound
Her sense; but most she loathed the hour
When the thick-moted sunbeam lay
Athwart the chambers, and the day
Was sloping toward his western bower.
    Then she said, "I am very dreary,
    He will not come," she said;
    She wept, "I am aweary, aweary,
    O God, that I were dead!"

5

It is ironical that, in this bad time, American poetry is of a higher qual-
ity than our criticism or teaching of poetry. Four major poets who
appear in this book—Elizabeth Bishop, James Merrill, Amy Clampitt,
and the still undervalued May Swenson—are gone, yet there are poems
here by Ashbery, Ammons, and at least a dozen others that I think will
endure, if only we can maintain a continuity of aesthetic appreciation
and cognitive understanding that more or less prevailed from Emerson
until the later 1960s, but that survives only in isolated pockets. While it
is true that several of the greatest American poets—Whitman, Dickin-
son, Stevens, Hart Crane—had either no or little authentic critical
response during their lifetimes, they at least did not have to endure a

cultural situation fundamentally hostile to aesthetic and cognitive standards of judgment. I marvel at the courage and desperate faith of our best younger poets, who have to withstand the indifference or hostility not just of society in general, but also of the supposed defenders of poetry, who now will advocate it only as an instrument of social change. If you urge political responsibilities upon a poet, then you are asking her to prefer to poetry what can destroy her poem. Emily Dickinson had the inner freedom to rethink everything for herself and so achieved a cognitive originality as absolute as William Blake's. She had economic and social advantages that Walt Whitman did not enjoy, yet like Whitman she did not have to confront ideological persuasions either irrelevant or inimical to aesthetic ambitions. Wallace Stevens could take for granted the autonomy of the aesthetic; how would *Harmonium* otherwise have been possible, or Hart Crane's first volume, *White Buildings*? I write this introduction out of the conviction that a literary critic has no political responsibilities, as a critic. My obligation is only to help (if that I can) make it possible for another Elizabeth Bishop or May Swenson or James Merrill to develop without being impeded by ideological demands. I am more than aware that the Resenters speak constantly of "the ideology of the aesthetic" and of "the Romantic ideology," but that is simply a playing with loaded dice. The only pragmatic aesthetic I know is that some poems intrinsically are better than others, while Romanticism, as I apprehend it, is a discipline in sensibility and in perception.

In his essay "Politics," Emerson provides a spark for these times:

> It makes no difference how many tons weight of atmosphere presses on our heads, so long as the same pressure resists it within the lungs. Augment the mass a thousand fold; it cannot begin to crush us, as long as reaction is equal to action.

The Resenters prate of power, as they do of race and gender: these are careerist stratagems and have nothing to do with the insulted and injured, whose lives will not be improved by our reading the bad verses of those who assert that they are the oppressed. Our schools as much as our universities are given away to these absurdities: replacing *Julius Caesar* by *The Color Purple* is hardly a royal road to enlightenment. A country where television, movies, computers, and Stephen King have replaced reading is already in acute danger of cultural collapse. That danger is dreadfully augmented by our yielding education to the ideologues whose deepest resentment is of poetry itself. What John Hollander remarks of Whitman—"The poetry, like its title, looks easy and proves hard"—is true of almost all great or very good poets. But there, I hope, will be one of the crucial uses for us of the best American poems: more than ever before, our situation *needs* aesthetic and cognitive difficulty. The mock poetry of Resentment looks easy and proves easy; unlike Whitman, it lacks mind. When I think of the American poets of this century whom I myself love best, I begin always with Wallace Stevens and with Hart Crane. Stevens subtly gives us what he calls "the hum of thoughts evaded in the mind," and Crane urges us to the most difficult transcendence ever visualized by any American poet. Their heirs, including Elizabeth Bishop, Merrill, Ashbery, and Ammons, have carried forward this mingled legacy of thoughts available to us only in poems, and yearnings made palpable only in complex imaginings. Mastery of metaphor and power of thinking are the true merits of the best American poetry of our time. I give the last words here to the sacred Emerson, from his Whitman-inspiring essay "The Poet," where the freedom of poetry is ascribed to "tropes" and to "thought":

> The poets are thus liberating gods. The ancient British bards had for the title of their order, "Those who are free throughout the world." They are free, and they make us free. An imaginative book renders us much more service at first, by stimulating us through its tropes, than afterward, when we arrive at the precise sense of the author. I think nothing is of any value in books, excepting the transcendental and extraordinary. If a man is inflamed and carried away by his thought, to that degree that he forgets the authors and the public, and heeds only this one dream, which holds him like an insanity, let me read his paper, and you may have all the arguments and histories and criticism. All the value which attaches to Pythagoras, Paracelsus, Cornelius Agrippa, Cardan, Kepler, Swedenborg, Schelling, Oken, or any other who introduces questionable facts into his cosmogony, as angels, devils, magic, astrology, palmistry, mesmerism, and so on, is the certificate we have of departure from routine, and that here is a new witness. That also is the best success in conversation, the magic of liberty, which puts the world, like a ball, in our hands. How cheap even the liberty then seems; how mean to study, when an emotion communicates to the intellect the power to sap and upheave nature: how great the perspective! nations, times, systems, enter and disappear, like threads in a tapestry of large figure and many colors; dream delivers us to dream, and, while the drunkenness lasts, we will sell our bed, our philosophy, our religion, in our opulence.

THE
BEST OF
THE BEST
AMERICAN
POETRY
1988–1997

◇ ◇ ◇

Dance Mania

◇　◇　◇

In 1027, not far from Bernburg,
eighteen peasants were seized
by a common delusion.
Holding hands, they circled for hours
in a churchyard, haunted by visions,
spirits whose names they called in terror or welcome,
until an angry priest cast a spell on them
for disrupting his Christmas service,
and they sank into the frozen earth
up to their knees. In 1227
on a road to Darmstadt, scores of children
danced and jumped in a shared delirium.
Some saw devils, others the Savior enthroned
in the open heavens. Those who survived
remained palsied for the rest of their days.
And in 1278, two hundred fanatics raved on a bridge
that spanned the Mosel near Koblenz.
A cleric passed carrying the host
to a devout parishioner, the bridge collapsed,
and the maniacs were swept away.
A hundred years later, in concert with
The Great Mortality, armies of dancers
roved in contortions all over Europe.
The clergy found them immune to exorcism,
gave in to their wishes and issued
decrees banning all but square-toed shoes,
the zealots having declared they hated
pointed ones. They disliked even more
the color red, suggesting

a connection between their malady
and the condition of certain infuriated
animals. Most of all they could not endure
the sight of people weeping.
The Swiss doctor Paracelsus was the first to call
the Church's theories of enchantment
nonsensical gossip. Human life is inseparable
from the life of the universe, he said.
Anybody's mortal clay is an extract
of all beings previously created. Illness
can be traced, he said,
to the failure of the Archaeus, a force
residing in the stomach and whose function
is to harmonize the mystic elements (salt,
sulphur, mercury) on which vitality depends.
He advocated direct measures, proposed remedies
fitting the degree of the affliction.
A patient could make a wax doll of himself,
invest his sins and blasphemies within the manikin,
then burn it with no further ceremony.
He could subject himself to ice-water baths,
or submit to starvation in solitary confinement.
Noted for his arrogance, vanity
and choler (his real name was Theophrastus Bombast
von Hohenheim), Paracelsus made enemies.
They discovered he held no academic degree
and caused him to be banished from Basle,
to become a wanderer who would die mysteriously
at the White Horse Inn in Salzburg in 1541.
After a drunken orgy, said one report.
The victim of thugs hired by jealous apothecaries,
said another. And the dance mania
found its own way through time to survive
among us, as untouched as ever by the wisdom of science.
Think of the strange, magnetic sleep
whole populations fall into every day,
in gymnasiums full of pounding darkness,
in the ballrooms of exclusive hotels,
on verandahs overlooking the ocean and played upon
by moonlight, in backyards, on the perfect lawns

30

of great estates, on city rooftops, in any brief field
the passing tourist sees as empty—
how many millions of us now, the living
and the dead, hand in hand as always,
approaching the brink of the millennium.

1992

A. R. AMMONS

Anxiety's Prosody

◊   ◊   ◊

Anxiety clears meat chunks out of the stew, carrots, takes
the skimmer to floats of greasy globules and with cheesecloth

filters the broth, looking for the transparent, the colorless
essential, the unbeginning and unending of consommé: the

open anxiety breezes through thick conceits, surface congestions
(it likes metaphors deep-lying, out of sight, their airs misting

up into, lighting up consciousness, unidentifiable presences),
it distills consonance and assonance, glottal thickets, brush

clusters, it thins the rhythms, rushing into longish gaits, more
distance in less material time: it hates clots, its stump-fires

level fields: patience and calm define borders and boundaries,
hedgerows, and sharp whirls: anxiety burns instrumentation

matterless, assimilates music into motion, sketches the high
suasive turnings, mild natures tangled still in knotted clumps.

1989

Garbage

◇ ◇ ◇

I

Creepy little creepers are insinuatingly
curling up my spine (bringing the message)

saying, Boy!, are you writing that great poem
the world's waiting for: don't you know you

have an unaccomplished mission unaccomplished;
someone somewhere may be at this very moment

dying for the lack of what W. C. Williams says
you could (or somebody could) be giving: yeah?

so, these messengers say, what do you
mean teaching school (teaching *poetry* and

poetry writing and wasting your time painting
sober little organic, meaningful pictures)

when values thought lost (but only scrambled into
disengagement) lie around demolished

and centerless because you (that's me, boy)
haven't elaborated everything in everybody's

face, yet: on the other hand (I say to myself,
receiving the messengers and cutting them down)

who has done anything or am I likely to do
anything the world won't twirl without: and

since SS's enough money (I hope) to live
from now on on in elegance and simplicity—

or, maybe, just simplicity—why shouldn't I
at my age (63) concentrate on chucking the

advancements and rehearsing the sweetnesses of
leisure, nonchalance, and small-time byways: couple

months ago, for example, I went all the way
from soy flakes (already roasted and pressed

and in need of an hour's simmering boil
to be cooked) all the way to soybeans, the

pure golden pearls themselves, 65¢ lb. dry: they
have to be soaked overnight in water and they

have to be boiled slowly for six hours—but
they're welfare cheap, are a complete protein,

more protein by weight than meat, more
calcium than milk, more lecithin than eggs,

and somewhere in there the oil that smoothes
stools, a great virtue: I need time and verve

to find out, now, about medicare/medicaid,
national osteoporosis week, gadabout tours,

hearing loss, homesharing programs, and choosing
good nutrition! for starters! why should I

be trying to write my flattest poem, now, for
whom, not for myself, for others?, posh, as I

have never said: Social Security can provide
the beans, soys enough: my house, paid for for

twenty years, is paid for: my young'un
is raised: nothing one can pay cash for seems

very valuable: that reaches a high enough
benchmark for me—high enough that I wouldn't

know what to do with anything beyond that, no
place to house it, park it, dock it, let it drift

down to: elegance and simplicity: I wonder
if we need those celestial guidance systems

striking mountaintops or if we need fuzzy
philosophy's abstruse failed reasonings: isn't

it simple and elegant enough to believe in
qualities, simplicity and elegance, pitch in a

little courage and generosity, a touch of
commitment, enough asceticism to prevent

fattening: moderation: elegant and simple
moderation: trees defined themselves (into

various definitions) through a dynamics of
struggle (hey, is the palaver rapping, yet?)

and so it is as if there were a genetic
recognition that a young tree would get up and

through only through taken space (parental
space not yielding at all, either) and, further:

so, trunks, accommodated to rising, to reaching
the high light and deep water, were slender

and fast moving, and this was okay because
one good thing about dense competition is that

if one succeeds with it one is buttressed by
crowding competitors; that is, there was little

room for branches, and just a tuft of green
possibility at the forest's roof: but, now,

I mean, take my yard maple—put out in the free
and open—has overgrown, its trunk

split down from a high fork: wind has
twisted off the biggest, bottom branch: there

was, in fact, hardly any crowding and competition,
and the fat tree, unable to stop pouring it on,

overfed and overgrew and, now, again, its skin's
broken into and disease may find it and bores

of one kind or another, and fungus: it just
goes to show you: moderation imposed is better

than no moderation at all: we tie into the
lives of those we love and our lives, then, go

as theirs go; their pain we can't shake off;
their choices, often harming to themselves,

pour through our agitated sleep, swirl up as
no-nos in our dreams; we rise several times

in a night to walk about; we rise in the morning
to a crusty world headed nowhere, doorless:

our chests burn with anxiety and a river of
anguish defines rapids and straits in the pit of

our stomachs: how can we intercede and not
interfere: how can our love move more surroundingly,

convincingly than our premonitory advice

II

garbage has to be the poem of our time because
garbage is spiritual, believable enough

to get our attention, getting in the way, piling
up, stinking, turning brooks brownish and

creamy white: what else deflects us from the
errors of our illusionary ways, not a temptation

to trashlessness, that is too far off, and,
anyway, unimaginable, unrealistic: I'm a

hole puncher or hole plugger: stick a finger
in the dame (*dam,* damn, dike), hold back the issue

of creativity's flood, the forthcoming, futuristic,
the origins feeding trash: down by I-95 in

Florida where flatland's ocean- and gulf-flat,
mounds of disposal rise (for if you dug

something up to make room for something to put
in, what about the something dug up, as with graves:)

the garbage trucks crawl as if in obeisance,
as if up ziggurats toward the high places gulls

and garbage keep alive, offerings to the gods
of garbage, of retribution, of realistic

expectation, the deities of unpleasant
necessities: refined, young earthworms,

drowned up in macadam pools by spring rains, moisten
out white in a day or so and, round spots,

look like sputum or creamy-rich, broken-up cold
clams: if this is not the best poem of the

century, can it be about the worst poem of the
century: it comes, at least, toward the end,

so a long tracing of bad stuff can swell
under its measure: but there on the heights

a small smoke wafts the sacrificial bounty
day and night to layer the sky brown, shut us

in as into a lidded kettle, the everlasting
flame these acres-deep of tendance keep: a

free offering of a crippled plastic chair:
a played-out sports outfit: a hill-myna

print stained with jelly: how to write this
poem, should it be short, a small popping of

duplexes, or long, hunting wide, coming home
late, losing the trail and recovering it:

should it act itself out, illustrations,
examples, colors, clothes or intensify

reductively into statement, bones any corpus
would do to surround, or should it be nothing

at all unless it finds itself: the poem,
which is about the pre-socratic idea of the

dispositional axis from stone to wind, wind
to stone (with my elaborations, if any)

is complete before it begins, so I needn't
myself hurry into brevity, though a weary reader

might briefly be done: the axis will be clear
enough daubed here and there with a little ink

or fined out into every shade and form of its
revelation: this is a scientific poem,

asserting that nature models values, that we
have invented little (copied), reflections of

possibilities already here, this where we came
to and how we came: a priestly director behind the

black-chuffing dozer leans the gleanings and
reads the birds, millions of loners circling

a common height, alighting to the meaty steaks
and puffy muffins (puffins?): there is a mound

too, in the poet's mind dead language is hauled
off to and burned down on, the energy held and

shaped into new turns and clusters, the mind
strengthened by what it strengthens for

where but in the very asshole of come-down is
redemption: as where but brought low, where

but in the grief of failure, loss, error do we
discern the savage afflictions that turn us around:

where but in the arrangements love crawls us
through, not a thing left in our self-display

unhumiliated, do we find the sweet seed of
new routes: but we are natural: nature, not

we, gave rise to us: we are not, though, though
natural, divorced from higher, finer configurations:

tissues and holograms and energy circulate in
us and seek and find representations of themselves

outside us, so that we can participate in
celebrations high and know reaches of feeling

and sight and thought that penetrate (really
penetrate) far, far beyond these our wet cells,

right on up past our stories, the planets, moons,
and other bodies locally to the other end of

the pole where matter's forms diffuse and
energy loses all means to express itself except

as spirit, there, oh, yes, in the abiding where
mind but nothing else abides, the eternal,

until it turns into another pear or sunfish,
that momentary glint in the fisheye having

been there so long, coming and going, it's
eternity's glint: it all wraps back round,

into and out of form, palpable and impalpable,
and in one phase, the one of grief and love,

we know the other, where everlastingness comes to
sway, okay and smooth: the heaven we mostly

want, though, is this jet-hoveled hell back,
heaven's daunting asshole: one must write and

rewrite till one writes it right: if I'm in
touch, she said, then I've got an edge: what

the hell kind of talk is that: I can't believe
I'm merely an old person: whose mother is dead,

whose father is gone and many of whose
friends and associates have wended away to the

ground, which is only heavy wind, or to ashes,
a lighter breeze: but it was all quite frankly

to be expected and not looked forward to: even
old trees, I remember some of them, where they

used to stand: pictures taken by some of them:
and old dogs, specially one imperial black one,

quad dogs with their hier*archies* (another *archie*)
one succeeding another, the barking and romping

sliding away like slides from a projector: what
were they then that are what they are now:

III

toxic waste, poison air, beach goo, eroded
roads draw nations together, whereas magnanimous

platitude and sweet semblance ease each nation
back into its comfort or despair: global crises

promote internationalist gettings-together,
problems the best procedure, whether they be in the

poet warps whose energy must be found and let
work or in the high windings of sulfur dioxide:

I say to my writing students—prize your flaws,
defects, behold your accidents, engage your

negative criticisms—these are the materials
of your ongoing—from these places you imagine,

find, or make the ways back to all of us, the figure,
keeping the aberrant periphery worked

clear so the central current may shift or slow
or rouse adjusting to the necessary dynamic:

in our error the defining energies of cure
errancy finds: suffering otherwises: but

no use to linger over beauty or simple effect:
this is just a poem with a job to do: and that

is to declare, however roundabout, sideways,
or meanderingly (or in those ways) the perfect

scientific and materialistic notion of the
spindle of energy: when energy is gross,

rocklike, it resembles the gross, and when
fine it mists away into mystical refinements,

sometimes passes right out of material
recognizability and becomes, what?, motion,

spirit, all forms translated into energy, as at
the bottom of Dante's hell all motion is

translated into form: so, in value systems,
physical systems, artistic systems, always this

same disposition from the heavy to the light,
and then the returns from the light downward

to the staid gross: stone to wind, wind to
stone: there is no need for "outside," hegemonic

derivations of value: nothing need be invented
or imposed: the aesthetic, scientific, moral

are organized like a muff along this spindle,
might as well relax: thus, the job done, the

mind having found its way through and marked
out the course, the intellect can be put by:

one can turn to tongue, crotch, boob, navel,
armpit, rock, slit, roseate rearend and

consider the perfumeries of slick exchange,
heaving breath, slouchy mouth, the mixed

means by which we stay attentive and keep to
the round of our ongoing: you wake up thrown

away and accommodation becomes the name of your
game: getting back, back into the structure

of protection, caring, warmth, numbers: one
and many, singles and groups, dissensions and

cooperations, takings and givings—the dynamic
of survival, still the same: but why thrown

out in the first place: because while the
prodigal stamps off and returns, the father goes

from iron directives that drove the son away
to rejoicing tears at his return: the safe

world of community, not safe, still needs
feelers sent out to test the environment, to

bring back news or no news; the central
mover, the huge river, needs, too, to bend,

and the son sent away is doubly welcomed home:
we deprive ourselves of, renounce, safety to seek

greater safety: but if we furnish a divine
sanction or theology to the disposition, we

must not think when the divine sanction shifts
that there is any alteration in the disposition:

the new's an angle of emphasis on the old:
new religions are surfaces, beliefs the shadows

of images trying to construe what needs no
belief: only born die, and if something is

born or new, then that is not it, that is not
the it: the it is the indifference of all the

differences, the nothingness of all the poised
somethings, the finest issue of energy in which

boulders and dead stars float: for what
if it were otherwise and the it turned out to

be *something,* damning and demanding, strict and
fierce, preventing and seizing: what range of

choice would be given up then and what value
could our partial, remnant choices acquire then:

with a high whine the garbage trucks slowly
circling the pyramid rising intone the morning

and atop the mound's plateau birds circling
hear and roil alive in winklings of wings

denser than windy forest shelves: and meanwhile
a truck already arrived spills its goods from

the back hatch and the birds as in a single computer
formed net plunge in celebrations, hallelujahs

of rejoicing: the driver gets out of his truck
and wanders over to the cliff on the spill and

looks off from the high point into the rosy-fine
rising of day, the air pure, the wings of the

birds white and clean as angel-food cake: holy, holy,
holy, the driver cries and flicks his cigarette

in a spiritual swoop that floats and floats before
it touches ground: here, the driver knows,

where the consummations gather, where the disposal
flows out of form, where the last translations

cast away their immutable bits and scraps,
flits of steel, shivers of bottle and tumbler,

here is the gateway to beginning, here the portal
of renewing change, the birdshit, even, melding

enrichingly in with debris, a loam for the roots
of placenta: oh, nature, the man on the edge

of the cardboard-laced cliff exclaims, that there
could be a straightaway from the toxic past into

the fusion-lit reaches of a coming time! our
sins are so many, here heaped, shapes given to

false matter, hamburger meat left out

IV

scientists plunge into matter looking for the
matter but the matter lessens and, looked too

far into, expands away: it was insubstantial all
along: that is, boulders bestir; they

are "alive" with motion and space: there is a
riddling reality where real hands grasp each

other in the muff but toward both extremes the
reality wears out, wears thin, becomes a reality

"realityless": this is satisfactory, providing
permanent movement and staying, providing the

stratum essential with an essential air, the
poles thick and thin, the middles, at interchange:

the spreader rakes a furrow open and lights a
drying edge: a priestly plume rises, a signal, smoke

like flies intermediating between orange peel
and buzzing blur: is a poem about garbage garbage

or will this abstract, hollow junk seem beautiful
and necessary as just another offering to the

high assimilations: (that means up on top where
the smoke is; the incinerations of sin,

corruption, misconstruction pass through the
purification of flame:) old deck chairs,

crippled aluminum lawn chairs, lemon crates
with busted slats or hinges, strollers with

whacking or spinningly idle wheels: stub ends
of hot dogs: clumps go out; rain sulls deep

coals; wind slams flickers so flat they lose
the upstanding of updraft and stifle to white

lingo—but oh, oh, in a sense, and in an
intention, the burning's forever, O eternal

flame, principle of the universe, without which
mere heaviness and gray rust prevail: dance

peopling the centers and distances, the faraway
galactic slurs even, luminescences, plasmas,

those burns, the same principle: but here on
the heights, terns and flies avoid the closest

precincts of flame, the terrifying transformations,
the disappearances of anything of interest,

morsel, gobbet, trace of maple syrup, fat
worm: addling intensity at the center

where only special clothes and designated
offices allay the risk, the pure center: but

down, down on the lowest appropinquations, the
laborsome, loaded vessels whine like sails in

too much wind up the long ledges, the whines
a harmony, singing away the end of the world

or spelling it in, a monstrous surrounding of
gathering—the putrid, the castoff, the used,

the mucked up—all arriving for final assessment,
for the toting up in tonnage, the separations

of wet and dry, returnable and gone for good:
the sanctifications, the burn-throughs, ash free

merely a permanent twang of light, a dwelling
music, remaining: how to be blessed are mechanisms,

procedures that carry such changes! the
garbage spreader gets off his bulldozer and

approaches the fire: he stares into it as into
eternity, the burning edge of beginning and

ending, the catalyst of going and becoming,
and all thoughts of his paycheck and beerbelly,

even all thoughts of his house and family and
the long way he has come to be worthy of his

watch, fall away, and he stands in the presence
of the momentarily everlasting, the air about

him sacrosanct, purged of the crawling vines
and dense vegetation of desire, nothing between

perception and consequence here: the arctic
terns move away from the still machine and

light strikes their wings in round, a fluttering,
a whirling rose of wings, and it seems that

terns' slender wings and finely tipped
tails look so airy and yet so capable that they

must have been designed after angels or angels
after them: the lizard family produced man in

the winged air! man as what he might be or might
have been, neuter, guileless, a feathery hymn:

the bulldozer man picks up a red bottle that
turns purple and green in the light and pours

out a few drops of stale wine, and yellow jackets
burr in the bottle, sung drunk, the singing

not even puzzled when he tosses the bottle way
down the slopes, the still air being flown in

in the bottle even as the bottle dives through
the air! the bulldozer man thinks about that

and concludes that everything is marvelous, what
he should conclude and what everything is: on

the deepdown slopes, he realizes, the light
inside the bottle will, over the weeks, change

the yellow jackets, unharmed, having left lost,
not an aromatic vapor of wine left, the air

percolating into and out of the neck as the sun's
heat rises and falls: all is one, one all:

hallelujah: he gets back up on his bulldozer
and shaking his locks backs the bulldozer up

V

dew shatters into rivulets on crunched cellophane
as the newly started bulldozer jars a furrow

off the mesa, smoothing and packing down:
flattening, the way combers break flat into

speed up the strand: unpleasant food strings down
the slopes and rats' hard tails whirl whacking

trash: I don't know anything much about garbage
dumps: I mean, I've never climbed one: I

don't know about the smells: do masks mask
scent: or is there a deodorizing mask: the

Commissioner of Sanitation in a bug-black caddy
hearse-long glisters creepy up the ziggurat: at

the top his chauffeur pops out and opens the
big back door for him: he goes over a few feet

away, puts a stiff, salute-hand to his forehead
and surveys the distances in all depths: the

birds' shadows lace his white sleeve: he
rises to his toes as a lifting zephyr from the

sea lofts a salt-shelf of scent: he approves: he
extends his arm in salute to the noisy dozer's

operator, waves back and forth canceling out
any intention to speak, re-beholds Florida's

longest vistas, gets back into the big buggy
and runs up all the windows, trapping, though,

a nuisance of flies: (or, would he have run
the windows down: or would anyone else have:

not out there: strike that:) rightness, at
any rate, like a benediction, settles on the

ambiance: all is proceeding: funding will be
continued: this work will not be abandoned:

this mound can rise higher: things are in order
when heights are acknowledged; the lows

ease into place; the wives get back from the laundromat,
the husbands hose down the hubcaps; and the

seeringly blank pressures of weekends crack
away hour by hour in established time: in your

end is my beginning: the operator waves back
to the Commissioner, acknowledging his understanding

and his submission to benign authority, and falls
to thinking of his wife, née Minnie Furher, a woman

of abrupt appetites and strict morals, a woman
who wants what she wants legally, largely as a

function of her husband's particulars: a closet
queen, Minnie hides her cardboard, gold-foiled

crown to wear in parade about the house when
nobody's home: she is so fat, fat people

like to be near her: and her husband loves
every bit of her, every bite (bit) round enough to get

to: and wherever his dinky won't reach, he finds
something else that will: I went up the road

a piece this morning at ten to Pleasant Grove
for the burial of Ted's ashes: those above

ground care; those below don't: the sun was
terribly hot, and the words of poems read out

loud settled down like minnows in a shallows
for the moment of silence and had their gaps

and fractures filled up and healed quiet: into
the posthole went the irises and hand-holds of dirt:

spring brings thaw and thaw brings the counterforce
of planted ashes which may not rise again,

not as anything recognizable as what they leach
away from: oh, yes, yes, the matter goes on,

turning into this and that, never the same thing
twice: but what about the spirit, does it die

in an instant, being nothing in an instant out of
matter, or does it hold on to some measure of

time, not just the eternity in which it is not,
but does death go on being death for a billion

years: this one fact put down is put down
forever, is it, or forever, forever to be a

part of the changes about it, switches in the
earth's magnetic field, asteroid collisions,

tectonic underplays, to be molten and then not
molten, again and again: when does a fact end:

what does one do with this gap from just yesterday
or just this morning to fifty-five billion

years—to infinity: the spirit was forever
and is forever, the residual and informing

energy, but here what concerns us is this
manifestation, this man, this incredible flavoring and

building up of character and éclat, gone,
though forever, in a moment only, a local

event, infinitely unrepeatable: the song of
the words subsides, the shallows drift away,

the people turn to each other and away: motors
start and the driveways clear, and the single

fact is left alone to itself to have its first
night under the stars but to be there now

for every star that comes: we go away who must
ourselves come back, at last to stay: tears

when we are helpless are our only joy: but
while I was away this morning, Mike, the young

kid who does things for us, cut down the
thrift with his weedeater, those little white

flowers more like weedsize more than likely:
sometimes called cliff rose: also got the grass

out of the front ditch now too wet to mow, slashed:
the dispositional axis is not supreme (how tedious)

and not a fiction (how clever) but plain (greatness
flows through the lowly) and a fact (like as not)

1993

From *Strip*

◇ ◇ ◇

1.

wdn't it be silly to be serious, now:
I mean, the hardheads and the eggheads

are agreed that we are an absurd
irrelevance on this slice of curvature

and that a boulder from the blue
could confirm it: imagine, mathematics

wiped out by a wandering stone, or
Grecian urns not forever fair when

the sun expands: can you imagine
cracking the story off we've built

up so long—the simian ancestries,
the lapses and leaps, the discovery

of life in the burial of grains:
the scratch of pictorial and syllabic

script, millennia of evenings around
the fires: nothing: meaninglessness

our only meaning: our deepest concerns
such as death or love or child-pain

arousing a belly laugh or a witty
dismissal: a bunch of baloney: it's

already starting to feel funny: I
think I may laugh: few of the dead

lie recalled, and they have not
cautioned us: we are rippers and

tearers and proceeders: restraint
stalls us still—we stand hands

empty, lip hung, dumb eyes struck
open: if we can't shove at the

trough, we don't understand: but is
it not careless to become too local

when there are four hundred billion
stars in our galaxy alone: at

least, that's what I heard: also,
that there are billions of such

systems spread about, some older,
some younger than ours: if the

elements are the elements throughout,
I daresay much remains to be learned:

however much we learn, tho, we may
grow daunted by our dismissibility

in so sizable a place: do our gods
penetrate those reaches, or do all

those other places have their godly
nativities: or if the greatest god

is the stillness all the motions add
up to, then we must ineluctably be

included: perhaps a dribble of
what-is is what what-is is: it is

nice to be included, especially from
so minor a pew: please turn, in yr

hymnals, to page "Archie carrying on
again:" he will have it his way

though he has no clue what his way
is: after such participation as

that with the shrill owl in the
spruce at four in the morning with

the snow ended and the moon come
out, how am I sagely to depart from

all being (universe and all—by
that I mean material and immaterial

stuff) without calling out—just a
minute, am I not to know at last

what lies over the hill: over the
ridge there, over the laps of the

ocean, and out beyond the plasmas
of the sun's winds, and way out

where the bang still bubbles in the
longest risings: no, no: I must

get peanut butter and soda crackers
and the right shoe soles (for ice)

and leave something for my son and
leave these lines, poor things, to

you, if you will have them, can they
do you any good, my trade for my

harm in the world: come, let's
celebrate: it will all be over

1997

Baked Alaska

◇ ◇ ◇

I

It will do. It's not
perfect, but it will do
until something better comes along.

It's not perfect.
It stinks. How are we
going to get out of having it
until something comes along, some ride
or other? That will return us
to the nominative case, shipshape and easy.

O but how long are you going to wait
for what you are waiting for, for
whatever is to come? Not
for long, you may be sure.
It may be here already.
Have you checked the mailbox today?

Sure I have, but listen.
I know what comes, comes.
I am prepared
to occupy my share of days,
knowing I can't have all of them. What is, is
coming over here to find you
missing, all or in part. Or you read me
one small item out of the newspaper
as though it would stand for today.

I refuse to open your box of crayons. Oh yes, I know
there may be something new in some combination
of styles, some gift in adding the addled
colors to our pate. But it's just too mush
for me. It isn't that I necessarily
set out on the trail of a new theory
that could liberate us from our shoes as we walked.
It's rather that the apartment comes to an end
in a small, pinched frown of shadow. He walked
through the wood, as a child. He will walk
on somebody's street in the days that come after.
He's noted as a problem child, an ignoramus;
therefore why can you not accept him in
your arms, girdled with silver-and-black
orchids, feed him everyday food?

Who says he likes cuttlebone?
But you get the idea, the idea
is to humor him for what vexations
may hatch from the stone attitude
that follows and clears the head, like a sneeze.
It's cozy to cuddle up to him,
not so much for warmth as that brains
are scarce, and two will have to do.
It takes two to tango,
it is written, and much
in the way of dragon's teeth after that,
and then the ad-hoc population that arises
on stilts, ready to greet or destroy us, it
doesn't matter which, not quite yet, at least.

Then when the spent avenger
turns tail you know it had all to do with
you, that discharge of fortunes
out of firecrackers, like farts. And who's to say
you don't get the one that belongs to you?
But he speaks, always, in terms of perfection,
of what we were going to have
if only he hadn't gotten busy and done something
    about it, yea,

and turned us back into ourselves
with something missing. And as oarsmen
paddle a scull downstream with phenomenal speed,
so he, in his cape, queries:
Is the last one all right? I know
I keep speaking of the last one, but is it all right?
For only after an infinite series
has eluded us does the portrait
of the boy make sense, and then such a triangular one:
he might have been a minaret, or a seagull.
He laid that on the car's radiator
and when you turned around it is gone.

II

Some time later, in Provence,
you waxed enthusiastic about the tail-
piece in a book, gosh how they
don't make them like that in this century, anymore.
They had a fibre then that doesn't exist now.
That's all you can do about it.
Sensing this, in the sopping diaspora, many a tanglefoot
waits, stars bloom at scalloped edges
of no thing, and it begins to
bleed, like a bomb or bordello.
The theme, unscathed,
with nothing to attach it to.

But like I was saying, probably some of us were
    encouraged
by a momentary freshness in the air
that proved attractive, once we had dwelt in
it, and bathed for many years our temples in its essence.
    Listen, memory:
Do this one thing for me
and I'll never ask you again for anything else—
just tell me how it began! What
were the weeds that got caught in the spokes
as it was starting up, the time the brake shaft split,

and what about all the little monsters that were willing to sit
on the top of your tit, or index finger.
How in the end sunshine prevailed—
but what was that welling in between?
Those bubbles
that proceeded from nowhere—surely there must be a
    source?
Because if there isn't it means that we haven't paid
for this ticket, and will be stopped at the exit gate
and sent back on a return journey through plowed fields
to not necessarily the starting place, that house
we can hardly remember, with the plangent
rose-patterned curtains.

And so in turn he who gets locked up is lost,
too, and must watch a boat nudge the pier
outside his window, forever, and for aye,
and the nose, the throat will be stopped
by absolutely correct memories of what did
we think we were doing when it all began happening,
down the lanes, across vales, out into the open city street.

And those it chooses can always say
it's easy, once you learn it, like a language,
and can't be dislodged thereafter.
In all your attractive worldliness, do you consider
the items crossed off the shopping list,
never to breathe again until the day
of bereavement stands open and naked like a woman
on a front porch, and do those you hobnob
with have any say or leverage in the matter?
Surely it feels like a child's feet propel us along

until everyone can explain.
Hell, it's only a ladder: structure
brought us here, and will be here when we're
honeycombs emptied of bees, and can say
That's all there is to say, babe, make it a good one
for me.

III

And when the hectic
light leaches upward into rolls of dark cloud
there will no longer be a contrast between thinking
and daily living. Light will be something even,
if remorseful, then. I say, swivel
your chair around, something cares, not the lamps
    purling
in the dark river, not the hot feet on the grass,
nor the cake emerging from the oven, nor the silver
trumpets on the sand: only a lining
that dictates the separation of this you from this some
    other,
and, in memorializing, drools. And if the hospice
gets over you this will be your magpie, this old hat,
when all is said, and done. No coffee, no rolls—
only a system of values, like the one printed
beside your height as it was measured as you grew
from child to urchin to young adult
and so on, back into the stitched wilderness
of sobs, sighs, songs, bells ringing, a thirst
for whatever could be discerned in the glacier—
tale, or tragedy, or talc—that backlit
these choices before we learned to talk
and so is a presence now, a posture like a chimney
that all men take to work with them
and that all see with our own eyes just
as the door is shutting, O shaft of light, O excellent,
    O irascible.

1993

Myrtle

◊　◊　◊

How funny your name would be
if you could follow it back to where
the first person thought of saying it,
naming himself that, or maybe
some other persons thought of it
and named that person. It would
be like following a river to its source,
which would be impossible. Rivers have no source.
They just automatically appear at a place
where they get wider, and soon a real
river comes along, with fish and debris,
regal as you please, and someone
has already given it a name: St. Benno
(saints are popular for this purpose) or, or
some other name, the name of his
long-lost girlfriend, who comes
at long last to impersonate that river,
on a stage, her voice clanking
like its bed, her clothing of sand
and pasted paper, a piece of real technology,
while all along she is thinking, I can
do what I want to do. But I want to stay here.

1994

The Problem of Anxiety

◇　◇　◇

Fifty years have passed
since I started living in those dark towns
I was telling you about.
Well, not much has changed. I still can't figure out
how to get from the post office to the swings in the park.
Apple trees blossom in the cold, not from conviction,
and my hair is the color of dandelion fuzz.

Suppose this poem were about you—would *you*
put in the things I've carefully left out:
descriptions of pain, and sex, and how shiftily
people behave toward each other? Naw, that's
all in some book it seems. For you
I've saved the descriptions of finger sandwiches,
and the glass eye that stares at me in amazement
from the bronze mantel, and will never be appeased.

1997

It Is Marvellous . . .

◇　◇　◇

It is marvellous to wake up together
At the same minute; marvellous to hear
The rain begin suddenly all over the roof,
To feel the air clear
As if electricity had passed through it
From a black mesh of wires in the sky.
All over the roof the rain hisses,
And below, the light falling of kisses.

An electrical storm is coming or moving away;
It is the prickling air that wakes us up.
If lightning struck the house now, it would run
From the four blue china balls on top
Down the roof and down the rods all around us,
And we imagine dreamily
How the whole house caught in a bird-cage of lightning
Would be quite delightful rather than frightening;

And from the same simplified point of view
Of night and lying flat on one's back
All things might change equally easily,
Since always to warn us there must be these black
Electrical wires dangling. Without surprise
The world might change to something quite different,
As the air changes or the lightning comes without our blinking,
Change as our kisses are changing without our thinking.

1989

The Fire Fetched Down

◊   ◊   ◊

When they knew what he had given them,
This florid colossus with the sunrise in his eyes
And skin the color of perfectly ripened fruit,
Understood what he had done in the name of freedom,
Of self-esteem, their first thought was to give it back,
Who had been happy in their miserable condition,
Had been content each hour to kill or cringe,
Pleased to end their days in the detached mercy
Of stupent sense, the sweet shock that flesh is air to;
When they saw what he intended, this monstrous
Avatar wrapped in conceits of agony, of honor,
Their every instinct (before such brute reflex
Was blunted by the dull weight of the abstract)
Was to spurn the bounty, slay the bearer, to destroy
The visiting light, its unwanted complication.
After all, his differences had not been theirs,
His absurd dispute with the divine, his squabble
About a sacred ox and some celestial secret;
His ambition for their state was nothing they could grasp,
And they wished only to be as they had been, dying
To extinguish the moted mazy rays that floated
Like gleaming locks on his titanic head, to blot out
The subtle moonbeams that shone so as he smiled. . . .
But the fire he brought was beautiful, a jewel
Of countless facets, a spectrum infinitely broad,
An aethereal motion they never tired of looking on;
The flame was gorgeous, and they were human,
And they took that gift, reaching to accept
The ember of ideas, the conflagration of tongues,

And then his name was their names (*Forethought,*
Premonition, how the word had frightened them!),
And his pain became theirs, too,
Chained in the rational abyss and torn
Time and again by cruel and busy claws, raked
By the razor bill of what they could conclude.

1994

Inevitably, She Declined

◊ ◊ ◊

On a bishop's backless chair, inevitably, upright she declined
Watching an empire flicker & die out. Morning, an anodyne
Of undrugged sleep, her attendant files the wedding ring embedded
In her flesh for half a century, an unhinged sapphire unmarrying
A monarch to this life of beautiful bastard sovereignty, unwedding
England's bloated hand. By evening an heirless country waits to bury
A distented queen with hawthorn boughs, bonfires blazing majusculed
Letters in the streets. She will go on watching them, upright & inevitable.
When Elizabeth sat dying, she would not lie down, for fear
She would never rise again, her high neck propped with molecules
Of lace, circling a countenance decked with the small queer
Embellishments of monarchy. In a breathless hour, her virguled
Breath, a speechless pilgrim grateful for a little death, minuscule
Between moments, squall of air reclining, upright bolt, declining vertical.

1992

ANNE CARSON

The Life of Towns

◇ ◇ ◇

Towns are the illusion that things hang together somehow, my pear, your winter.

I am a scholar of towns, let God commend that. To explain what I do is simple enough. A scholar is someone who takes a position. From which position, certain lines become visible. You will at first think I am painting the lines myself; it's not so. I merely know where to stand to see the lines that are there. And the mysterious thing, it seems a very mysterious thing, is how these lines do paint themselves. Before there was any up or down, any bright or dark, any edges or angles or virtue—who was there to ask the questions? Well, let's not get carried away with exegesis. A scholar is someone who knows how to limit oneself to the matter at hand.

Matter which has painted itself within lines constitutes a town. Viewed in this way the world is, as we say, an open book. But what about variant readings? For example, consider the town defined for us by Lao Tzu in the twenty-third chapter of the Tao Te Ching:

> *A man of the way conforms to the way; a man of virtue*
> *conforms to virtue; a man of loss conforms to loss.*
> *He who conforms to the way is gladly accepted by the way;*
> *he who conforms to virtue is gladly accepted by virtue;*
> *he who conforms to loss is gladly accepted by loss.*

This sounds like a town of some importance, where a person could reach beyond himself, or meet himself, as he chose. But another scholar (Kao) takes a different position on the Town of Lao Tzu. "The word translated 'loss' throughout this section does not make much sense," admonishes Kao. "It is possible that it is a graphic error for 'heaven.' " Now, in order for you or I to quit living here and go there—either to the Town of Lao Tzu or to the Town of Kao—we have to get certain details clear, like Kao's tone. Is he impatient or deeply sad or merely droll? The position you take on this may pull you separate from me. Hence, towns. And then, scholars.

I am not being trivial. Your separateness could kill you unless I take it from you as a sickness. What if you get stranded in the town where pears and winter are variants for one another? Can you eat winter? No. Can you live six months inside a frozen pear? No. But there is a place, I know the place, where you will stand and see pear and winter side by side as walls stand by silence. Can you punctuate yourself as silence? You will see the edges cut away from you, back into a world of another kind—back into real emptiness, some would say. Well, we are objects in a wind that stopped, is my view. There are regular towns and irregular towns, there are wounded towns and sober towns and fiercely remembered towns, there are useless but passionate towns that battle on, there are towns where the snow slides from the roofs of the houses with such force that victims are killed, but there are no empty towns (just empty scholars) and there is no regret.

APOSTLE TOWN

After your death.
It was windy every day.
Every day.
Opposed us like a wall.
We went.
Shouting sideways at one another.
Along the road.
It was useless.
The spaces between us.
Got hard.
They are empty spaces.
And yet they are solid.
And black and grievous.
As gaps between the teeth.
Of an old woman.
You knew years ago.
When she was.
Beautiful the nerves pouring around in her like palace fire.

TOWN OF SPRING ONCE AGAIN

"Spring is always like what it used to be."
Said an old Chinese man.
Rain hissed down the windows.
Longings from a great distance.
Reached us.

LEAR TOWN

Clamor the bells falling bells.
Precede silence of bells.
As madness precedes.
Winter as childhood.
Precedes father.
Into the kill-hole.

DESERT TOWN

When the sage came back in.
From the desert.
He propped the disciples up again like sparrows.
On a clothesline.
Some had fallen into despair this puzzled him.
In the desert.
Where he baked his heart.
Were no shadows no up and down to remind him.
How they depended on him a boy died.
In his arms.
It is very expensive he thought.
To come back.
He began to conform.
To the cutting away ways.
Of this world a fire was roaring up.
Inside him his bones by now liquid and he saw.
Ahead of him.
Waiting nothing else.
Waiting itself.

HÖLDERLIN TOWN

You are mad to mourn alone.
With the wells gone dry.
Starlight lying at the bottom.
Like a piece of sound.
You are stranded.
Props hurtle past you.
One last thing you may believe.
Before the lights go out is.
That the mourning is at fault.
Then the sin of wishing to die.
Collapses behind you like a lung.
Night.
The night itself.

A TOWN I HAVE HEARD OF

"In the middle of nowhere."
Where.
Would that be?
Nice and quiet.
A rabbit.
Hopping across.
Nothing.
On the stove.

TOWN OF THE DEATH OF SIN

What is sin?
You asked.
The moon screamed past us.
All at once I saw you.
Just drop sin and go.
Flashing after the moon.
Black as a wind over the forests.

LOVE TOWN

She ran in.
Wet corn.
Yellow braid.
Down her back.

TOWN OF THE SOUND OF A TWIG BREAKING

Their faces I thought were knives.
The way they pointed them at me.
And waited.
A hunter is someone who listens.
So hard to his prey it pulls the weapon.
Out of his hand and impales.
Itself.

TOWN OF THE MAN IN THE MIND AT NIGHT

Twenty-five.
To four blackness no.
Waking thing no voice no wind huge.
Wads of silence stuff.
The air outside the room blackness.
Outside the streets blackness outside.
The world blackness outside blackness I wonder.
As hard as it can.
Press from deep.
In here to far.
Out there farther.
Farthest pressing out.
Where black.
Winds drop from star.
To star where the deep.
Tinkle of the moon grazes.
It knocks.
It.
Off.

The blade.
Of night like a.
Paring if a man.
Falls off the world in the dark.
Because he doesn't.
Know it is there does that mean it.
Is?

TOWN ON THE WAY THROUGH GOD'S WOODS

Tell me.
Have you ever seen woods so.
Deep so.
Every tree a word does your heart stop?
Once I saw a cloud over Bolivia so deep.
Mountains were cowering do you ever?
Look in so quick you see the secret.
Word inside the word?
As in an abandoned railway car.
One winter afternoon I saw.
The word for "God's woods."

PUSHKIN TOWN

When I live I live in the ancient future.
Deep rivers run to it angel pavements are in use.
It has rules.
And love.
And the first rule is.
The love of chance.
Some words of yours are very probably ore there.
Or will be by the time our eyes are ember.

TOWN OF FINDING OUT ABOUT THE LOVE OF GOD

I had made a mistake.
Before this day.
Now my suitcase is ready.
Two hardboiled eggs.
For the journey are stored.
In the places where.
My eyes were.
How could it be otherwise?
Like a current.
Carrying a twig.
The sobbing made me.
Audible to you.

DEATH TOWN

This day.
Whenever I pause.
The noise of the town.

LUCK TOWN

Digging a hole.
To bury his child alive.
So that he could buy food for his aged mother.
One day.
A man struck gold.

MEMORY TOWN

In each one of you I paint.
I find.
A buried site of radioactive material.
You think 8 miles down is enough?
15 miles?
140 miles?

September Town

One fear is that.
The sound of the cicadas.
Out in the blackness zone is going to crush my head.
Flat as a piece of paper some night.
Then I'll be expected.
To go ahead with normal tasks anyway just because.
Your head is crushed flat.
As a piece of paper doesn't mean.
You can get out of going to work.
Mending the screen door hiding.
Your brother from the police.

Entgegenwärtigung Town

I heard you coming after me.
Like a lion through the underbrush.
And I was afraid.
I heard you.
Crashing down over flagpoles.
And I covered my ears.
I felt the walls of the buildings.
Sway once all along the street.
And I crouched low on my heels.
In the middle of the room.
Staring hard.
Then the stitches came open.
You went past.

Wolf Town

Let tigers.
Kill them let bears.
Kill them let tapeworms and roundworms and heartworms.
Kill them let them.
Kill each other let porcupine quills.
Kill them let salmon poisoning.

Kill them let them cut their tongue on a bone and bleed.
To death let them.
Freeze let them.
Starve let them get.
Rickets let them get.
Arthritis let them have.
Epilepsy let them get.
Cataracts and go blind let them.
Run themselves to death let eagles.
Snatch them when young let a windblown seed.
Bury itself in their inner ear destroying equilibrium let them have.
Very good ears let them yes.
Hear a cloud pass.
Overhead.

EMILY TOWN

"Riches in a little room."
Is a phrase that haunts.
Her since the voltage of you.
Left.
Snow or a library.
Or a band of angels.
With a message is.
Not what.
It meant to.
Her.

TOWN OF THE DRAGON VEIN

If you wake up too early listen for it.
A sort of inverted whistling the sound of sound.
Being withdrawn after all where?
Does all the sound in the world.
Come from day after day?
From mountains but.
They have to give it back.
At night just.

As your nightly dreams.
Are taps.
Open reversely.
In.
To.
Time.

SYLVIA TOWN

The burners and the starvers.
Came green April.
Drank their hearts came.
Burning and starving her.
Eyes pulled up like roots.
Lay on the desk.

TOWN OF MY FAREWELL TO YOU

Look what a thousand blue thousand white.
Thousand blue thousand white thousand.
Blue thousand white thousand blue thousand.
White thousand blue wind today and two arms.
Blowing down the road.

TOWN JUST BEFORE THE LIGHTNING FLASH

"Nuances not effective in point form."
Wrote Paul Klee (1923).

TOWN GONE TO SLEEP

There was distant thunder that was its.
Voice there was blood.
Hitting the ground that was.
A Creature's life melting.
In its time there.

Was air forcing.
Out to the edges of that garden as.
Veins of a diver who.
Shoots toward the surface that was a Creature's.
Hope in it just before turning to see.
Ah there we lay.
There the desert.
Of the world immense and sad as hell.
That *was* hell that.
Was a Creature's heart.
Plunged.

TOWN OF BATHSHEBA'S CROSSING

Inside a room in Amsterdam.
Rembrandt painted a drop of life inside.
The drop he painted Rembrandt's stranger.
Dressed as a woman rippling.
With nakedness she has.
A letter in her hand she is.
Traveling.
Out of a thought toward us.
And has not yet.
Arrived even when he.
Paints Rembrandt's stranger.
As Rembrandt he shows.
Him bewildered and tousled.
As if just in.
From journeys.
On tracks and sideroads.

ANNA TOWN

What an anxious existence I led.
And it went on for years it was years.
Before I noticed the life of objects one day.
Anna gazed down at her.
Sword I saw the sword yield up.

To her all that had been accumulated.
Within it all that strange.
World where an apple weighs more.
Than a mountain then.
We set off.
For bitter warfare.
Is dear to us.

TOWN OF THE WRONG QUESTIONS

How.
Walls are built why.
I am in here what.
Pulleys and skin when.
The panels roll back what.
Aching what.
Do they eat—light?

FREUD TOWN

Devil say I am an unlocated.
Window of myself devil.
Say nobody sit.
There nobody light.
The lamp devil.
Say one glimpse of it.
From outside do the trick do.
The trick devil.
Say smell this devil say.
Raw bones devil say the mind.
Is an alien guest I say.
Devil outlived devil in.

Town of the Little Mouthful

Without arrows how?
Do I know if I hit.
The target he said smiling from ear.
To cut.
Through by the bowstring.

Bride Town

Hanging on the daylight black.
As an overcoat with no man in it one cold bright.
Noon the Demander was waiting for me.

Judas Town

Not a late hour not unlit rows.
Not olive trees not locks not heart.
Not moon not dark wood.
Not morsel not I.

1990

My Cousin Muriel

◇   ◇   ◇

From Manhattan, a glittering shambles
of enthrallments and futilities, of leapers
in leotards, scissoring vortices blurred,
this spring evening, by the *punto in aria*
of hybrid pear trees in bloom (no troublesome
fruit to follow) my own eyes are drawn to—
childless spinner of metaphor, in touch
by way of switchboard and satellite, for
the last time ever, with my cousin Muriel:

mother of four, worn down by arthritis,
her kidneys wasting, alone in a hospital
somewhere in California: in that worn voice,
the redhead's sassy timbre eroded from it,
while the unspeakable stirs like a stone,
a strange half-absence and a tone of weakness
(Wordsworth's discharged soldier comes to mind)
as she inquires, fatigued past irony, "How's
your work going?" As for what was hers—

nursing-home steam-table clamor, scummed
soup fat, scrubbed tubers, bones, knives,
viscera, cooking odors lived with till
they live with you, a settlement in the
olfactory tissue—well, it's my function
to imagine scenes, try for connections
as I'm trying now: a grope for words,
the numb, all but immobilized trajectory
to where my cousin, whom I've seen just once

since she went there to live, lies dying:
part of the long-drawn larger movement
that lured the Reverend Charles Wadsworth
to San Francisco, followed in imagination
from the cupola of the shuttered homestead
in Amherst where a childless recluse,
on a spring evening a century ago, A.D.
(so to speak) 1886, would cease to breathe
the air of rural Protestant New England—

an atmosphere and a condition which,
by stages, wagon trains, tent meetings,
the Revival, infused the hinterland
my cousin Muriel and I both hailed from:
a farmhouse childhood, kerosene-lit,
tatting-and-mahogany genteel. "You
were the smart one," she'd later say.
Arrant I no doubt was; as for imagining
scenes it must be she'd forgotten

the melodramas she once improvised above
the dolls' tea table: "For the pity's sake!
How could you get us all in such a fix?
Well, I s'pose we'll just have to make
the best of it"—the whole trajectory of
being female, while I played the dullard,
presaged. She bloomed, knew how to flirt,
acquired admirers. I didn't. In what I now
recall as a last teen-age heart-to-heart,

I'm saying I don't plan on getting married.
"Not ever?" "Not ever"—then, craven, "Oh,
I'd like to be *engaged*." Which is what she
would have been, by then, to Dorwin Voss,
whom I'd been sweet on in fifth grade (last
painless crush before the crash of puberty)—
blue-eyed, black-haired, good-looking Dorwin,
who'd later walk out on her and their kids,
moving on again, part of the larger exodus

from the evangel-haunted prairie hinterland.
Some stayed; the more intemperate of us
headed East—a Village basement, uptown
lunch hours, vertiginous delusions of
autonomy, the bar crowd; waiting for
some well-heeled dullard of a male to
deign to phone, or for a stumbling-
drunk, two-timing spouse's key to turn
the small-hour dark into another fracas—

others for California: the lettuce fields,
Knott's Berry Farm, the studios; palms,
slums, sprinklers, canyon landslides,
fuchsia hedges hung with hummingbirds,
the condominium's kempt squalor: whatever
Charles Wadsworth, out there, foresaw
as consolation for anyone at all—attached,
estranged, or merely marking time—little
is left, these days, these times, to say

when the unspeakable stirs like a stone.
Pulled threads, the shared fabric of a
summer memory: the state-fair campground,
pump water, morning light through tent flaps,
the promenade among the booths: blue-ribbon
zinnias and baby beeves, the cooled marvel
of a cow, life-size, carved out of butter;
a gypsy congeries without a shadow on it
but the domed torpor of the capitol

ballooning, ill at ease, egregious
souvenir of pomp among the cornfields;
Kewpie-doll lowlife along the midway,
the bleachers after dark, where, sick
with mirth, under the wanton stars,
for the ineptitude of clowns, we soared
in arabesques of phosphorus, and saw—
O dread and wonder, O initiating taste
of ecstasy—a man shot from a cannon.

Too young then to know how much we knew
already of experience, how little of
its wider paradigm, enthralled by that
punto in aria of sheer excitement, we who
are neither leaf nor bole—O hybrid
pear tree, cloned fruitless blossomer!—
suspend, uprooted from the hinterland,
this last gray filament across a continent
where the unspeakable stirs like a stone.

1990

DOUGLAS CRASE

True Solar Holiday

◇ ◇ ◇

Out of the whim of data,
Out of binary contests driven and stored,
By the law of large numbers and subject to that law
Which in time will correct us like an event,
And from bounce and toss of things that aren't even things,
I've determined the trend I call "you" and know you are real,
Your unwillingness to appear
In all but the least likely worlds, as in this world
Here. In spite of excursions, despite my expenditures
Ever more anxiously matrixed, ever baroque,
I can prove we have met and I've proved we can do it again
By each error I make where otherwise one couldn't be
Because only an actual randomness
Never admits a mistake. It's for your sake,
Then (*though the stars get lost from the bottle,*
Though the bottle unwind), if I linger around in the wrong
Ringing up details, pixel by high bit by bit,
In hopes of you not as integer but at least as the sum
Of all my near misses, divisible,
Once there is time, to an average that poses you perfectly
Like a surprise, unaccidentally credible
Perfectly like a surprise. Am I really too patient
When this is the only program from which you derive?
Not if you knew how beautiful you will be,
How important it is your discovery dawn on me,
How as long as I keep my attention trained
Then finally the days
Will bow every morning in your direction

As they do to the sun that hosannas upon that horizon
Of which I am witness and not the one farther on:
Set to let me elect you as if there were no other choice,
Choice made like temperature, trend I can actually feel.

1989

litany

◊ ◊ ◊

Tom, will you let me love you in your restaurant?
i will let you make me a sandwich of your invention and i will
    eat it and call
it a carolyn sandwich. then you will kiss my lips and taste the
    mayonnaise and
that is how you shall love me in my restaurant

Tom, will you come to my empty beige apartment and help me
    set up my daybed?
yes, and i will put the screws in loosely so that when we move
    on it, later,
it will rock like a cradle and then you will know you are my
    baby

Tom, I am sitting on my dirt bike on the deck. Will you come
    out from the kitchen
and watch the people with me?
yes, and then we will race to your bedroom. i will win and we
    will tangle up
on your comforter while the sweat rains from our stomachs and
    foreheads

Tom, the stars are sitting in tonight like gumball gems in a little
    girl's
jewelry box. Later can we walk to the duck pond?
yes, and we can even go the long way past the jungle gym. i
    will push you on
the swing, but promise me you'll hold tight. if you fall i might
    disappear

Tom, can we make a baby together? I want to be a big pregnant
        woman with a
loved face and give you a squalling red daughter.
no, but i will come inside you and you will be my daughter

Tom, will you stay the night with me and sleep so close that we
        are one person?
no, but i will lay down on your sheets and taste you. there will
        be feathers
of you on my tongue and then i will never forget you

Tom, when we are in line at the convenience store can I put my
        hands in your
back pockets and my lips and nose in your baseball shirt and feel
        the crook
of your shoulder blade?
no, but later you can lay against me and almost touch me and
        when i go i will
leave my shirt for you to sleep in so that always at night you
        will be pressed
up against the thought of me

Tom, if I weep and want to wait until you need me will you
        promise that someday
you will need me?
no, but i will sit in silence while you rage, you can knock the
        chairs down
any mountain. i will always be the same and you will always
        wait

Tom, will you climb on top of the dumpster and steal the sun
        for me? It's just
hanging there and I want it.
no, it will burn my fingers. no one can have the sun: it's on loan
        from god.
but i will draw a picture of it and send it to you from richmond
        and then you
can smooth out the paper and you will have a piece of me as
        well as the sun

Tom, it's so hot here, and I think I'm being born. Will you
    come back from
Richmond and baptise me with sex and cool water?
i will come back from richmond. i will smooth the damp spiky
    hairs from the
back of your wet neck and then i will lick the salt off it. then i
    will leave

Tom, Richmond is so far away. How will I know how you love
    me?
i have left you. that is how you will know

1993

THOMAS M. DISCH

The Cardinal Detoxes:
A Play in One Act

◇   ◇   ◇

We are a sinful church. We are naked. Our anger, our pain,
our anguish, our shame, are clear to the whole world.
> —The Most Reverend Alphonsus L. Penney,
> D.D., Archbishop of St. John's,
> Newfoundland, in his statement of
> resignation July 18, 1990

The scene is a monastically bare cell in a Catholic detox center run by the Broth-
ers of the Most Holy Blood. There is a bed, a small night table beside it, a desk and
chair, and a prie-dieu. On the wall above the bed, a crucifix, flanked by pictures of
the Sacred Heart and Mater Dolorosa.

The Cardinal and a Brother of the Most Holy Blood are discovered as the lights come
up. The Cardinal in a state of nerves; the Brother stands by the door, attentive but
inexpressive, except at rare moments when the Cardinal has said something par-
ticularly offensive to conventional piety or pious convention. After any action he has
been called to perform, the Brother returns to his post of duty before the door.

THE CARDINAL:

> God. For the most part I do without
> Him. Don't we all. He leaves us no choice,
> Having left us, bereft us, at some point
> In pre-history—say, at the moment Christ

Particularly complained of. Was that before
Or after the gall was proffered him? Say what?
Oh, yes, I know, it is your vow to say
Nothing at all. The merest sponge for all
My vinegar. And speaking of vinegar . . . ?

*The Brother nods, leaves the room a moment and returns with a bottle of white
wine and a wineglass on a tray. He places this on the night table, fills the glass
half-full, and gives it to the Cardinal, who takes a sip and makes a sour face.*

THE CARDINAL:

Where do you find this wine? The tears of Christ,
Indeed! He would have died before he drank
This piss. But piss is sacred, too, if it
Is His, and I consume it reverently,
Having—had you supposed?—whispered the words,
The abracadabra, of consecration.
What priest, what Catholic, does not imagine
Every drop as somehow holy? Dregs
Of the wedding feast, lees of the Last Supper: this
Is my blood—
                    [*sips*]
                              —or soon enough will be.
It is kind of the Abbot to accommodate
My evening need to transubstantiate.
He doubtless sees it as the loosener of
My tongue. Is the recorder on? I know
I'm being bugged, but that's all one to me.
So long as you employ corkscrews and not
Thumbscrews, I will unfold my heresies
With all due pomp, a true heresiarch.
But the Abbot ought to know I'm not
The sort of heretic the Church is prone
To burn. In matters that concern the Faith
I am as orthodox as any pope.
The Trinity, the Virgin Birth, the fall
Of Adam and the fault of Eve,
The fleshy Resurrection of the Dead,

Whatever's set down in the Creed, or been
Decreed by any Vicar of the Church—
In all this I have Faith. What I believe's
Another thing. Belief's involuntary;
Faith's an act of will, more powerful
As it demands credence in what we can't
Believe. Were I the Pope, I'd elevate
The Shroud of Turin to an article
Of Faith; I would declare the round world flat
And build basilicas on Ararat.
So much for Faith; in morals, as well, I am
Ultra-montane. Priestly celibacy?
I agree. No contraception but
By abstinence. No sodomy. You look
Askance? Surely we must seal the back door,
If we lock up the front. Carnality will out,
No doubt, even among our holy few,
But all in cloistered silence, stealthily.
AIDS, alas, has made it hard to keep
Our sepulchres properly spotless. Even
Among you Brothers of the Holy Blood,
I hear, there have been actuarial
Anomalies. One abbot dead, another
Ailing, or so it's said. Well, there have been
Plagues before, and there'll be plagues again.
Please don't suppose I'm being holier
Than thou and thine. Would I be serving time
In detox if I hadn't erred as well?

He sits down on the bed and looks to the Brother for a glance of permission, then pours another glass of wine.

THE CARDINAL:

I *do* repent me of the woman's death:
Mother of four and pregnant with a fifth;
A Catholic to boot. Had I had doubts
Of God's ambition as a dramatist,
They'd be resolved with this: CARDINAL FLYNN,

93

INTOXICATED, REAR-ENDS PREGNANT MOM—

They're always "Moms" in newspapers—a Mom,
What's more, who was my own parishioner.
It is deplorable, and I deplore it.
Do I, as well, blame God? Who iced the road
And sent her Chevy somersaulting? No.
I doubt that God's as meddlesome as that.
Newton's laws of motion did the job
Without His intervention. God, if He's
Not dead, is deaf, indifferent, or asleep.
For me, for most of us, God is a sham—
An ancient Poetry: I Am That I Am,
As who is not? I'm what I am, too—a priest,
A whited sepulchre, a drunken beast—
According to the *Times-Despatch* and *Sun*—
A criminal, though yet, with any luck,
The diocese will pay whatever price
The prosecution asks to drop the charge.
It wouldn't do, would it, to have My Grace
Be sent away, however many drinks
I may have had. Archbishops are not put
In jail. I wonder what they *will* have done
With me. You wouldn't know? Or wouldn't say.
Yours is the vow *I* ought to take—Silence!
But silence never was my forte. My forte
Is speech, and I will use it if I must.
I trust the tape recorder is still on?
Then this is what I mean to do, the same
As any minor mafioso caught
And facing time: I'll sing. I'll tell those things
We Cardinals and Archbishops say
Among ourselves, the secret wisdom of
The Church, its policies and stratagems,
Beginning with the obvious. Just guess.

He pours more wine, savoring the Brother's baleful looks.

THE CARDINAL:

Abortion, naturally. It is the cause
To knit our ever fewer faithful few
By giving them an enemy to fight,
Those murderous liberal bitches who refuse
To be a Mom. It is the wolf who herds
The sheep; the shepherd but assists, and sheep
Know this. Wolfless, they'll stray beyond the reach
Of hook and crook. Just look at the mess we're in.
No one attends Mass but the senile poor.
Detroit has simply given up the ghost
And closed its churches as the surest way
To stanch the flow of cash. Even where there
Is money, Faith's extinct—and Brotherhood,
The kind that's formed by cotes and ghetto walls.
Consider Poland, Northern Ireland,
Or *my* Archdiocese before this age
Of wishy-washy tolerance, when we
Were wops and micks and spics and krauts and built
The churches that stand empty now. The WASP
Majority was our oppressor then,
But now? Who hates us? Whom have we to fear?
Jews served the purpose for a while, and still
One meets the odd parishioner who feels
A pang of loss for Father Coughlin. Glemp,
In Poland, still baits Jews—the five or six
Surviving there. But after Auschwitz, how
Shall Holy Mother Church pursue that course?
The Jews, in any case, are not our problem:
Our problem's women. Ah-ha! Your eyes agree.
It's something every cleric understands.
It's what we mean by harping on the theme
Of family values and the sanctity
Of life, i.e., a way of bringing up
Men to be men, women to be slaves,
And priests to be their overseers. Think
Of Italy. For centuries the Church
Beneficently engineered the codes
Of gender so each Giacomo would have

His Jill, his family fiefdom, and his fill
Of sex, or if not quite his fill, his bare
Sufficiency, while she, the Mom, kept dumb
Or mumbled rosaries. Beyond the pale
Of family, the convent and the brothel
Took up the overflow of those who balked
At their Madonnament. The benefit
To all men of sufficient strength of mind
Should be self-evident; the rest could join
The Church, and practice harsh austerities
Expressive of a holy impotence,
Or else become the system's managers.
Of course, it's not just Italy of which
I speak: it's you and me. It's Fatherhood
In all the Mother Church's Fatherlands.
And it's *women* who've rebelled, thrown off
The yoke of meek subservience becoming
Handmaids of the Lord Their Spouse, who would address
The Angel of Annunciation: "No,
I've better things to do just now than bear
A child. When I am ready, *I'll* tell you."
Women demand equality, and no one
Has been able to gainsay them. They have
The vote, the pill, the freedom of the street.
Now they'd be priests! They do not understand
When they have won their last demand, there'll be
No Church but just Detroit writ large. For why
Should men go on pretending they believe
In all our Bulls, if somehow they don't stand
To benefit? They will walk out the door.
Not all of them and all at once, of course.
Some unisex parents for a while will rear
Mini-families of one or two,
As now the wealthier Protestants do.
What's to be done? Redraw the line again?
Admit the ladies and admit the Church
Was wrong? Declare the Fathers of the Church
This age's Ptolemys, ruled out-of-date
By schoolmarm Galileos? Rather turn
Our churches into mosques! Islam, at least

Holds firm in keeping women in their place.
Within her chadhor, every Moslem Mom's
A nun, while *our* nuns change their habits for
A warrior garb of pants and pantyhose.
What we must do, what we have long discussed,
Is to relight the Inquisition's torch
For the instruction and delight of those
Who still can be relied on to attend
Autos-da-fé. Burn down the clinics of
Planned Parenthood. Make foetuscide a crime
Punishable, like homicide, by death,
And if the civil power's craven courts
Should balk, if legislation's voted down
Or overthrown, then we must urge our flocks
To act upon their own. One simple, just
Expedient would be to institute
Homes where reluctant mothers might be brought
To term; initially, for Catholic girls
Whose parents can coerce such penitence,
As once defiant daughters might be placed
In convents; then, that precedent secure,
Encourage a clandestine brotherhood
To save those foetuses whose mothers may
Reject more mild persuasion. Civil crimes
Are justified—read any casuist—
When one is acting in a Higher Cause.
Not that such deeds would make states change their laws:
We would be martyred, made pariahs, sent
To jail—but what a triumph for the rights
Of foetuses, and what a way to weed
The Church's fields of tares. You think I jest:
So did the bishops gathered in St. Louis,
Though after the formalities, Malone
Of Boston and Passaic's Muggerone
Took me aside and asked to know if such
A league of fetal-rights revengers had
Been formed, assuring me that when it was,
They could supply recruits. Then Muggerone
Bewailed the evils of the media,
Who had exposed his till-then secret charity

In bailing out three youths who'd raped and stabbed
A cyclist in the park. The Bishop swears
He acted only in the interest
Of inter-racial harmony, a cause
That also prompted him to champion
St. Athanasius' Orphanage
For Children Born with AIDS, a charity
That has been universally acclaimed
Except by Bishop Muggerone's *bête noir,*
The *Jersey Star,* which claims the charges paid
To the contracting firm of Muggerone
And Sons for laying the foundation of
The orphanage would have sufficed to build
A concrete pyramid upon the site.
It seems the Bishop's outlays for cement
Exceed the county's. He was furious.
"The media!" he roared—and you could see
His chins all in a tremble—"The media
Is killing us. It's Jews is what it is.
Jews hate Italians and control the news.
If you're Italian then you're in the mob.
There is no mob, the mob's a media myth!"
And all the while he fulminates and rants,
His limousine is waiting in the lot,
His chauffeur sinister as some Ton-ton
Macoute. What is so wonderful about
The Bishop is the man's unswerving and
Unnerving righteousness, his perfect Faith
That his shit and the shit of all his kin
Must smell like roses. God, what strength of mind!
Can you suppose that like aggressiveness
Would not more suit the present circumstance
Than to require this pusillanimity
Of me, those mewling statements to the press,
My sanctuary in a drying tank:
As well embroider double A's on alb,
Dalmatic, chasuble, and pallium.
Does Rome believe such sops will satisfy
The public's appetite for blood? I face

A statutory minimum of ten!
And what is being done? I must put by
My crozier, to preach from my own pulpit,
Surrender the archdiocese accounts,
As though I were another Muggerone,
Fold my hands and wait for sentencing!
I may not even speak in privacy
With my attorneys, but the legate's spy
Is crouching in the corner taking notes.
You keep me virtually a prisoner:
No telephone, no visitors, no mail
That doesn't bear the Abbot's imprimatur.
And then you counsel me to fast and pray!
Well, I'll be damned if I'll be put away
As docilely as that. I'll bleat before
I bleed. You think *my* case is scandalous?
Wait till the papers get on yours, my boys!
I trust this is a live broadcast, and that
The Abbot's at his intercom—with whom
Else? Let me guess: Monsignor Mallachy;
My Deputy-Archbishop Sneed; and Rome's
Own damage control team, nameless to me.
If I'm not addressing empty air,
And if you'd like to hear the aria
Through to the end, I would appreciate
A dollop of some better lubricant.
I wait Your Graces' pleasure, and my own.

He finishes the last of the wine in the bottle on the tray, then goes to the prie-dieu, kneels, and folds his hands in prayer. The Brother regards him balefully; the Cardinal lowers his eyes. The Brother cocks his head, and presses his hand to his cowl, as though better to listen to earphones. With a look of disgruntlement, he nods and takes the tray with bottle and glass from the room.

Almost as soon as the Brother is out the door, the Cardinal gets the hiccoughs. He goes through various contortions trying to stop hiccoughing, sucking in his gut, holding his breath. He still has the hiccoughs when the Brother returns with a new bottle. The hiccoughs continue for a while even after his first careful sip of wine—each one being indicated by an asterisk within parentheses in the text he speaks: (*).

THE CARDINAL:

Hiccoughs always make me (⋆) think of Gene
Pacelli, Pius Twelfth, who died of them
And now is offered as a candidate
For sainthood. A saint who can't stop (⋆) hiccoughing!
As well a holy arsonist, a saint
With clap, a blessed ex(⋆)ecutioner.
The present Abbot's predecessor felt
A special reverence for his (⋆) witheredness,
I understand, and entertained the hope
Of a mir(⋆)aculous remission. Yes?
It must be either Pius has no pull
With God, or sodomites can't win (⋆) his ear.
Imagine if his prayer'd been answered and
Instead of (⋆) what it is, a jail for drunks
In Roman collars, the Abbey here became
The (⋆) Lourdes of AIDS-infected clergymen.
I see them now, coming to hang ex (⋆) votos
At Pius's shrine. The statue's right hand holds
A model of a concentration camp;
The left, a water glass symbolic of
His (⋆) sufferings.

*In the course of these blasphemies against Pius XII, the Brother has approached
the Cardinal to refill his quickly emptying glass. His indignation finally is too
much for him, and he slaps the Cardinal across the face, knocking off his glasses.
Immediately, remorseful, he is on his knees to retrieve the glasses and return them
to the Cardinal, who after his initial shock seems pleased to have made a dent in
the Brother's composure.*

THE CARDINAL:

I think I touched a nerve.
And you did, too: I've stopped the hiccoughing.
I wonder if you might have saved the Pope,
If you'd been there in 1958?
Now don't explode again: keep beating me,
I may seize up, or modify my tune

To something maddeningly bland, as: jazz,
And its potential for the liturgy,
Or else a homily on nuclear arms
And how the bishops must speak up for peace.
Oh, I have bromides in reserve that could
Sedate entire senates and have done so.
It's one of a bishop's most important jobs
To demonstrate to those who wield real power
The Church's ineffectuality
In matters of much consequence. We scold
Bad boys if they make noise, but otherwise
We turn our eyes away. What if the Church
Were to attack the mafia, instead
Of sub-contracting with it, snuggling up
On St. Columbus Day, and saying Mass
At mobsters' funerals? You know as well
As I, the mafia would attack right back
As ruthlessly as any sovereign state.
Look at the drug lords of Colombia,
Where crime and law at last officially
Are one, the shotgun wedding of all time.
Do you think those drug lords don't intend
To decorate their polity with priests?
Their haciendas have not only taps
Of solid gold, but chapels, too, wherein
The Virgin Mother is particularly
Venerated, and with perfect piety.
For in all things relating to the heart
Criminals, poets, madmen, and lovers
Are more in touch with what they feel than we
Whose lives are ruled by prudence. I have been
Assured by Muggerone that Domenic,
His brother, is as staunchly orthodox
As Ratzinger in Rome—the same "Fat Nick"
Who holds the strings to half the rackets on
The Jersey docks. A scandal? Not at all.
Or not according to His Eminence,
Who takes a high, Dantean view of sin.
As, in the *Inferno,* lustful lovers
Are tumble-dried forever in gusts of flame,

Which *are* the lusts that sucked them down to hell,
So Muggerone insists that every crime
Is its own punishment, and prisons are
Superfluous, especially for the rich,
Whose very riches are more punitive,
In a Dantean sense, than time served in
The cloister of a penitentiary.
A lovely theory, is it not, because
Perfectly self-contained: whatever is
Is right, even if it's wrong. Much more than I,
The Bishop's of a sanguine temperament,
Disposed to find in any seeming ill
The silvery linings of Our Savior's will.
In AIDS he sees a triple blessing: First,
As a plague selective of those most accurst;
And then in that it affords a lingering death,
Time for a true repentance to take root,
And for a good confession at the end;
And lastly, he rejoices in its horror,
Betokening the horror of lust itself,
Which violates the temple of the flesh
And now is seen to do so visibly
For the enlightenment of all who might
Be tempted to the sin of sodomy.
The bishop is no less inventive in
Finding a moral advantage in the plague,
So rampant in his own community,
Of drugs. Not only alcohol.

The Cardinal holds out his cup and as the Brother fills it, continues speaking.

THE CARDINAL:

                         We all,
Who celebrate the Mass, find comfort in
The wine that is our Savior's blood. But crack,
As well. In terms of moral theology,
Drugs are a bit of a conundrum—Cheers!—
Since nowhere in the older Tablets of

The Law are drugs, as such, proscribed. Indeed,
Good Catholics imbibed with not a twinge
Of guilt in Prohibition days, and what
Is alcohol if not a drug? This bottle's
Better, by the by. My compliments
To the cellarer. So, where were we?
Oh, yes: is heroin or ecstasy
Or crack *essentially* more wrong than, say,
A bottle of Chardonnay? Not logically:
It is the use to which it's put. And that,
Among the younger felons of our age
Is to release a murderous rage, and rage
Is anger heightened exponentially,
And anger is, like lust, a deadly sin,
Whose deadliness the plague of AIDS reveals.
This can't be the official view of AIDS,
Of course; it wouldn't play well in the press.
Sufficient that we interdict the use
Of prophylactics; sin and nature can
Be counted on to do the rest. The Church
In this is like those foresters who let
A fire sweep unchecked through timberlands,
Then, when the ashes cool, move in to sow
The seedlings they have kept in readiness.
The Church's view is long as His who formed
The rivers, canyons, reefs, and limestone cliffs,
Taught bees, by trial and error, to mold their nests
In tidy hexagons, and teaches man,
As patiently, to follow Natural Law.
I've read somewhere there are historians
Who call the new age dawning on us now
Post-History, a pregnant phrase, and one
Suggestive of that Thousand Years of Peace
St. John foresaw in his Apocalypse.
If this is so, the Church must reassert
Its claim, based on its own long stability,
To be the stabilizer of the new
Homeostatic state, the *Pax vobiscum*
At the end of time. Oh my, this wine
Is mellower than the first. I hope I may

Interpret it as tender of a more
Merciful, accommodating view
Toward the disposition of my case.
The laurels of authorship as little tempt
Me as the palm of martyrdom, but if
I am thrown to the wolves and made to serve
That statutory minimum, I will
Write such a book the Vatican will wish
I'd never sat at her consistories,
Had not been privy to the audits of
The Banco Ambrosiano, nor been sent
On secret missions to the President.
Oh, I have tales to tell, and they exist
Not only in my mortal memory
But in a still unpolished form in vaults
To which my legal counsel has the key—
In the event of my untimely death
They will be published in their present form,
And I assure you, there'll be such a storm
As has not rocked the Church's holy boat
Since presses multiplied what Luther wrote
Like basketfuls of poisoned loaves and fish.
Such cannot be the Hierarchy's wish.
These are my terms: I must retain my See,
My freedom and my Cardinality.
As to the means, ask Bishop Muggerone
What judges currently are selling for.
Now, if you please, I'd like to use a phone.

*The Cardinal comes to stand directly in front of the Brother, who moves away
from the door. The Cardinal tries the door and finds it locked. He stands for a
while, resting his forehead against the locked door, defeated—and unaware that
the Brother, after receiving another message through his earphones, employs this
moment of inattention to introduce poison into the opened bottle of wine.*

THE CARDINAL:

I see. It is a kind of miracle
When those who have been blind are made to see.
Attorneys can be bought for half the cost
Of the judiciary. Muggerone
Would have known that. My aide-memoire
Can't help me now, if it is where I think.
            (faces round, smiling)
Well, then, let me drown myself in drink.

*The Brother pours a full glass of the poisoned wine, which the Cardinal accepts after
a moment of hesitation. As at his first taste of the earlier bottle, he makes a sour face.*

THE CARDINAL:

Between the first glass and this next, the wine
Would seem to have turned sour. Would you agree?
Ah, I forget—you're sworn to abstinence.
My tongue should have been wise as yours. And mute.

*He tosses back all the wine in the glass and holds it out to be refilled. The last of
the wine is poured in the glass.*

THE CARDINAL:

A toast: to my successful autopsy
And to the holy and redeeming blood
Of Christ. May it provide the evidence
To hang the lot of you! In youth I prayed
I might become a martyr for the Faith.
God has too long a memory, too cruel
A wit—which makes Him, come to think of it,
A God that I deserve, and vice versa.

*He flinches with the first effect of the poison. The Brother helps him to sit on the
edge of the bed. He begins, again, to hiccough, and makes a desperate effort to stop.*

THE CARDINAL:

Water, damn you! Get me a glass of (*)

The Brother takes the wineglass, goes to the door, unlocks it, leaves the room, and returns with the glass full of water. The Cardinal, who is doubled with cramps, and hiccoughing, closes his eyes, holds his breath, growing red in the face and takes twenty sips of water. To no avail. The hiccoughing persists. The Cardinal smashes the glass on the floor. He pulls himself to his feet by clawing at the Brother's habit.

THE CARDINAL:

Cure me! You did before, you (*) must again:
I will not die like that damned (*) wop!

The Brother strikes him across the face, knocking off his glasses, but the blow has no effect against the hiccoughs.

THE CARDINAL:

Again!

The Brother uses all his force. The Cardinal falls back across the bed. His face is bloody. His hiccoughs are gone. He is dead. The Brother kneels at the foot of the bed and makes the sign of the cross.

Curtain

1994

Terminal Laughs

◇　◇　◇

Thirty years ago the young Corso in his cups
—*my* cups, in fact, my booze, too, on which, a gulp
away from getting smashed, he was loading up.
First, tagging along, he'd crashed the party,
then was everywhere making his presence felt,
depositing impartially—on rug, on couch,
on the proffered hand and the affable lap—
steaming little signatures of self.
Introduced to me, his next-to-unknown
and near-anonymous host, Gregory exclaimed,
" 'Irving Feldman?' 'Irving *Feldman*?' '*Oiving* Feldman?'
—what kind of name is that for a poet?"
He probably intended well: you know
—Touring Star Instructs Benighted Yokel In
the finer perks of fame, its *droit de seigneur:*
since one never knows who'll get the last laugh,
Maestro will make sure he grabs the first sneer.
Caught redhanded being *myself,* naked in quotes,
I contemplated the awfulness of my name
—undistinguished, uneuphonious, a joke.
What vocal apparatus would not collapse in
a fatal fibrillation of runaway yuks,
intoning those syllables with suitable awe?
Well, then, spare the world apocalypse by laughter
—just shut up, Irving, shut down, back off!
Oh, but now " 'Gregorio Nunzio Corso!' "
he tarantara-ed, nose loftily rising to
this high occasion, as if summoned upward by
the fanfaronade of its fantastic fanfare,

"now *that,* Oiving, is a name for a poet!"
Second paeon, dactyl, dactyl catalectic
—his name itself, alone, had heft and breath
enough to launch and swell a mighty fine line.
No way to know *this* poet from his poem!
—who, an hour later, crossed one line too many.
Ralph (redfaced, Anglophile), taking his measure,
tapped out deeDUM, the old iambic one-TWO,
and did a number on Gregory's nose.

It took a day or so, but finally,
gestating the guy's manners, mien, mug
while licking at my wounds, my "staircase wit,"
laggard though it was and lost in transit usually,
gagged up a furball part blood, mostly spit:
"As the poet said, Gregory, What is *in*
a name? By any other you'd be as Coarso."
The party, fortunately, had long been over,
and, bolstered by two tenderhearted ladies
covering his flanks as he retreated, while
his nose autographed in red a borrowed hanky,
the poet, faring forward, had stumbled downstairs
—to pipe his old tune in pastures not greener,
perhaps, but, for sure, far far grassier.

Skip thirty years. An eye's blink. The interim?
Some books. Some other books. Fade swiftly to:
Another party now (my son's). Another coast.
Same hubbub. Each newcomer turns the volume up.
Whom the gods would mock they first make famous.
Enter Thad. Young actor here in Hollywood,
dying for parts, money, acclaim, the glamour and
groveling and intoxication due to fame,
to be something more, but not necessarily
much more, than "just another pretty face."
He spots me there, singled out from the crowd
by the sudden celebrity that follows me
around, or maybe is leading me on:
this year's MacLaurels penciled in on my brow.
"Hey, Irving Feldman," he shouts across the tumult

of everyone madly talking all at once,
"you are a goddamn star of poetry!"
Has he ever read a word I wrote?
Still, I glow for a moment in his glee.
But somewhere behind my back I sort of hear
how Gregory, our Chatterton, our wingèd boy,
sloshed out of his cups now and into his saucer,
stubblebearded, his underwear stained with pee,
his nose no straighter for being out of joints
though longer perhaps by a thousand lines,
half toothless, and slowed to a sub-pubcrawl
—just the type, immortality's mortal bouncer,
to i.d. the gaggle at Parnassus Gate,—
I seem to hear how, guarding the lowest stair,
he mutters in his despondency (*his*, truly,
having kept his lost promise all these years),
" 'Irving Feldman,' huh? Just another pretty name."

1995

The Printer's Error

◇ ◇ ◇

Fellow compositors
and pressworkers!

I, Chief Printer
Frank Steinman,
having worked fifty-seven
years at my trade,
and served for five years
as president
of the Holliston
Printers' Council,
being of sound mind
though near death,
leave this testimonial
concerning the nature
of printers' errors.

First: I hold that
all books and all
printed matter have
errors, obvious or no,
and that these are
their most significant moments,
not to be tampered with
by the vanity and folly
of ignorant, academic
textual editors.
Second: I hold that there are
three types of errors, in ascending

order of importance:
One: chance errors
of the printer's trembling hand
not to be corrected incautiously
by foolish scholars
and other such rabble
because trembling is part
of divine creation itself.
Two: silent, cool sabotage
by the printer,
the manual laborer
whose protests
have at times taken this
historical form,
covert interferences
not to be corrected
censoriously by the hand
of the second and far
more ignorant saboteur,
the textual editor.
Three: errors
from the touch of God,
divine and often
obscure corrections
of whole books by
nearly unnoticed changes
of single letters
sometimes meaningful but
about which the less said
by preemptive commentary
the better.
Third: I hold that all three
sorts of error,
errors by chance,
errors by workers' protest,
and errors by
God's work,
are in practice the
same and indistinguishable.

Therefore I,
Frank Steinman,
typographer
for thirty-seven years,
and cooperative Master
of the Holliston Guild
eight years,
being of sound mind and body
though near death
urge the abolition
of all editorial work
whatsoever
and manumission
from all textual editing
to leave what was
as it was, and
as it became,
except insofar as editing
is itself an error, and

therefore also divine.

1995

Powers of Congress

◇ ◇ ◇

How the lightstruck trees change sun
to flamepaths: veins, sap, stem, all
on brief loan, set to give all
their spooled, coded heat to stoves called
Resolute: wet steel diecast
by heat themselves. Tree, beast, bug—
the worldclass bit parts in this
world—flit and skid through it; the
powers of congress tax, spend, law
what lives to pure crisp form
then break forms' lock, stock, and hold
on flesh. All night couples pledge
to stay flux, the hit-run stuff
of cracked homes. Men trim their quick
lawns each weekend, trailing power
mowers. Heartslaves, you've seen them: wives
with flexed hair, hitched to bored kids,
twiddling in good living rooms,
their twin beds slept in, changed, made.

1989

ALLEN GINSBERG

Salutations to Fernando Pessoa

◇ ◇ ◇

Everytime I read Pessoa I think
I'm better than he is I do the same thing
more extravagantly—he's only from Portugal,
I'm American greatest Country in the world
right now End of XX Century tho Portugal
had a big empire in the 15th century never mind
now shrunk to a Corner of Iberian peninsula
whereas New York take New York for instance
tho Mexico City's bigger N.Y.'s richer think of Empire State
Building not long ago world empire's biggest skyscraper—
be that as't may I've experienced 61 years' XX Century
Pessoa walked down Rua do Ouro only till 1936
He entered Whitman so I enter Pessoa no
matter what they say besides dead he wouldn't object.

What way'm I better than Pessoa?
Known on 4 Continents I have 25 English books he only 3
his mostly Portuguese, but that's not his fault—
U.S.A.'s a bigger Country
merely 2 Trillion in debt a passing freakout,
Reagan's dirty work an American Century aberration
unrepresenting our Nation Whitman sang in Epic manner
tho worried about in Democratic Vistas
As a Buddhist not proud my superiority to Pessoa
I'm humble Pessoa was nuts big difference,
tho apparently gay—same as Socrates,
consider Michelangelo DaVinci Shakespeare
inestimable comrado Walt
True I was tainted Pinko at an early age a mere trifle

Science itself destroys ozone layers this era antiStalinists
poison entire earth with radioactive anticommunism
Maybe I lied somewhat
rarely in verse, only protecting others' reputations
Frankly too Candid about my mother tho meant well
Did Pessoa mention his mother? she's interesting,
powerful to birth sextuplets
Alberto Cairo Alvaro de Campos Ricardo Reis Bernardo Soares
      & Alexander Search simultaneously
with Fernando Pessoa himself a classic sexophrenic
Confusing personae not so popular
outside Portugal's tiny kingdom (till recently a secondrate police state)
Let me get to the point er I forget what it was
but certainly enjoy making comparisons between this Ginsberg
      & Pessoa
people talk about in Iberia hardly any books in English
presently the world's major diplomatic language extended throughout
      China.
Besides he was a shrimp, himself admits in interminable "Salutations
      to Walt Whitman"
Whereas 5′ 7½″ height
somewhat above world average, no immodesty,
I'm speaking seriously about me & Pessoa.
Anyway he never influenced me, never read Pessoa
before I wrote my celebrated "Howl" already translated into 24
      languages,
not to this day's Pessoa influence an anxiety
Midnight April 12 88 merely glancing his book
certainly influences me in passing, only reasonable
but reading a page in translation hardly proves "Influence."
Turning to Pessoa, what'd he write about? Whitman,
(Lisbon, the sea etc.) method peculiarly longwinded,
diarrhea mouth some people say—Pessoa Schmessoa.

1995

LOUISE GLÜCK

Celestial Music

◊ ◊ ◊

I have a friend who still believes in heaven.
Not a stupid person, yet with all she knows, she literally talks
    to god,
she thinks someone listens in heaven.
On earth, she's unusually competent.
Brave, too, able to face unpleasantness.

We found a caterpillar dying in the dirt, greedy ants crawling
    over it.
I'm always moved by weakness, by disaster, always eager to
    oppose vitality.
But timid, also, quick to shut my eyes.
Whereas my friend was able to watch, to let events play out
according to nature. For my sake, she intervened,
brushing a few ants off the torn thing, and set it down
    across the road.

My friend says I shut my eyes to god, that nothing else
    explains
my aversion to reality. She says I'm like the child who buries
    her head in the pillow
so as not to see, the child who tells herself
that light causes sadness—
My friend is like the mother. Patient, urging me
to wake up an adult like herself, a courageous person—

In my dreams, my friend reproaches me. We're walking
on the same road, except it's winter now;

she's telling me that when you love the world you hear celestial
        music:
look up, she says. When I look up, nothing.
Only clouds, snow, a white business in the trees
like brides leaping to a great height—
Then I'm afraid for her; I see her
caught in a net deliberately cast over the earth—

In reality, we sit by the side of the road, watching the sun set;
from time to time, the silence pierced by a birdcall.
It's this moment we're both trying to explain, the fact
that we're at ease with death, with solitude.
My friend draws a circle in the dirt; inside, the caterpillar
        doesn't move.
She's always trying to make something whole, something
        beautiful, an image
capable of life apart from her.
We're very quiet. It's peaceful sitting here, not speaking, the
        composition
fixed, the road turning suddenly dark, the air
going cool, here and there the rocks shining and glittering—
it's this stillness that we both love.
The love of form is a love of endings.

1991

LOUISE GLÜCK

Vespers

◇ ◇ ◇

In your extended absence, you permit me
use of earth, anticipating
some return on investment. I must report
failure in my assignment, principally
regarding the tomato plants.
I think I should not be encouraged to grow
tomatoes. Or, if I am, you should withhold
the heavy rains, the cold nights that come
so often here, while other regions get
twelve weeks of summer. All this
belongs to you: on the other hand,
I planted the seeds, I watched the first shoots
like wings tearing the soil, and it was my heart
broken by the blight, the black spot so quickly
multiplying in the rows. I doubt
you have a heart, in our understanding of
that term. You who do not discriminate
between the dead and the living, who are, in consequence,
immune to foreshadowing, you may not know
how much terror we bear, the spotted leaf,
the red leaves of the maple falling
even in August, in early darkness: I am responsible
for these vines.

1992

Manifest Destiny

◇ ◇ ◇

(Note: Rebibbia is the name of the women's jail in Rome.)

(Fabrice Hélion, 1947–1990)

Northbound, on the way to the station, through the narrow
                                                            rutted
place in the patch of woods,
    the dust from the car ahead rose up
into the wide still shafts of morning-light the trees let
    through,
its revolutionary swirls uplifted in some kind of
    cosmic merriment, up

    all round the sleek whiskey-colored slice
of time
    passing—though perfectly still to our eyes, passengers—
a blade of stillness, the intravenous access
    of the unearthly
into this soil.
    The dust rose into it. No, the dust

    slapped round, falling, a thick curiosity, shabby but
extravagant, crazy pulverized soliloquy, furled up, feathery,
    around the
metronome, raking, as if to transfuse itself onto what won't be
    touched,
a thick precipitate, feudal, a glossary of possible entrances
                                                            replete

with every conceivable version of
change.
    Change! it seemed to almost screech as it rose again and
                                          again
out of our drought into the stiff and
    prosperous stillness—*change, change*—into, onto
that shaft driven in firm,

    steely backbone of the imperial
invisible.
    I watched the stationary golden avenue. At every curve
watched the dust
    thrown up like some mad prophet taking on
all the shapes, all the contortions of the
    human form—bent over, flayed, curled back

onto itself.
    It was hard not to see the grief in it, the
cowardice—
    this carnage of fictive
possibilities, this prolonged
    carnage.
The gold bars gleam.
    The money is put down on the gleaming platter
like an eyelid forced back down,
    and another bill, and another bill, down,
onto the open hand, onto the open,

    —how long till the blazing gaze is dulled, the wide
need, bristling with light,
    unwavering, shimmering with rightfulness, god,
so still!—
    and the dusty money coming down onto it.

We rose from the table having paid our bill.

    Rome stepped back all round us as we rose up

—colonnades, promenades, porticoes,
    shadows of warriors, lovers and the various queens of

heaven—
    arms raised holding the stone fruit, lips parted uttering the
stone word—the stone child in the stone arms—the stone

    sword held up into the stone
cry—.
    I look into the air
for your face—
    a fold in the invisible out of which features
slip—
    until you put it on again, there, in the dusty air, the
expression you wore, click,
    among the shadows of the sculptures in the

Vatican arcade—3 miles of corridor we hurry through
    to reach the reliquary before it shuts,
to see the Veronica,
    your hands pressed to the glass till the guard
speaks—
    and the eyes in brine,
and the index finger of Aquinas,
    and the burned head of Lawrence so black it seems
to face on all four

sides—then back out into the noon
    sun. *Rome.* And the word pulverizes. In the restaurant
you were gone so long I
    came to look for you.
Your face started up from the two arms below you—
    one holding the needle into the other—

white kiss on the brow of the forever waiting white maiden,
    forever and forever, forever and forever.
We paid up and left there too.
    The city even whiter now. White noise. White light.

    Walking the back way we passed the length of Rebibbia.
Cooler down there. Riverside traffic above to the left.
    We were used to them, the women's shrieks—hanging their arms,
hundreds of them, out through the bars into the steamy

heat—pointing, cursing, all the fingers in the dark noonlight
     screaming down the stories—who was killed, why, where
the children are, will you take a message, I'd do it again,
     I'd do it to you, come on, let me give it to you—thousands
of white fingers all over the dark façade, no faces
                                        visible—just

listen, listen and I'll make you
     come they'd shriek, trellis of iron and white fleshgrowth,
3 blocks long this queen of the skies—huntress—no face—

     all stone and fingerclutch, white, raking the air.
You stood below looking up,
     the thing which is your laugh sucked up like a small down-
payment—so small—
     then taking my arm, hard, forced me to stand there
before them, below them—*here, do you want her, will she do* you
                                        screamed—
     thousands of fingers moving—*tell me, will she do*—

screech of muscle,
     throbbing façade,
how should we make her you screamed
     do her time, drunk too I thought, the clamp of your hand
hard on my upper arm,
     the light down harder on my face, something rising in me
                                        as they
screamed down give her to us, let us have her,
     their one scream going in through
the hole where your hand gripped, the narrow opening
     through which I knew
that you would not believe in life,
     that you would hand the piece you were holding back up,
the debt too heavy to carry,
     up to the balcony there, in full sun,

like a caress on the infinite
     this handing up of the full amount,
a handful of cloth, cash, skin—
     2:53 pm—Rome time—
in the marketplace now, in the arcade,

arms waving the flies off
over the cut meats, beside the statue of Caesar—
    two dancers with a hat out for change—
the swallower of flames, the fabric merchant

    holding the star-spangled yardage out on her arms,
and singing the price out—loud, clear,
    —*what is love what is creation what is longing what*
is a star—
    behold I show you the last man—
the price rising up on the gold track of its note,
    the cloth on her arms lifting,

catching the light, dustmotes in the light,
    and the voice thrusting round it,
and the unalterable amount—
    high, hard, doth she and did she and shall she ever more—
sleeps she a thousand years and then and then—
    a motorcycle through it now then a dog—
the last man grows, lives longest,
    is ineradicable—blink—
"we have invented happiness" he says—
    meats sizzling on the silver spit,
price aloft,

    perfect price in the dusty air,
us swirling round its upwardmoving note,
    milling, taking this shape then that, hot wind,

until I have to turn to let her voice in,
    to feel the blue velveteen spangly brocade,
the invisible sum with its blazing zero ajar, there, midair—

    and something so quick darting through it—
what will my coin repair? what does my meaning mend?

    I pay her now. I pay her again. Again.
Gold open mouth hovering—no face.
    Until you're pulling me away. Saying *love*.
As if to find me with that.

But I want to pay her again.
To keep the hole open.
    The zero. The gold lidless pupil.
She will not look away.
    Change change it shrieks   the last man blinks   we have invented,
                                                            invented—

Oh why are you here on this earth, you—*you*—swarming, swirling,
    carrying valises, standing on line,
ready to change your name if need be—?

1992

JORIE GRAHAM

What the Instant Contains

◇　◇　◇

(Lyle Van Waning, 1922–1988)

Presently Lyle gets into bed.
The amaryllis on the sill hum.
The dust starts inventing the afterwards.
He is not getting up again.

The dust starts inventing the afterwards.
The whole thing from the ground up.
The *presently*. The *Lyle gets into bed*.
The amaryllis on the sill hum.

The roses on the wall grow virulent.
Then dreadful in increasing dimness.
Then even the wicked no longer matter.
Even the one who would steal the water of life goes under,

even the unread last 49 pages
of the mystery novel on the kitchen table,
(the sill under the amaryllis hums),
even the ancient family name,

even the woman he never found.
If you sit there, near him, in the sofa chair,
if you look at him and he's sleeping now, curled,
the oxygen furious in its blank tubes,

you can hear the wind as it touches the panes,
then, as the wind drops, bushtips brushing the panes,
buds on the tips,
then, as the wind stills altogether,

the weight of the air on the panes,
the face of the air not moving,
the time of day adhering to the panes,
the density of the light where the glass fits the frame

of the windows Lyle built
in the walls Lyle built,
all of it adhering—glass to light, light to time—
all of it unable to advance any further,

here now, arrived. If you sit here,
if you sit in your attention watching him sleep,
if it is still sleep,
looking past the vials and the industrial oxygen tanks,

hearing the tap at the pane,
hearing the tap, click, as the wildgrasses rap
as the wind picks up,

looking into his closed face for the gaze,

you will see, if you can posit the stillness
that beats on its pendulum at the heart of the room,
x beats per minute,
if you can place it at the center,

the beat of the stillness swinging on its tiny firm arc,
like a face on a string, perfect, back and forth,
to permit the center of the center to glow,
you will see the distance start to grow

on the shore of the endlessly lain-down face,
yellow shore which the wide hand holds—
right there on the pinpoint of the face in the room . . .

When he wakes I will give him some water.
I will try to feed him some soup.
We will try to drive back into the body
what roves around it,

will try to darken the body with a red flush,
make it affirm itself in relation to the light again,
make it *know* something, make it grow dull again,
instead of this translucence, this mirror becoming glass,

dents in it, sockets, tape on the left cheek
pulling the papery skinfolds back
to hold the nostril open
to fit the radiant tube inside.

But now the face is going faster, faster

—*floor sills dust* going the other way,
the whole marriage pulling apart—his dream from the drawer,
waiting from skin—
Now he opens his eyes and looks across *the room* at me,

now there are men on the bed with him, many men, naked,

one puts his fist in another's mouth,
one puts his fingers in another's ears,
another's fingers are in there now too,

they put their hands on each other's feet, they roil,
there's a shield in the air but you cannot see it,
it's the thing the dust makes when it's cast up,
there are elements from *history*,

the air hums, edges, undersides, bevelled lips,
shadows behind the edges, ears, fingers,
Circe there on her throne in her shining robe
with golden mantle and the place was lovely

and nymphs and naiads waiting on her
carding no fleece, spinning no wool, but only
sorting, arranging from confusion
in separate baskets the bright-colored flowers,

the different herbs,
and where we had shoulders we have no shoulders
and where our arms were in their right places
there are no arms, there are no right places,

her song would move the wood, would stop the
streams, would stay the wandering birds,
her song would move the wood
would stop the stream

would stay the wandering *afterwards.* Tap tap.
Presently the cast-iron stove,
with metal fruit upon its wondrous flanks, is cold,
grapes swelling there, and apples, pears.

I put my hand on them.
I press my palm onto the icy fruit.
Tap tap the flowertips.
The heart of waiting. Tap.

There are two directions—fast—in the instant,
two, tangled up into each other, blurred, bled,
two motions in every stillness,
to make a body, a waiting—

the motion into here, the firming up,
chest paper book face leaf branch drawer,
the order of events, days, days,

something like a head at the top, stiff,
the minutes flowing off into limbs, fingertips,
the trunk made of actions-that-can't-be-undone,
shield high,

the first minute of existence ruffling like feathers or hair
at the top of his crown, stilling,
the next minute arriving, stilling,
all of him standing there on his crucial deeds, on the out-

come, growing ever more still.
And then, faster and faster—the other direction: *her,*
the silvery thing which is the absence of properties,
the enchantment of itself with itself whirling,

both itself and the hole it leaves—fed by dream—
fed by each glance in the mirror however swift in passing,
moving suddenly in limbs that are not limbs,
moving with a will not yet an individual will—

and the room containing this flow or being contained
                                        by it,
and Lyle momentarily on the crest till the wave breaks again,

and Lyle being distributed partly to him partly to her,
torn up and thrust,
(I want to forget it, I want to forget what I saw),
the face riding for a moment longer on the spray,

the *look* on the face riding after the face has
                        dissolved,
for just a moment longer the gaze in the eye looking out,
                                tossed out—

dust lifting and drifting—
specks and sparkles of dust in the empty room—
then us walking by a mirror on our way out and looking in,
and us being fooled for a moment longer

before we realize what's in there, look,
does not belong to us at all
but is an argument tossed out
                        in that instant
for the sake of discussion

by the queen on the other side
on her throne with shining robes and golden mantle
(and the place lovely)
towards him whom she loves

to convince him, to undo him.
I look in there at it a moment longer—my face—my expression—
flung out into the room by her for the sake of discussion—

the features on there a phrase—not even—the lilt in, the

intonation of, a phrase, brisk, a tactic, quick,
from her in the room where the cloth is not woven
only colors sorted back into that separateness

the earth in its fields has momentarily blurred—
columbine, fire-on-the-mountain, vetch and iris—

                                  the iris
so early this year as we leave, and waving in patches of sun—

and then the blue vase I'll put them in for a time.

1993

ALLEN GROSSMAN

The Piano Player Explains Himself

◊ ◊ ◊

When the corpse revived at the funeral,
The outraged mourners killed it; and the soul
Of the revenant passed into the body
Of the poet because it had more to say.
He sat down at the piano no one could play
Called Messiah, or The Regulator of the World,
Which had stood for fifty years, to my knowledge,
Beneath a painting of a red-haired woman
In a loose gown with one bared breast, and played
A posthumous work of the composer S——
About the impotence of God (I believe)
Who has no power not to create everything.
It was the Autumn of the year and wet,
When the music started. The musician was
Skillful but the Messiah was out of tune
And bent the time and the tone. For a long hour
The poet played The Regulator of the World
As the spirit prompted, and entered upon
The pathways of His power—while the mourners
Stood with slow blood on their hands
Astonished by the weird processional
And the undertaker figured his bill.
—We have in mind an unplayed instrument
Which stands apart in a memorial air
Where the room darkens toward its inmost wall
And a lady hangs in her autumnal hair

At evening of the November rains; and winds
Sublime out of the North, and North by West,
Are sowing from the death-sack of the seed
The burden of her cloudy hip. Behold,
I send the demon I know to relieve your need,
An imperfect player at the perfect instrument
Who takes in hand The Regulator of the World
To keep the splendor from destroying us.
Lady! The last virtuoso of the composer S——
Darkens your parlor with the music of the Law.
When I was green and blossomed in the Spring
I was mute wood. Now I am dead I sing.

1988

Prophecy

◇ ◇ ◇

I will strike down wooden houses; I will burn aluminum
clapboard skin; I will strike down garages
where crimson Toyotas sleep side by side; I will explode
palaces of gold, silver, and alabaster:—the summer
great house and its folly together. Where shopping malls
spread plywood and plaster out, and roadhouses
serve steak and potatoskins beside Alaska King Crab;
where triangular flags proclaim tribes of identical campers;
where airplanes nose to tail exhale kerosene,
weeds and ashes will drowse in continual twilight.

I reject the old house and the new car; I reject
Tory and Whig together; I reject the argument
that modesty of ambition is sensible because the bigger
they are the harder they fall; I reject Waterford;
I reject the five-and-dime; I reject Romulus and Remus;
I reject Martha's Vineyard and the slamdunk contest;
I reject leaded panes; I reject the appointment made
at the tennis net or on the seventeenth green; I reject
the Professional Bowling Tour; I reject matchboxes;
I reject purple bathrooms with purple soap in them.

Men who lie awake worrying about taxes, vomiting
at dawn, whose hands shake as they administer Valium,—
skin will peel from the meat of their thighs.
Armies that march all day with elephants past pyramids
and roll pulling missiles past Generals weary of saluting
and past President-Emperors splendid in cloth-of-gold,—
soft rumps of armies will dissipate in rain. Where square

miles of corn waver in Minnesota, where tobacco ripens
in Carolina and apples in New Hampshire, where wheat
turns Kansas green, where pulpmills stink in Oregon,

dust will blow in the darkness and cactus die
before it flowers. Where skiers wait for chairlifts,
wearing money, low raspberries will part rib-bones.
Where the drive-in church raises a chromium cross,
dandelions and milkweed will straggle through blacktop.
I will strike from the ocean with waves afire;
I will strike from the hill with rainclouds of lava;
I will strike from darkened air
with melanoma in the shape of decorative hexagonals.
I will strike down embezzlers and eaters of snails.

I reject Japanese smoked oysters, potted chrysanthemums
allowed to die, Tupperware parties, Ronald McDonald,
Karposi's sarcoma, the Taj Mahal, holsteins wearing
electronic necklaces, the Algonquin, Tunisian aqueducts,
Phi Beta Kappa keys, the Hyatt Embarcadero, carpenters
jogging on the median, and betrayal that engorges
the corrupt heart longing for criminal surrender:
I reject shadows in the corner of the atrium
where Phyllis or Phoebe speaks with Billy or Marc
who says that afternoons are best although not reliable.

Your children will wander looting the shopping malls
for forty years, suffering for your idleness,
until the last dwarf body rots in a parking lot.
I will strike down lobbies and restaurants in motels
carpeted with shaggy petrochemicals
from Maine to Hilton Head, from the Skagit to Tucson.
I will strike down hanggliders, wiry adventurous boys;
their thighbones will snap, their brains
slide from their skulls. I will strike down
families cooking wildboar in New Mexico backyards.

Then landscape will clutter with incapable machinery,
acres of vacant airplanes and schoolbuses, ploughs
with seedlings sprouting and turning brown through colters.

Unlettered dwarves will burrow for warmth and shelter
in the caves of dynamos and Plymouths, dying
of old age at seventeen. Tribes wandering
in the wilderness of their ignorant desolation,
who suffer from your idleness, will burn your illuminated
missals to warm their rickety bodies.
Terrorists assemble plutonium because you are idle

and industrious. The whip-poor-will shrivels and the pickerel
chokes under the government of self-love. Vacancy burns
air so that you strangle without oxygen like rats
in a biologist's bell jar. The living god sharpens
the scythe of my prophecy to strike down red poppies
and blue cornflowers. When priests and policemen
strike my body's match, Jehovah will flame out;
Jehovah will suck air from the vents of bombshelters.
Therefore let the Buick swell until it explodes;
therefore let anorexia starve and bulimia engorge.

When Elzira leaves the house wearing her tennis dress
and drives her black Porsche to meet Abraham,
quarrels, returns to husband and children, and sobs
asleep, drunk, unable to choose among them,—
lawns and carpets will turn into tar together
with lovers, husbands, and children.
Fat will boil in the sacs of children's clear skin.
I will strike down the nations, astronauts and judges;
I will strike down Babylon, I will strike acrobats,
I will strike algae and the white birches.

Because Professors of Law teach ethics in dumbshow,
let the Colonel become President; because Chief Executive
Officers and Commissars collect down for pillows,
let the injustice of cities burn city and suburb;
let the countryside burn; let the pineforests of Maine
explode like a kitchenmatch and the Book of Kells turn
ash in a microsecond; let oxen and athletes
flash into grease:—I return to Appalachian rocks;
I shall eat bread; I shall prophesy through millennia
of Jehovah's day until the sky reddens over cities:

Then houses will burn, even houses of alabaster;
the sky will disappear like a scroll rolled up
and hidden in a cave from the industries of idleness.
Mountains will erupt and vanish, becoming deserts,
and the sea wash over the sea's lost islands
and the earth split open like a corpse's gassy
stomach and the sun turn as black as a widow's skirt
and the full moon grow red with blood swollen inside it
and stars fall from the sky like wind-blown apples,—
while Babylon's managers burn in the rage of the Lamb.

1988

The Porcelain Couple

◇　◇　◇

When Jane felt well enough for me to leave her
for a whole day, I drove south by the river
to empty my mother Lucy's house in Connecticut.
I hurried from room to room, cellar to attic,
opening a crammed closet, then turning
to discover a chest with five full drawers.
I labelled for shipping sofas and chairs,
bedroom sets, and tables; I wrapped figurines
and fancy teacups in paper, preserving things
she cherished—and dreaded, in her last years,
might go for a nickel on the Spring Glen lawn.
Everywhere I looked I saw shelves and tabletops
covered with Lucy's glass animals and music boxes.
Everywhere in closets, decades of dresses hung
in dead air. I carried garbage bags in one hand,
and with the other swept my mother's leftover
possessions into sacks for the Hamden dump.
I stuffed bags full of blouses, handkerchiefs,
and the green-gold dress she wore to Bermuda.
At the last moment I discovered and saved
a cut-glass tumbler, stained red at the top,
Lucy 1905 scripted on the stain. In the garage
I piled the clanking bags, then drove four hours
north with my hands tight on the Honda's wheel,
drank a beer looking through Saturday's mail,
pitched into bed beside Jane fitfully asleep,
and woke exhausted from rolling unendable
nightmares of traffic and fire. In my dreams
I grieved or mourned interchangeably for Lucy,

for Lucy's things, for Jane, and for me.
When I woke, I rose as if from a drunken sleep
after looting a city and burning its temples.
All day as I ate lunch or counted out pills,
or as we lay weeping, hugging in bed together,
I counted precious things from our twenty years:
a blue vase, a candelabrum Jane carried on her lap
from the Baja, and the small porcelain box
from France I found under the tree one Christmas
where a couple in relief stretch out asleep,
like a catafalque, on the pastel double bed
of the box's top, both wearing pretty nightcaps.

1997

St. Luke Painting the Virgin

◇ ◇ ◇

St. Luke's eyes are steady on the babe.
I, insufficiently transfixed,
Am led inexorably beyond
Van der Weyden's (you call him "Roger,"
Just as you ought)—beyond the window
Roger has set behind radiant
St. Luke, peaceful knower, to gardens,
And beyond them
                to find in the clear
Distance the delicate city street
Where the figures of humanity
Consult the ground, their eyes helplessly
On the details of history that
Hold them there in the street as the laws
Of perspective, not imperfectly,
Hold the infant before the St.'s eyes.

It is the beauty of these figures
As background, as reinterpreted
Landscape I cry for; to be landscape
Is not to be at the center, not
The first thing the painter, seizing his
Focus, illuminated, and what
Are we, unilluminated? What,
To go on, is illumination
For? In the painting, for instance,
The atrocity is not in fact
Visible on the streets but in the eyes
Of the painter—St. Luke. The painter,

Gazing only on the bright infant,
Instead of out the window, reaches
A conclusion not plainly implied
In infant glee. Yet St. Luke's face is plainly
Illuminated by what he sees
Directly before him, while I look
Over Roger's shoulder and out the
Window. And weep, to see the city
So delicate and outside, though
I grant the mistake, the mistake of
Weeping, that is, when perhaps I could
Move subtly into the paint and stand
Behind St. Luke. He looks calm enough.
But I, seeing what he sees, would have
No thought of Fridays, or windows, or

Outsides of any sort; this is
The essential weakness of eyes like
Mine, to see, faced with a divine light,
Nothing but divine light, which is why
Landscapes, or whatever you paint
Beyond the garden, become so central,
Not to the conception, which is all
Complete in what the St. sees, but
To the training of the eye that is,
After all, an action of painting

And illuminations. There are those
That descend to the street while the bright
Neon sign above the square that says
True Cigarets glows undiminished
As the hosts of heaven. In Boston,
Standing before this painting I thought,
Even as I was transported, of
Streets in general, the subway ride home,
And the expanse of walks, all crowded,
That lay between you and me at that
Moment. I thought, in short, of you. We

Have Roger to thank for this. With just
The Infant before me I might have
Stepped out of all those streets directly
Into the light—only in my mind,
Of course, thus forgetting the way

Home. As it was I found my way through
The shadows and arrived in your arms
Only slightly bruised, and all because
Roger kindly refrained from making
A portrait of Christ in unrelieved
Brilliance. Light is light. We are guided,
Sometimes, more easily by the faint
Revelations in the shapes shadows
Suggest than by the blank expanses
On the faces of stars. I find some
Guidance, anyway, in my dark fears
Of what lurks in the streets and come to
See the light more clearly because I
Have missed it so many times, many
Hours. Gaze at the ground, then look up,
Is my advice, and see light, at last,
As precious because we find it
In the darkness outside a garden
Between the light and the world.

1992

Prospects

◊ ◊ ◊

We have set out from here for the sublime
Pastures of summer shade and mountain stream;
I have no doubt we shall arrive on time.

Is all the green of that enamelled prime
A snapshot recollection or a dream?
We have set out from here for the sublime

Without provisions, without one thin dime,
And yet, for all our clumsiness, I deem
It certain that we shall arrive on time.

No guidebook tells you if you'll have to climb
Or swim. However foolish we may seem,
We have set out from here for the sublime

And must get past the scene of an old crime
Before we falter and run out of steam,
Riddled by doubt that we'll arrive on time.

Yet even in winter a pale paradigm
Of birdsong utters its obsessive theme.
We have set out from here for the sublime;
I have no doubt we shall arrive on time.

1995

Man on a Fire Escape

◊ ◊ ◊

He couldn't remember what propelled him
out of the bedroom window onto the fire escape
of his fifth-floor walkup on the river,

so that he could see, as if for the first time,
sunset settling down on the dazed cityscape
and tugboats pulling barges up the river.

There were barred windows glaring at him
from the other side of the street
while the sun deepened into a smoky flare

that scalded the clouds gold-vermillion.
It was just an ordinary autumn twilight—
the kind he had witnessed often before—

but then the day brightened almost unnaturally
into a rusting, burnished, purplish-red haze
and everything burst into flame;

the factories pouring smoke into the sky,
the trees and shrubs, the shadows,
of pedestrians scorched and rushing home. . . .

There were storefronts going blind and cars
burning on the parkway and steel girders
collapsing into the polluted waves.

Even the latticed fretwork of stairs
where he was standing, even the first stars
climbing out of their sunlit graves

were branded and lifted up, consumed by fire.
It was like watching the start of Armageddon,
like seeing his mother dipped in flame. . . .

And then he closed his eyes and it was over.
Just like that. When he opened them again
the world had reassembled beyond harm.

So where had he crossed to? Nowhere.
And what had he seen? Nothing. No foghorns
called out to each other, as if in a dream,

and no moon rose over the dark river
like a warning—icy, long forgotten—
while he turned back to an empty room.

1992

Kinneret

◇ ◇ ◇

As the dry, red sun set we sat and watched
   Them bring the fish in from the harp-shaped lake.
At night my life, whose every task is botched,
   Dreams of far distant places, by mistake.

They tunnelled through the mountains to connect
   The raging ocean with the inland sea.
Dreaming of you, I wander through some wrecked
   Historic region of antiquity.

We played unknowing for the highest stakes
   All day, then lost when night was "drawing nigh."
The dark pale of surrounding hemlocks makes
   Stabs at transcendence in the evening sky.

Out on the lake at night one understands
   How the far shore's more distant than a star.
The music playing right into my hands,
   I took the measure of my dark guitar.

Beauty? the dolphins leap. But for the truth,
   The filtering baleen of the great whale.
Age? it's more gullible than flashing youth:
   The ending swallows the beginning's tale.

Far from the freeway and its hoarse, sick roaring,
   He can still listen to the wildwood's sigh.
Across the world the shattering rain was pouring:
   Tears merely glistened in my childhood's eye.

Out of the depths I call for you: the water
   Drowns it, as if that sound were its own name.
Enisled in height, she learned what had been taught her:
   From closer up, the sky was more of the same.

Her thought was silent, but the darkness rang
   With the strong questions of a headlight's beam.
He walked around the lake: the water sang
   An undersong as if it were a stream.

The wind was working on the laughing waves,
   Washing a shore that was not wholly land.
I give life to dead letters: from their graves
   Come leaping even X and ampersand.

Below, the dialect of the market-place,
   All dark *o*'s, narrowed *i*'s and widened *e*'s.
Above, through a low gate, this silent space:
   The whitened tomb of wise Maimonides.

Only a *y*, stupidly questioning,
   Separates what is yours from what is ours.
Only mute aspiration now can sing
   Our few brief moments into endless hours.

The merest puddle by the lowest hill
   Answers the flashing sunlight none the less.
I harp on the two flowing themes of still
   Water and jagged disconnectedness.

I lay in a long field; eleven sheep
   Leapt from a barge onto the grass, and fed.
She cleared the wall and leapt into my sleep,
   Riding her piebald mare of night and dread.

Dressed like their foes, nomadic and unkempt,
   The emperor's legion crept across the stream.
Only as her great rival could she attempt
   The soft parapets of her lover's dream.

The voice of the Commander rang in us;
  Our hearts in stony ranks echoed his shout.
The cold, bare hills have no cause to discuss
  What the thunder among them is about.

Musing at sundown, I recall the long
  Voyages across shoreless seas of sand.
Shuddering at dawn, I call out for your song,
  O isle of water in the broad main of land.

What speck of dust fell on my page of strife
  And mixed its coughing with the prose of breath?
The pensive comma, hanging on to life?
  The full stop that sentences us to death.

From his blue tomb the young sun rises and
  The marble whitecaps pass like dancing stones.
A boy, somewhere in an old, arid land,
  Sat carving spoons out of his father's bones.

Windward, the sun; a galley on our lee
  Rolls gently homeward; now its sail is gone.
This miracle the moonlight once gave me:
  The sky lay still; the broad water walked on.

What cannot be seen in us as we stare
  At the same stretch of ordinary bay?
Her constant dreaming of the Immermeer,
  My half-lost moment on the Harfensee.

In bright, chaste sunlight only forms are seen:
  Off-color language gives the world its hue.
Only in English does the grass grow green;
  In ancient Greece the dogs were almost blue.

The bitten-into fig does, without doubt,
  Show forth that blushing part of which we've heard.
Resemblance turns our language inside-out:
  Pudenda is a self-descriptive word.

He fought Sloth in her arbitrary den,
    And grew bored long before he could defeat her.
I stop—something is too pedestrian
    About the iambs in this kind of meter.

Footsore, his argument gave out and slept
    In the unmeasured vale of meditation.
In marked but quiet waves the water kept
    Time with the heartbeats of an old elation.

This night in which all pages are the same
    Black: the Hegelians must shut up shop.
It seemed when, smiling, you called out my name
    The humor of the noon would never stop.

He parsed his schoolboy Greek, the future more
    Vivid, where rich, strange verbs display emotion.
My glass of dark wine drained, from the dim shore
    I scan the surface of a sparse, gray ocean.

They built beside a chilly mountain lake
    The prison of particularity.
The sun is blind now; only the stars awake
    To see the whole world mirrored in the sea.

The sea's a mere mirror wherein you see
    Something of the gray face of the high sky.
Far from shore, the dark lake relays to me
    The lie of the old, silent land nearby.

The everlastingness of childhood's summer
    Evenings itself skyrockets and is gone.
As if great age would evermore become her
    The far-lit winter night reigns on and on.

Snows on the far, long mountain in the north,
    Seen from the lake, are never reflected there.
Gazing at distance, I keep setting forth
    Unwittingly into the thoughtless air.

We stand our ungiving ground, our unpaid mission
    To creep through fields or scamper across the town.
Still at last, supine, we learn what position
    Earth took on the great issues of up and down.

A kingfisher flashed by them on their lee
    To lead their thoughts toward a blue yet once more.
My tears blur world and water and I see
    Each seed of flickering lake, each drop of shore.

The dry, unsinging river that runs south:
    Somewhere along it we must some day cross.
The memory of music in my mouth
    Sticks to my silence now like leaves, like moss.

Some husbandman will plow where now I row;
    My lively wake will be the long dead road.
Drowning our songs, the river will flood and go
    Mad, as if flowing were itself a goad.

My mind's eye, wearied of distrust, soon turned
    To surfaces, of which it then grew fond.
She meditated on the mud that churned
    Up from the fruitful bottom of the pond.

Down in undreaming deeps the heavy carp
    Fed, while above the shining surface trembled.
Was it my voice that spoke for the bright harp?
    Or was it a heart the singing lake resembled?

Some say I mutter; some, that I reconditely
    Shout: but meanings, like words, like air, expand.
Some fragments hurt you when you grasp them tightly,
    Some feel as if they were part of your hand.

Every dog has his day, and the worm turns
    Nasty within the hard, absorbing grave.
The heat of August threatens as it burns
    Our hearts with the dead cold of winter's cave.

The wind turned to the hard hills and wondered
  At their cold heads and then began to hum.
My white and faulty mortar should not have sundered
  Under the grinding of this cardamom.

Pale cliffs descend below the sea and steep
  In the full silence, calm and unconfounded.
He broke through the thrumming surface of his sleep
  As if some lake-shaped instrument had sounded.

1989

JOHN HOLLANDER

An Old-Fashioned Song

◇ ◇ ◇

("Nous n'irons plus au bois")

No more walks in the wood:
The trees have all been cut
Down, and where once they stood
Not even a wagon rut
Appears along the path
Low brush is taking over.

No more walks in the wood;
This is the aftermath
Of afternoons in the clover
Fields where we once made love
Then wandered home together
Where the trees arched above,
Where we made our own weather
When branches were the sky.
Now they are gone for good,
And you, for ill, and I
Am only a passer-by.

We and the trees and the way
Back from the fields of play
Lasted as long as we could.
No more walks in the wood.

1990

JOHN HOLLANDER

The See-Saw

◊　◊　◊

Of the remedies acting primarily on the body, the see-saw especially has proved efficacious, especially with raving lunatics. The see-saw movement induces giddiness in the patient and loosens his fixed idea.

G. W. F. Hegel, Zusatz to section 408
of the *Encyclopedia of the Philosophical Sciences*
(trans. A. V. Miller)

Margery daw.
And up she went as I went down
And up she went and then I saw
The hair between her legs was brown.

Hold the handle with just your thumbs
And flap your fingers. Smile and frown
And giggle and sigh . . . we know what comes
Up must come down.

Up! and the end of the tip of me thrills:
Now I see over
The playground fence to the lovely hills,
The shadowy dales, the meadows of clover.

Down! and I bump . . . a hardened cough . . .
Against the place where I have a tail
(Do I have a tail? If I do, then they'll
Cut it all off.)

Mechanical Operations of
The Spirit oscillate between

The high of hate, the low of love,
As we have seen;

As we have sawn
So shall we rip, this way and that
Way, up and down, and my peace has gone
Off to war in a funny hat.

Two bolts on the handle dream of me
Like eyes (those very eyes I see
Saw something dirty they did to you,
Margery Doo)

A fulcrum with an idée fixe
(Hear how it creaks!)
Won't be shaken, *Balance is all.*
I'm unbalanced, a head-shaped ball.

Margery Dall:
I'd fill her up but my thing's too small,
She'd fill me down with her legs apart.
Every stopper gives me a start.

Here I come and she goes there,
Each of us President of the Air,
Slave of the Ground.
It's square that makes the world go round.

Toes just touch the ground, she and I,
Gravel and sky,
Balanced now in the midst of flight
Listen for yesterday, wait for night.

Something bad back-and-forth was there
Under Grandmother's rocking chair,
With his hanging weights and his swinging cock,
Grandfather Clock

Punishes Pa,
Ravishes Ma, and ticks the tock

Of now and then and the Time they mock.
Und ich bin hier und Margery da.

And she goes low and I go high
By an inexorable law:
See me be born? I saw Margery die,
Margery Daw.

See saw.

My wooden slope can't get to sleep,
The peaks are sunken, the moon down deep,
The desert damp and the sea sere
Margery Dear
I'm here there, and you're there here.
Margery Day,
Sold her old bed to lie on straw
To die on straw on the Days of Awe;
Margery Daw on the Days of Play
Goes up and down in the same old way

Und ich bin hier und Margery da
Tra la la la.

Out and down and up and back,
All comes on now faster and faster
When will I rest? and when will Jack
"Have a new master?"

I watch the light by which I see
Saw away at my wooden head,
Living or dead?
I haven't been told and I'll never be.

Who is it calls us home from play?
That nurse of darkness with Nothing to say.
One last up and down. And then
Never again.

1991

154

Like Most Revelations

◇ ◇ ◇

after Morris Louis

It is the movement that incites the form,
discovered as a downward rapture—yes,
it is the movement that delights the form,
sustained by its own velocity. And yet

it is the movement that delays the form
while darkness slows and encumbers; in fact
it is the movement that betrays the form,
baffled in such toils of ease, until

it is the movement that deceives the form,
beguiling our attention—we supposed
it is the movement that achieves the form.
Were we mistaken? What does it matter if

it is the movement that negates the form?
Even though we give (give up) ourselves
to this mortal process of continuing,
it is the movement that creates the form.

1992

Nostalgia of the Lakefronts

◊ ◊ ◊

Cities burn behind us; the lake glitters.
A tall loudspeaker is announcing prizes;
Another, by the lake, the times of cruises.
Childhood, once vast with terrors and surprises,
Is fading to a landscape deep with distance—
And always the sad piano in the distance,

Faintly in the distance, a ghostly tinkling
(O indecipherable blurred harmonies)
Or some far horn repeating over water
Its high lost note, cut loose from all harmonies.
At such times, wakeful, a child will dream the world,
And this is the world we run to from the world.

Or the two worlds come together and are one
On dark sweet afternoons of storm and of rain,
And stereopticons brought out and dusted,
Stacks of old *Geographics*, or, through the rain,
A mad wet dash to the local movie palace
And the shriek, perhaps, of Kane's white cockatoo.
(Would this have been summer, 1942?)

By June the city seems to grow neurotic.
But lakes are good all summer for reflection,
And ours is famed among painters for its blues,
Yet not entirely sad, upon reflection.

Why sad at all? Is their wish not unique—
To anthropomorphize the inanimate
With a love that masquerades as pure technique?

O art and the child are innocent together!
But landscapes grow abstract, like aging parents;
Soon now the war will shutter the grand hotels;
And we, when we come back, must come as parents.
There are no lanterns now strung between pines—
Only, like history, the stark bare northern pines.

And after a time the lakefront disappears
Into the stubborn verses of its exiles
Or a few gifted sketches of old piers.
It rains perhaps on the other side of the heart;
Then we remember, whether we would or no.
—Nostalgia comes with the smell of rain, you know.

1988

DONALD JUSTICE

Invitation to a Ghost

◇ ◇ ◇

for Henri Coulette (1927–1988)

I ask you to come back now as you were in youth,
Confident, eager, and the silver brushed from your temples.
Let it be as though a man could go backwards through death,
Erasing the years that did not much count,
Or that added up perhaps to no more than a single brilliant forenoon.

Sit with us. Let it be as it was in those days
When alcohol brought our tongues the first sweet foretaste of oblivion
And what should we speak of but verse? For who would speak of
      such things now but among friends?
(A bad line, an atrocious line, could make you wince: we have all seen it.)

I see you again turn toward the cold and battering sea.
Gull shadows darken the skylight; a wind keens among the chimney pots;
Your hand trembles a little.
                What year was that?

Correct me if I remember it badly,
But was there not a dream, sweet but also terrible,
In which Eurydice, strangely, preceded *you*?
And you followed, knowing exactly what to expect, and of course she
      did turn.
Come back now and help me with these verses.
Whisper to me some beautiful secret that you remember from life.

1993

158

The White Pilgrim:
Old Christian Cemetery

◇   ◇   ◇

The cicadas were loud and what looked like a child's
Bracelet was coiled at the base of the Pilgrim.
It was a snake. Red and black.   The cemetery
Is haunted. Perhaps by the Pilgrim. Perhaps
By another.   We were looking for names
For the baby. My daughter liked Achsa and Luke
And John Jacob. She was dragging her rope
Through the grass. It was hot. The insect
Racket was loud and there was that snake.
It made me nervous. I almost picked it up
Because it was so pretty. Just like a bracelet.
And I thought, Oh the child will be a girl,
But it was not.   This was around the time
Of the dream.   Dreams come from somewhere.
There is this argument about nowhere,
But it is not true.   I dreamed that some boys
Knocked down all the stones in the cemetery,
And then it happened. It was six months later
In early December. Dead cold. Just before
Dawn. We live a long way off so I slept
Right through it. But I read about it the next
Day in the Johnsonburg paper.   There is
This argument about the dead, but that is not
Right either. The dead keep working. If
You listen you can hear them.   It was hot
When we walked in the cemetery. And my daughter,

159

Told me the story of the White Pilgrim.
She likes the story. Yes, it is a good one.
A man left his home in Ohio and came East,
Dreaming he could be the dreamed-of Rider
in St. John's *Revelations.* He was called
The White Pilgrim because he dressed all
In white like a rodeo cowboy and rode a white
Horse. He preached that the end was coming soon.
And it was. He died a month later of the fever.
The ground here is unhealthy. And the insects
Grind on and on.   Now the Pilgrim is a legend.
I know your works, God said, and that is what
I am afraid of.   It was very hot that summer.
The birds were too quiet.   *God's eyes are like
A flame of fire,* St. John said, *and the armies
Of heaven . . .* But these I cannot imagine.
Many dreams come true. But mostly it isn't
The good ones.   That night in December
The boys were bored. They were pained to the teeth
With boredom. You can hardly blame them.
They had been out all night breaking trashcans
And mailboxes with their baseball bats. They
Hang from their pickups by the knees and
Pound the boxes as they drive by. The ground
Here is unhealthy, but that is not it.
Their satisfaction just ends too quickly.
They need something better to break. They
Need something holy. But there is not much left,
So that night they went to the cemetery.
It was cold, but they were drunk and perhaps
They did not feel it. The cemetery is close
To town, but no one heard them.   The boys are part
Of a larger destruction, but this is beyond
What they can imagine. War in heaven
And the damage is ours. The birds come to feed
On what is left. You can see them always
Around Old Christian. As if the bodies of the dead
Were lying out exposed. But of course they are
Not.   St. John the Evangelist dreamed of birds
And of the White Rider. That is the one

The Ohio preacher wanted to be. He dressed
All in white leather and rode a white horse.
His own life in the Midwest was not enough,
And who can blame him?   My daughter thinks
That all cemeteries have a White Pilgrim.
She said that her teacher told her this. I said
This makes no sense but she would not listen.
There was a pack of dogs loose in my dream
Or it could have been dark angels. They were
Taking the names off the stones.   St. John said
An angel will be the one who invites the birds
To God's Last Supper, when he eats the flesh
Of all the kings and princes.   Perhaps God
Is a bird. Sometimes I think this. The thought
Is as good as another.   The boys shouldered
Over the big stones first, save for the Pilgrim.
And then worked their way down to the child-
Sized markers. These they punted like footballs.
The cemetery is close to town but no one
Heard them. They left the Pilgrim for last
Because he is a legend, although only local.
My daughter thinks that all cemeteries
Have a White Pilgrim, ghost and stone, and that
The stone is always placed dead in the center
Of the cemetery ground. In Old Christian
This is true. The Ohio Pilgrim was a rich man
And before he died he sunk his wealth into
The marble obelisk called by his name. We saw
The snake curled around it. Pretty as a bracelet.
But the child was not a girl.   The boys left
The Pilgrim till last, and then took it down,
Too.   The Preacher had a dream but it was not
Of a larger order so it led to little. Just
A stone broken like a tooth, and a ghost story
For children.   God says the damage will be
Restored. Among other things.   At least
They repaired Old Christian. The Historical
Society raised a collection and the town's
Big men came out to hoist the stones. The boys
Got probation, but they won't keep it.   I

Don't go to the cemetery anymore. But once
I drove past and my babysitter's family
Was out working. Her father and mother were
Cutting back the rose of Sharon, and my red-haired
Sitter, who is plain and good-hearted, was
Pushing a lawn mower. Her beautiful younger
Sister sat on the grass beside the Pilgrim
Pretending to clip some weeds. She never works.
She has asthma and everybody loves her.
I imagined that the stones must have fine seams
Where they had been broken. But otherwise
Everything looked the same. Maybe better . . .
The summer we walked in the cemetery it was hot.
We were looking for names for the baby
And my daughter told me the story of the White
Pilgrim. This was before the stones fell
And before the worked-for restoration.
I know your works, says God, and talks of
The armies of heaven. They are not very friendly.
Some dreams hold and I am afraid that this
May be one of them. The White Rider may come
With his secret name inscribed on his thigh,
King of Kings, Lord of Lords, and the child
Is large now . . . but who will be left standing?

1993

JANE KENYON

Three Songs at the End of Summer

◇　◇　◇

A second crop of hay lies cut
and turned. Five gleaming crows
search and peck between the rows.
They make a low, companionable squawk,
and like midwives and undertakers
possess a weird authority.

Crickets leap from the stubble,
parting before me like the Red Sea.
The garden sprawls and spoils.

Across the lake the campers have learned
to water-ski. They have, or they haven't.
Sounds of the instructor's megaphone
suffuse the hazy air. "Relax! Relax!"

Cloud shadows rush over drying hay,
fences, dusty lane, and railroad ravine.
The first yellowing fronds of goldenrod
brighten the margins of the woods.

Schoolbooks, carpools, pleated skirts;
water, silver-still, and a vee of geese.

★

The cicada's monotony breaks
over me. The days are bright
and free, bright and free.

Then why did I cry today
the way babies cry, for
an hour, with my whole body?

★

A white, indifferent morning sky,
and a crow, hectoring from its nest
high in the hemlock, a nest as big
as a laundry basket. . . .
                              In my childhood
I stood under a dripping oak,
while autumnal fog eddied around my feet,
waiting for the school bus
with a dread that took my breath away.

The damp dirt road gave off
this same complex organic scent.

I had my new books—words, numbers
and operations with numbers I did not
comprehend—and crayons unspoiled
by use, in a blue canvas satchel
with red leather straps.

Spruce, inadequate, and alien,
I stood at the side of the road.
It was the only life I had.

1989

When One Has Lived a Long Time Alone

◇ ◇ ◇

1

When one has lived a long time alone,
one refrains from swatting the fly
and lets him go, and one hesitates to strike
the mosquito, though more than willing to slap
the flesh under her, and one lifts the toad
from the pit too deep for him to hop out of
and carries him to the grass, without minding
the toxic urine he slicks his body with,
and one envelops, in a towel, the swift
who fell down the chimney and knocks herself
against the window glass and releases her outside
and watches her fly free, a life line flung at reality,
when one has lived a long time alone.

2

When one has lived a long time alone,
one grabs the snake behind the head
and holds him until he stops trying to stick
the orange tongue, which splits at the end
into two black filaments and jumps out
like a fire-eater's belches and has little
in common with the pimpled pink lump that shapes

sounds and sleeps inside the human mouth,
into one's flesh, and clamps it between his jaws,
letting the gaudy tips show, as children do
when concentrating, and as very likely
one does oneself, without knowing it,
when one has lived a long time alone.

3

When one has lived a long time alone,
among regrets so immense the past occupies
nearly all the room there is in consciousness,
one notices in the snake's eyes, which look back
without paying less attention to the future,
the first coating of the opaque milky-blue
leucoma snakes get when about to throw
their skins and become new—meanwhile continuing,
of course, to grow old—the exact *bleu passé*
that discolors the corneas of the blue-eyed
when they lie back at last and look for heaven,
a blurring one can see means they will never find it,
when one has lived a long time alone.

4

When one has lived a long time alone,
one holds the snake near a loudspeaker disgorging
gorgeous sound and watches him crook
his forepart into four right angles
as though trying to slow down the music
flowing through him, in order to absorb it
like milk of paradise into the flesh,
and now a glimmering appears at his mouth,
such a drop of intense fluid as, among humans,
could form after long exciting at the tip
of the penis, and as he straightens himself out
he has the pathos one finds in the penis,
when one has lived a long time alone.

When one has lived a long time alone,
one can fall to poring upon a creature,
contrasting its eternity's-face to one's own
full of hours, taking note of each difference,
exaggerating it, making it everything,
until the other is utterly other, and then,
with hard effort, possibly with tongue sticking out,
going back over each one once again
and cancelling it, seeing nothing now
but likeness, until . . . half an hour later
one starts awake, taken aback at how eagerly
one swoons into the happiness of kinship,
when one has lived a long time alone.

6

When one has lived a long time alone
and listens at morning to mourning doves
sound their *kyrie eleison,* or the small thing
spiritualizing onto one's shoulder cry "pewit-phoebe!"
or peabody-sparrows at midday send schoolboys'
whistlings across the field, or at dusk, undamped,
unforgiving clinks, as from stonemasons' chisels,
or on trees' backs tree frogs scratch the thighs'
needfire awake, or from the frog pond pond frogs
raise their *ave verum corpus*—listens to those
who hop or fly call down upon us the mercy
of other tongues—one hears them as inner voices,
when one has lived a long time alone.

7

When one has lived a long time alone,
one knows only consciousness consummates,
and as the conscious one among these others
uttering compulsory cries of being here—

the least flycatcher witching up "che-bec,"
or redheaded woodpecker clanging out his
music from a metal drainpipe, or ruffed grouse
drumming "thrump thrump thrump thrump-thrump-
thrump-thrump-rup-rup-rup-rup-rup-r-r-r-r-r-r"
through the trees, all of them in time's
unfolding trying to cry themselves into self-knowing—
one knows one is here to hear them into shining,
when one has lived a long time alone.

8

When one has lived a long time alone,
one likes alike the pig, who brooks no deferment
of gratification, and the porcupine, or thorned pig,
who enters the cellar but not the house itself
because of eating down the cellar stairs on the way up,
and one likes the worm, who by bunching herself together
and expanding rubs her way through the ground,
no less than the butterfly, who totters full of worry
among the day-lilies, as they darken,
and more and more one finds one likes
any other species better than one's own,
which has gone amok, making one self-estranged,
when one has lived a long time alone.

9

When one has lived a long time alone,
sour, misanthropic, one fits to one's defiance
the satanic boast—*It is better to reign
in hell than to submit on earth*—
and forgets one's kind, as does the snake,
who has stopped trying to escape and moves
at ease across one's body, slumping into its contours,
adopting its temperature, and abandons hope
of the sweetness of friendship or love
—before long can barely remember what they are—

and covets the stillness in inorganic matter,
in a self-dissolution one may not know how to halt,
when one has lived a long time alone.

10

When one has lived a long time alone,
and the hermit thrush calls and there is an answer,
and the bullfrog, head half out of water, remembers
the exact sexual cantillations of his first spring,
and the snake slides over the threshold and disappears
among the stones, one sees they all live
to mate with their kind, and one knows,
after a long time of solitude, after the many steps taken
away from one's kind, toward the kingdom of strangers,
the hard prayer inside one's own singing
is to come back, if one can, to one's own,
a world almost lost, in the exile that deepens,
when one has lived a long time alone.

11

When one has lived a long time alone,
one wants to live again among men and women,
to return to that place where one's ties with the human
broke, where the disquiet of death and now
also of history glimmers its firelight on faces,
where the gaze of the new baby looks past the gaze
of the great-granny, and where lovers speak,
on lips blowsy from kissing, that language
the same in each mouth, and like birds at daybreak
blether the song that is both earth's and heaven's,
until the sun has risen, and they stand
in a light of being united: kingdom come,
when one has lived a long time alone.

1990

Sonogram

◇　◇　◇

Something of desk work and pornography,
through succulences of conducting gel.
Vector: creation (in a partial view),

held in the half-dark of the examination room,
just as a wishbone of base mineral
holds pomegranate seed or emerald

or alveolus in a narthex rose.
God's image lies couched safe in blood and matter,
where an ionic snow falls lightly, hushed

into the deep calm of the body's gulf.
The channel-changer skates . . . tiny hot springs
of the beating heart, or sinuses of thought

like Siracusa's limestone quarries, where
an army of seven thousand starved to death.
The world of line and measure somewhat darkly

honors you in this glass, child: all your hands
will make, all your body will savor,
your mind consider, or your heart regret,

seeking your whole life for such immanence.

1995

KENNETH KOCH

One Train
May Hide Another

◊ ◊ ◊

(sign at a railroad crossing in Kenya)

In a poem, one line may hide another line,
As at a crossing, one train may hide another train.
That is, if you are waiting to cross
The tracks, wait to do it for one moment at
Least after the first train is gone. And so when you read
Wait until you have read the next line—
Then it is safe to go on reading.
In a family one sister may conceal another,
So, when you are courting, it's best to have them all in view
Otherwise in coming to find one you may love another.
One father or one brother may hide the man,
If you are a woman, whom you have been waiting to love.
So always standing in front of something the other
As words stand in front of objects, feelings, and ideas.
One wish may hide another. And one person's reputation may hide
The reputation of another. One dog may conceal another
On a lawn, so if you escape the first one you're not necessarily safe;
One lilac may hide another and then a lot of lilacs and on the Appia
         Antica one tomb
May hide a number of other tombs. In love, one reproach may hide
         another,
One small complaint may hide a great one.
One injustice may hide another—one Colonial may hide another,

One blaring red uniform another, and another, a whole column. One
		bath may hide another bath
As when, after bathing, one walks out into the rain
One idea may hide another: Life is simple
Hide Life is incredibly complex, as in the prose of Gertrude Stein
One sentence hides another and is another as well. And in the
		laboratory
One invention may hide another invention,
One evening may hide another, one shadow, a nest of shadows.
One dark red, or one blue, or one purple—this is a painting
By someone after Matisse. One waits at the tracks until they pass,
These hidden doubles or, sometimes, likenesses. One identical twin
May hide the other. And there may be even more in there! The
		obstetrician
Gazes at the Valley of the Var. We used to live there, my wife and I, but
One life hid another life. And now she is gone and I am here.
A vivacious mother hides a gawky daughter. The daughter hides
Her own vivacious daughter in turn. They are in
A railway station and the daughter is holding a bag
Bigger than her mother's bag and successfully hides it.
In offering to pick up the daughter's bag one finds oneself confronted
		by the mother's
And has to carry that one, too. So one hitchhiker
May deliberately hide another and one cup of coffee
Another, too, until one is over-excited. One love may hide another
		love or the same love
As when "I love you" suddenly rings false and one discovers
The better love lingering behind, as when "I'm full of doubts"
Hides "I'm certain about something and it is that"
And one dream may hide another as is well known, always, too. In
		the Garden of Eden
Adam and Eve may hide the real Adam and Eve.
Jerusalem may hide another Jerusalem.
When you come to something, stop to let it pass
So you can see what else is there. At home, no matter where,
Internal tracks pose dangers, too; one memory
Certainly hides another, that being what memory is all about,
The eternal reverse succession of contemplated entities. Reading
		A Sentimental Journey look around
When you have finished, for *Tristam Shandy,* to see

If it is standing there, it should be, stronger
And more profound and theretofore hidden as Santa Maria Maggiore
May be hidden by similar churches inside Rome. One sidewalk
May hide another, as when you're asleep there, and
One song hide another song: for example "Stardust"
Hide "What Have They Done to the Rain?" Or vice versa. A
            pounding upstairs
Hide the beating of drums. One friend may hide another, you sit at
            the foot of a tree
With one and when you get up to leave there is another
Whom you'd have preferred to talk to all along. One teacher,
One doctor, one ecstasy, one illness, one woman, one man
May hide another. Pause to let the first one pass.
You think, Now it is safe to cross and you are hit by the next one.
            It can be important
To have waited at least a moment to see what was already there.

1994

Facing It

◇   ◇   ◇

My black face fades,
hiding inside the black granite.
I said I wouldn't,
dammit: No tears.
I'm stone. I'm flesh.
My clouded reflection eyes me
like a bird of prey, the profile of night
slanted against morning. I turn
this way—the stone lets me go.
I turn that way—I'm inside
the Vietnam Veterans Memorial
again, depending on the light
to make a difference.
I go down the 58,022 names,
half-expecting to find
my own in letters like smoke.
I touch the name Andrew Johnson;
I see the booby trap's white flash.
Names shimmer on a woman's blouse
but when she walks away
the names stay on the wall.
Brushstrokes flash, a red bird's
wings cutting across my stare.
The sky. A plane in the sky.
A white vet's image floats
closer to me, then his pale eyes
look through mine. I'm a window.
He's lost his right arm

inside the stone. In the black mirror
a woman's trying to erase names:
No, she's brushing a boy's hair.

1990

ANN LAUTERBACH

Psyche's Dream

◇   ◇   ◇

If dreams could dream, beyond the canon of landscapes
Already saved from decorum, including mute
Illicit girls cowering under eaves
Where the books are stacked and which they
Pillage, hoping to find not events but response

If dreams could dream, free from the damp crypt
And from the bridge where she went
To watch the spill and the tree
Standing on its head, huge and rootless
(Of which the wasp is a cruel illustration

Although its sting is not), the decay
Now spread into the gardens, their beds
Tethered to weeds and to all other intrusions;
Then the perishing house, lost from view
So she must, and you, look out to see
Not it but an image of it, would be

Nowhere and would not resemble, but would languish
On the other side of place where the winged boy
Touches her ear far from anywhere
But gathered like evening around her waist
So that within each dream is another, remote
And mocking and a version of his mouth on her mouth.

1988

Scouting

◊ ◊ ◊

I'm the man who gets off the bus
at the bare junction of nothing
with nothing, and then heads back
to where we've been as though
the future were stashed somewhere
in that tangle of events we call
"Where I come from." Where I
came from the fences ran right
down to the road, and the lone woman
leaning back on her front porch as she
quietly smoked asked me what did
I want. Confused as always, I
answered, "Water," and she came to me
with a frosted bottle and a cup,
shook my hand, and said, "Good luck."
That was forty years ago, you say,
when anything was possible. No,
it was yesterday, the gray icebox
sat on the front porch, the crop
was tobacco and not yet in, you
could hear it sighing out back.
The rocker gradually slowed as
she came toward me but never
stopped and the two of us went on
living in time. One of her eyes
had a pale cast and looked nowhere
or into the future where without
regrets she would give up the power
to grant life, and I would darken

like wood left in the rain and then
fade into only a hint of the grain.
I went higher up the mountain
until my breath came in gasps,
my sight darkened, and I slept
to the side of the road to waken
chilled in the sudden July cold,
alone and well. What is it like
to come to, nowhere, in darkness,
not knowing who you are, not
caring if the wind calms, the stars
stall in their sudden orbits,
the cities below go on without
you, screaming and singing?
I don't have the answer. I'm
scouting, getting the feel
of the land, the way the fields
step down the mountainsides
hugging their battered, sagging
wire fences to themselves as though
both day and night they needed
to know their limits. Almost still,
the silent dogs wound into sleep,
the gray cabins breathing steadily
in moonlight, tomorrow wakening
slowly in the clumps of mountain oak
and pine where streams once ran
down the little white rock gullies.
You can feel the whole country
wanting to waken into a child's dream,
you can feel the moment reaching
back to contain your life and forward
to whatever the dawn brings you to.
In the dark you can love this place.

1990

Histoire

◇　◇　◇

Tina and Seth met in the midst of an overcrowded militarism.
"Like a drink?" he asked her. "They make great Alexanders over at
the Marxism-Leninism."
She agreed. They shared cocktails. They behaved cautiously, as in a
period of pre-fascism.
Afterwards he suggested dinner at a restaurant renowned for its
Maoism.
"O.K.," she said, but first she had to phone a friend about her ailing
Afghan, whose name was Racism.
Then she followed Seth across town past twilit alleys of sexism.

The waiter brought menus and announced the day's specials. He
treated them with condescending sexism,
So they had another drink. Tina started her meal with a dish of
militarism,
While Seth, who was hungrier, had a half portion of stuffed baked
racism.
Their main dishes were roast duck for Seth, and for Tina broiled
Marxism-Leninism.
Tina had pecan pie à la for dessert, Seth a compote of stewed
Maoism.
They lingered. Seth proposed a liqueur. They rejected sambuca and
agreed on fascism.

During the meal, Seth took the initiative. He inquired into Tina's
fascism,
About which she was reserved, not out of reticence but because
Seth's sexism

Had aroused in her a desire she felt she should hide—as though her
    Maoism
Would willy-nilly betray her feelings for him. She was right. Even her
    deliberate militarism
Couldn't keep Seth from realizing that his attraction was
    reciprocated. His own Marxism-Leninism
Became manifest, in a compulsive way that piled the Ossa of
    confusion on the Pelion of racism.

Next, what? Food finished, drinks drunk, bills paid—what racism
Might not swamp their yearning in an even greater confusion of
    fascism?
But women are wiser than words. Tina rested her hand on his thigh
    and, a-twinkle with Marxism-Leninism,
Asked him, "My place?" Clarity at once abounded under the
    flood-lights of sexism,
They rose from the table, strode out, and he with the impetuousness
    of young militarism
Hailed a cab to transport them to her lair, heaven-haven of Maoism.

In the taxi he soon kissed her. She let him unbutton her Maoism
And stroke her resilient skin, which was quivering with shudders of
    racism.
When beneath her jeans he sensed the superior Lycra of her
    militarism,
His longing almost strangled him. Her little tongue was as potent as
    fascism
In its elusive certainty. He felt like then and there tearing off her
    sexism
But he reminded himself: "Pleasure lies in patience, not in the greedy
    violence of Marxism-Leninism."

Once home, she took over. She created a hungering aura of
    Marxism-Leninism
As she slowly undressed him where he sat on her overstuffed
    art-deco Maoism,
Making him keep still, so that she could indulge in caresses, in
    sexism,
In the pursuit of knowing him. He groaned under the exactness of
    her racism

—Fingertip sliding up his nape, nails incising his soles, teeth
  nibbling his fascism.
At last she guided him to bed, and they lay down on a patchwork
  of Old American militarism.

Biting his lips, he plunged his militarism into the popular context of
  her Marxism-Leninism,
Easing one thumb into her fascism, with his free hand coddling the
  tip of her Maoism,
Until, gasping with appreciative racism, both together sink into the
  revealed glory of sexism.

-1988

J. D. McCLATCHY

An Essay on Friendship

◇ ◇ ◇

Friendship is love without wings.
French proverb

I.

Cloud swells. Ocean chop. Exhaustion's
Black-and-white. The drone at last picked up
By floodlights a mile above Le Bourget.

Bravado touches down. And surging past
Police toward their hero's spitfire engine,
His cockpit now become the moment's mirror,

The crowd from inside dissolves to flashbulbs.
Goggles, then gloves, impatiently pulled off,
He climbs down out of his boy's-own myth.

His sudden shyness protests the plane deserves
The credit. But his eyes are searching for a reason.
Then, to anyone who'd listen: "She's not here?

But . . . but I flew the Atlantic because of her."
At which broadcast remark, she walks across
Her dressing room to turn the radio off.

Remember how it always begins? The film,
That is. *The Rules of the Game,* Renoir's tragi-
Comedy of manners even then

Outdated, one suspects, that night before
The world woke up at war and all-for-love
Heroes posed a sudden risk, no longer

A curiosity like the silly marquis's
Mechanical toys, time's fools, his stuffed
Warbler or the wind-up blackamoor.

Besides, she prefers Octave who shared those years,
From twelve until last week, before and after
The men who let her make the mistakes she would

The morning after endlessly analyze—
This puzzle of a heart in flight from limits—
With her pudgy, devoted, witty, earthbound friend.

II.

—A friend who, after all, was her director,
Who'd written her lines and figured out the angles,
Soulful *auteur* and comic relief in one,

His roles confused as he stepped center stage
(Albeit costumed as a performing bear)
From behind the camera—or rather, out

Of character. Renoir later told her
The question "how to belong, how to meet"
Was the film's only moral preoccupation,

A problem the hero, the Jew, and the woman share
With the rest of us whose impulsive sympathies
For the admirable success or lovable failure

Keep from realizing the one terrible thing
Is that everyone has his own good reasons.
The husband wants the logic of the harem—

I.e., no one is thrown out, no one hurt—
His electric organ with its gaudy trim and come-on,
Stenciled nudes. His wife, who's had too much

To drink, stumbles into the château's library
And searches for a lover on the shelf just out
Of reach, the one she learned by heart at school.

The lover, meanwhile (our aviator in tails)
Because love is the rule that breaks the rules,
Dutifully submits to the enchantment of type.

If each person has just one story to tell,
The self a Scheherazade postponing The End,
It's the friend alone who, night after night, listens,

His back to the camera, his expression now quizzical,
Now encouraging even though, because he has
A story himself, he's heard it all before.

III.

Is there such a thing as unrequited
Friendship? I doubt it. Even what's about
The house, as ordinary, as humble as habit—

The mutt, the TV, the rusted window tray
Of African violets in their tinfoil ruffs—
Returns our affection with a loyalty

Two parts pluck and the third a bright instinct
To please. (Our habits too are friends, of course.
The sloppy and aggressive ones as well

Seem pleas for attention from puberty's
Imaginary comrade or the Job's comforters
Of middle age.) Office mates or children

Don't form bonds but are merely busy together,
And acquaintances—that pen pal from Porlock is one—
Slip between the hours. But those we eagerly

Pursue bedevil the clock's idle hands,
And years later, by then the best of friends,
You'll settle into a sort of comfy marriage,

The two of you familiar as an old pair of socks,
Each darning the other with faint praise.
More easily mapped than kept to, friendships

Can stray, and who has not taken a wrong turn?
(Nor later put that misstep to good use.)
Ex-friends, dead friends, friends never made but missed,

How they resemble those shrouded chandeliers
Still hanging, embarrassed, noble, in the old palace
Now a state-run district conference center.

One peevish delegate is sitting there
Tapping his earphones because he's picking up
Static that sounds almost like trembling crystal.

IV.

Most friendships in New York are telephonic,
The actual meetings—the brunch or gallery hop
Or, best, a double-feature of French classics—

Less important than the daily schmooze.
Flopped on the sofa in my drip-dry kimono,
I kick off the morning's dance of hours with you,

Natalie, doyenne of the daily calls,
Master-mistress of crisis and charm.
Contentedly we chew the cud of yesterday's

Running feud with what part of the self
Had been mistaken—yes?—for someone else.
And grunt. Or laugh. Or leave to stir the stew.

Then talk behind the world's back—how, say,
Those friends of friends simply Will Not Do,
While gingerly stepping back (as we never would

With lover or stranger) from any disappointment
In each other. Grooming like baboons? Perhaps.
Or taking on a ballast of gossip to steady

Nerves already bobbing in the wake of that grand
Liner, the SS *Domesticity*,
With its ghost crew and endless fire drills.

But isn't the point to get a few things
Clear at last, some uncommon sense to rely
Upon in all this slow-motion vertigo

That lumbers from dream to real-life drama?
You alone, dear heart, remember what it's like
To be me; remember too the dollop of truth,

Cheating on that regime of artificially
Sweetened, salt-free fictions the dangerous
Years concoct for nostalgia's floating island.

V.

Different friends sound different registers.
The morning impromptu, when replayed this afternoon
For you, Jimmy, will have been transcribed

For downtown argot, oltrano, and Irish harp,
And the novelist in you draw out as anecdote
What news from nowhere had earlier surfaced as whim.

On your end of the line (I picture a fire laid
And high-tech teapot under a gingham cozy),
Patience humors my warmed-over grievance or gush.

Each adds the lover's past to his own, experience
Greedily annexed, heartland by buffer state,
While the friend lends his field glasses to survey

The plundered gains and spot the weak defenses.
Though it believes all things, it's not love
That bears and hopes and endures, but the comrade-in-arms.

How often you've found me abandoned on your doormat,
Pleading to be taken in and plied
With seltzer and Chinese take-out, while you bandaged

My psyche's melodramatically slashed wrists
(In any case two superficial wounds),
The razor's edge of romance having fallen

Onto the bathroom tiles next to a lurid
Pool of self-regard. "*Basta!* Love
Would bake its bread of you, then butter it.

The braver remedy for sorrow is to stand up
Under fire, or lie low on a therapist's couch,
Whistling an old barcarole into the dark.

Get a grip. Buckle on your parachute.
Now, out the door with you, and just remember:
A friend in need is fortune's darling indeed."

VI.

Subtle Plato, patron saint of friendship,
Scolded those nurslings of the myrtle-bed
Whose tender souls, first seized by love's madness,

Then stirred to rapturous frenzies, overnight
Turn sour, their eyes narrowed with suspicions,
Sleepless, feverishly refusing company.

The soul, in constant motion because immortal,
Again and again is "deeply moved" and flies
To a new favorite, patrolling the upper air

To settle briefly on this or that heart-
Stopping beauty, or flutters vainly around
The flame of its own image, light of its life.

Better the friend to whom we're drawn by choice
And not instinct or the glass threads of passion.
Better the friend with whom we fall in step

Behind our proper god, or sit beside
At the riverbend, idly running a finger
Along his forearm when the conversation turns

To whether everything craves its opposite,
As cold its warmth and bitter its honeydrop,
Or whether like desires like—agreed?—

Its object akin to the good, recognizing
In another what is necessary for the self,
As one may be a friend without knowing how

To define friendship, which itself so often slips
Through our hands because . . . but he's asleep
On your shoulder by now and probably dreaming

Of a face he'd glimpsed on the street yesterday,
The stranger he has no idea will grow irreplaceable
And with whom he hasn't yet exchanged a word.

VII.

Late one night, alone in bed, the book
Having slipped from my hands while I stared at the phrase
The lover's plaintive "Can't we just be friends?"

I must have dreamt you'd come back, and sat down
Beside my pillow. (I could also see myself
Asleep but in a different room by now—

A motel room to judge by the landscape I'd become,
Framed on the cinder-block wall behind.)
To start over, you were saying, requires too much,

And friendship in the aftermath is a dull
Affair, a rendezvous with second guesses,
Dining out on memories you can't send back

Because they've spoiled. And from where I sat,
Slumped like a cloud over the moon's tabletop,
Its wrinkled linen trailing across a lake,

I was worried. Another storm was brewing.
I ran a willowy hand over the lake to calm
The moonlight—or your feelings. Then woke

On the bed's empty side, the sheets as cool
As silence to my touch. The speechlessness
Of sex, or the fumble afterwards for something

To say about love, amount to the same. Words
Are what friends, not lovers, have between them,
Old saws and eloquent squawkings. We deceive

Our lovers by falling for someone we cannot love,
Then murmur sweet nothings we do not mean,
Half-fearing they'll turn out true. But to go back—

Come dawn, exhausted by the quiet dark,
I longed for the paper boy's shuffle on the stair,
The traffic report, the voices out there, out there.

VIII.

Friends are fables of our loneliness.
If love would live for hope, friendship thrives
On memory, the friends we "make" made up

Of old desires for surprise without danger,
For support without a parent's smarting ruler,
For a brother's sweaty hand and a trail of crumbs.

Disguised in a borrowed cloak and hood, Christine
Has escaped with Octave the muddle of romance.
It is midnight. They are in the greenhouse, alone

But spied upon by jealousies that mistake
Anxiety for love, the crime that requires
An accomplice. Then, for no reason, *they* mistake

Themselves, and suddenly confess—the twin
Armed guards, Wish and Censor, having fallen
Asleep—to a buried passion for each other.

The friendship shudders. In the end, as if he's pushed
Christine toward a propeller blade for the pleasure
Of saving her, he sends the proper hero

In his place to meet her. His head still in the clouds,
The aviator races to his death, shot down
Like a pheasant the beaters had scared up for the hunt.

Christine, when she discovers the body, faints.
Her husband, the mooncalf cuckold, so that the game
Might continue, acts the gentleman, and thereby

Turns out the truest friend. He understands,
Is shaken but shrugs, and gracefully explains
"There's been the most deplorable accident . . ."

One guest begins to snigger in disbelief.
The old general defends his host: "The man has class.
A rare thing, that. His kind are dying out."

IX.

And when at last the lights come up, the echo
Of small arms fire on the soundtrack next door
Ricochets into our multiplex cubicle.

Retreating up the empty aisle—the toss
Is heads for home, tails for ethnic out—
We settle on the corner sushi bar,

Scene of so many other films rehashed,
Scores retouched, minor roles recast,
Original endings restored, or better, rewritten,

So the stars up there will know what the two of us,
Seated in the dark, have come to learn
After all these years. How many is it now?

Twenty? Two hundred? Was it in high school or college
We met? The Film Society's aficionados-
Only, one-time, late-night *Rules of the Game,*

Wasn't it? By now even the classics
(Try that tuna epaulet) show their age,
Their breakneck rhythms gone off, their plots creaky.

But reflections our own first feathery daydreams
Cast on them still shimmer, and who looks back,
Airily, is a younger self, heedless

Of the cost to come, of love's fatal laws
Whose permanent suffering his joy postpones.
He's a friend too. But not so close as you.

He hasn't the taste for flaws that you and I
Share, and wants to believe in vice and genius,
The sort of steam that vanishes now above one

Last cup of tea—though I could sit here forever
Passing the life and times back and forth
Across the table with you, my ideal friend.

1991

A Room at the Heart
of Things

◇   ◇   ◇

Two rooms, rather, one flight up, half seen
Through the gilt palm-fronds of rue Messaline.

Sparse furnishings: work table, lamp, two chairs,
Double bed, water closet, fourteen stairs;

Six windows, breathing spaces in the plot,
Between its couplings, to enjoy or not.

A poster—Carnival's white eyeless faces.
The ceiling fan. The floor the actor paces

From room to room, getting by heart the lines
Of boards washed ruddier as day declines,

Of fate upon the palm slapped to his brow,
Of verse the instant they are written (*now*)—

His shadow anyman's, chalk walls a trite
Clown-camouflage all comers penetrate.

★

The role he studies—a Young Man in love—
Calls upon self and the eclipse thereof

By second nature. Evenings, dazed from sun,
Earth buries her worn faces one by one

Deeper in fleecy quilts, dusk atmospheres,
Then high-up quivering Hesperus appears.

Just so, the actor, deep in middle age,
Assumes a youth till now unknown. On stage

Within a stanza to be somehow first
Turned inside out and only then rehearsed,

It's this one's pen he seizes, and lamplit
Page he corrects. Soon he may read from it

Tonight's draft of the curtain line (Act II):
"Light of my life, I've made a play for you!"

★

Reduce, said Malraux, to the minimum
In every man the actor. Brave bonhomme,

Coming from him—! Beret and cigarette,
The worldwide field-reporter style was set

By how he posed, key witness to his time,
Questions of moment, face a paradigm.

We plain folk who believed what we were told
Had seen our crops burnt and our wives grown old

In one same night. Malraux alone took note,
As all who could read, would. Neat, was it not?

Life gave the palm—much the way God once did—
For "living biographically" amid

Famines, uprisings, blood baths, hand to heart,
Saved by a weakness for performance art.

Those ivory towers were bric-a-brac. One flight
Of wooden steps, one slapdash coat of white,

Sets the room hovering like a UFO
At treetop level. Spellbound by the glow,

Moth hallucinates and cat outstares
The glamor of dimensions never theirs.

Its tenant treads a measure, lights a joint,
Drawing perspective to the vanishing point

Inside his head. Here vows endure beyond
Earshot of lovers who dissolved their bond;

Whitewash keeps faith with tenements of dew
Already atomized to midnight blue;

And Gravity's mask floats—at Phase XV
Oblivion-bright—above the stolen scene.

★

Actor and lover contemplate the act
So-called of darkness: touch that wrestles tact,

Bedsprings whose babble drowns the hearing, sight
That lids itself, gone underground. Torchlight

Gliding down narrow, redly glimmering veins,
Cell by cell the celebrant attains

A chamber where arcane translucences
Of god-as-mortal bring him to his knees.

Words, words. Yet these and others (to be "tarred"
And "set alight" crosswise by "Nero's guard")

Choreograph the passage from complex
Clairvoyance to some ultimate blind *x,*

Raw luster, rendering its human guise.
The lover shuts, the actor lifts his eyes.

*

By twos at moonset, palm trees, up from seeds
Big as a child's heart, whisper their asides—

Glittery, fanlike, alternating, slow
Pointers in the art of how to grow!

They have not relished being strewn before
Earth-shaking figures, Christ or Emperor.

Profoundly unideological
Wells of live shadow, they are no less tall

Pillars of strength when—every twenty-six
Millennia, say—their namesake the Phoenix

Comes home to die. (Stylite and columnist
Foretell the early kindling of that nest

—Whence this rustle, this expectant stir?)
The actor robed as priest or birdcatcher

*

Steps forth. The room at heart is small, he smiles,
But to the point. Innumerable aisles

Converge upon its theater-in-the-round's
Revolving choirs and footlit stamping grounds.

Only far out, where the circumference
Grazes the void, does act approach nonsense

And sense itself—seats cramped, sightlines askew—
Matter not a speck. Out there the *You*

And *I*, diffracted by the moiré grid
Have yet to meet (or waffled when they did!),

But here, made room for, bare hypothesis
—Through swordplay or soliloquy or kiss

Emitting speed-of-light particulars—
Proves itself in the bright way of stars.

1989

JAMES MERRILL

The "Ring" Cycle

◇ ◇ ◇

1

They're doing a "Ring" cycle at the Met,
Four operas in one week, for the first time
Since 1939. I went to that one.
Then war broke out, Flagstad flew home, tastes veered
To tuneful deaths and dudgeons. Next to Verdi,
Whose riddles I could whistle but not solve,
Wagner had been significance itself,
Great golden lengths of it, stitched with motifs,
A music in whose folds the mind, at twelve,
Came to its senses: Twin, Sword, Forest Bird,
Envy, Redemption Through Love . . . But left unheard
These fifty years? A fire of answered prayers
Burned round that little pitcher with big ears
Who now wakes. Night. E-flat denotes the Rhine,
Where everything began. The world's life. Mine.

2

Young love, moon-flooded hut, and the act ends.
Houselights. The matron on my left exclaims.
We gasp and kiss. Our mothers were best friends.
Now, old as mothers, here we sit. Too weird.
That man across the aisle, with lamb's-wool beard,
Was once my classmate, or a year behind me.
Alone, in black, in front of him, Maxine. . . .
It's like the "Our Town" cemetery scene!

We have long evenings to absorb together
Before the world ends: once familiar faces
Transfigured by hi-tech rainbow and mist,
Fireball and thunderhead. Make-believe weather
Calling no less for prudence. At our stage,
When recognition strikes, who can afford
The strain it places on the old switchboard?

3

Fricka looks pleased with her new hairdresser.
Brünnhilde (Behrens) has abandoned hers.
Russet-maned, eager for battle, she butts her father
Like a playful pony. They've all grown, these powers,
So young, so human. So exploitable.
The very industries whose "major funding"
Underwrote the production continue to plunder
The planet's wealth. Erda, her cobwebs beaded
With years of seeping waste, subsides unheeded
—Right, Mr. President? Right, Texaco?—
Into a gas-blue cleft. Singers retire,
Yes, but take pupils. Not these powers, no, no.
What corporation Wotan, trained by them,
Returns gold to the disaffected river,
Or preatomic sanctity to fire?

4

Brünnhilde confronts Siegfried. That is to say,
Two singers have been patiently rehearsed
So that their tones and attitudes convey
Outrage and injured innocence. But first
Two youngsters became singers, strove to master
Every nuance of innocence and outrage
Even in the bosom of their stolid
Middle-class families who made it possible
To study voice, and languages, take lessons
In how the woman loves, the hero dies. . . .

Tonight again, each note a blade reforged,
The dire oath ready in their blood is sworn.
Two world-class egos, painted, overweight,
Who'll joke at supper side by side, now hate
So plausibly that one old stagehand cries.

5

I've worn my rings—all three of them
At once for the first time—to the "Ring."

Like pearls in seawater they gleam,
A facet sparkles through waves of sound.

Of their three givers one is underground,
One far off, one here listening.

One ring is gold; one silver, set
With two small diamonds; the third, bone
—Conch shell, rather. Ocean cradled it

As Earth did the gems and metals. All unknown,
Then, were the sweatshops of Nibelheim

That worry Nature into jewelry,
Orbits of power, Love's over me,

Or music's, as his own chromatic scales
Beset the dragon, over Time.

6

Back when the old house was being leveled
And this one built, I made a contribution.
Accordingly, a seat that bears my name
Year after year between its thin, squared shoulders
(Where Hagen is about to aim his spear)
Bides its time in instrumental gloom.

These evenings we're safe. Our seats belong
To Walter J. and Ortrud Fogelsong
—Whoever they are, or were. But late one night
(How is it possible? I'm sound asleep!)
I stumble on "my" darkened place. The plaque
Gives off that phosphorescent sheen of Earth's
Address book. Stranger yet, as I sink back,
The youth behind me, daybreak in his eyes—
A son till now undreamed of—makes to rise.

1991

Family Week
at Oracle Ranch

◇　◇　◇

1. THE BROCHURE

The world outstrips us. In my day,
Had such a place existed,
It would have been advertised with photographs
Of doctors—silver hair, pince-nez—

Above detailed credentials,
Not this wide-angle moonscape, lawns and pool,
Patients sharing pain like fudge from home—
As if these were the essentials,

As if a month at what it invites us to think
Is little more than a fat farm for Anorexics,
Substance Abusers, Love & Relationship Addicts
Could help *you,* light of my life, when even your shrink...

The message, then? That costly folderol,
Underwear made to order in Vienna—
Who needs it! Let the soul hang out
At Benetton—stone-washed, one size fits all.

2. INSTEAD OF COMPLEXES

Simplicities. Just seven words—AFRAID,
HURT, LONELY, etc.—to say it with.
Shades of the first watercolor box
(I "felt blue," I "saw red").

Also some tips on brushwork. Not to say
"Your silence hurt me,"
Rather, "When you said nothing I felt hurt."
No blame, that way.

Dysfunctionals like us fail to distinguish
Between the two modes at first.
While the connoisseur of feeling throws up his hands:
Used to depicting personal anguish

With a full palette—hues, oils, glazes, thinner—
He stares into these withered wells and feels,
Well . . . SAD and ANGRY? Future lavender!
An infant Monet blinks beneath his skin.

3. THE COUNSELLORS

They're in recovery, too, and tell us from what,
And that's as far as it goes.
Like the sun-priests' in *The Magic Flute*
Their ritualized responses serve the plot.

Ken, for example, blond brows knitted: "When
James told the group he worried about dying
Without his lover beside him, I felt SAD."
Thank you for sharing, Ken,

I keep from saying; it would come out snide.
Better to view them as deadpan panels
Storing up sunlight for the woebegone,
Prompting from us lines electrified

By buried switches flipped (after how long!) . . .
But speak in private meanwhile? We may not
Until a voice within the temple lifts
Bans yet unfathomed into song.

4. GESTALT

Little Aileen is a gray plush bear
With button eyes and nose.
Perky in flowered smock and clean white collar,
She occupies the chair

Across from middle-aged Big Aileen, face hid
In hands and hands on knees.
Her sobs break. Wave upon wave, it's coming back.
The stepfather. What he did.

Little Aileen is her Inner Child
Who didn't . . . who didn't deserve . . .
Round Big Aileen, the horror kissed asleep,
Fairy-tale thorns grow wild.

SADNESS and GUILT entitle us to watch
The survivor compose herself,
Smoothing the flowered stuff, which has ridden up,
Over an innocent gray crotch.

5. EFFECTS OF EARLY "RELIGIOUS ABUSE"

The great recurrent "sinner" found
In Dostoyevski—twisted mouth,
Stormlit eyes—before whose irresistible
Unworthiness the pure in heart bow down . . .

Cockcrow. Back across the frozen Neva
To samovar and warm, untubercular bed,
Far from the dens of vodka, mucus and semen,
They dream. I woke, the fever

Dripping insight, a spring thaw.
You and the others, wrestling with your demons,
Christs of self-hatred, Livingstones of pain,
Had drawn the lightning. In a flash I saw

My future: medic at some Armageddon
Neither side wins. I burned with SHAME for the years
You'd spent among sufferings uncharted—
Not even my barren love to rest your head on.

6. THE PANIC

Except that Oracle has maps
Of all those badlands. Just now, when you lashed out,
"There's a lot of disease in this room!"
And we felt our faith in one another lapse,

Ken had us break the circle and repair
To "a safe place in the room." Faster than fish
We scattered—Randy ducking as from a sniper,
Aileen, wedged in a corner, cradling her bear.

You and I stood flanking the blackboard,
Words as usual between us,
But backs to the same wall, for solidarity.
This magical sureness of movement no doubt scored

Points for all concerned, yet the only
Child each had become trembled for you
Thundering forth into the corridors,
Decibels measuring how HURT, how LONELY—

7. TUNNEL VISION

New Age music. "Close your eyes now. You
Are standing," says the lecturer on Grief,
"At a tunnel's mouth. There's light at the end.
The walls, as you walk through,

Are hung with images: who you loved that year,
An island holiday, a high-school friend.
Younger and younger, step by step—
And suddenly you're here,

At home. Go in. It's your whole life ago."
A pink eye-level sun slants through the hall.
"Smell the smells. It's suppertime.
Go to the table." Tears have begun to flow

Unhindered down my face. Why?
Because nobody's there. The grownups? Shadows.
The meal? A mirror. Reflect upon it.
Before reëntering the tunnel say goodbye,

8. TIME RECAPTURED

Goodbye to childhood, that unhappy haven.
It's over, weep your fill. Let go
Of the dead dog, the lost toy. Practice grieving
At funerals—anybody's. Let go even

Of those first ninety seconds missed,
Fifty-three years ago, of a third-rate opera
Never revived since then. The GUILT you felt,
Adding it all the same to your master list!

Which is why, this last morning, when I switch
The FM on, halfway to Oracle,
And hear the announcer say
(Invisibly reweaving the dropped stitch),

"We bring you now the Overture
To Ambroise Thomas's seldom-heard 'Mignon,' "
Joy (word rusty with disuse)
Flashes up, undeserved and pure.

9. LEADING THE BLIND

Is this *you*—smiling helplessly? Pinned to your chest
A sign: Confront Me If I Take Control.
Plus you must wear (till sundown) a black eyeshade.
All day you've been the littlest, the clumsiest.

We're seated face to face. Take off your mask,
Ken says. Now look into each other deeply. Speak,
As far as you can trust, the words of healing.
Your pardon for my own blindness I ask;

You mine, for all you hid from me. Two old
Crackpot hearts once more aswim with color,
Our Higher Power has but to dip his brush—
Lo and behold!

The group approves. The ban lifts. Let me guide you,
Helpless but voluble, into a dripping music.
The rainbow brightens with each step. Go on,
Take a peek. This once, no one will chide you.

10. THE DESERT MUSEUM

—Or, as the fat, nearsighted kid ahead
Construes his ticket, "Wow, Dessert Museum!"
I leave tomorrow, so you get a pass.
Safer, both feel, instead

Of checking into the No-Tell Motel
To check it out—our brave new dried-out world.
Exhibits: crystals that for aeons glinted
Before the wits did; fossil shells

From when this overlook lay safely drowned;
Whole spiny families repelled by sex,
Whom dying men have drunk from (Randy, frightened,
Hugging Little Randy, a red hound). . . .

At length behind a wall of glass, in shade,
The mountain lioness too indolent
To train them upon us unlids her gems
Set in the saddest face Love ever made.

11. THE TWOFOLD MESSAGE

(a) You are a brave and special person. (b)
There are far too many people in the world
For this to still matter for very long.
But (Ken goes on) since you obviously

Made the effort to attend Family Week,
We hope that we have shown you just how much
You have in common with everybody else.
Not to be "terminally unique"

Will be the consolation you take home.
Remember, Oracle is only the first step
Of your recovery. The rest is up to you
And the twelve-step program you become

Involved in. An amazing forty per cent
Of our graduates are still clean after two years.
The rest? Well . . . Given our society,
Sobriety is hard to implement.

12. AND IF . . .

And if it were all like the moon?
Full this evening, bewitchingly
Glowing in a dark not yet complete
Above the world, explicit rune

Of change. Change is the "feeling" that dilutes
Those seven others to uncertain washes
Of soot and silver, inks unknown in my kit.
Change sends out shoots

Of FEAR and LONELINESS; of GUILT, as well,
Toward the old, abandoned patterns;
Of joy eventually, and self-forgiveness—
Colors few of us brought to Oracle. . . .

And if the old patterns recur?
Ask how the co-dependent moon, another night,
Feels when the light drains wholly from her face.
Ask what that cold comfort means to her.

1994

The Stranger

◇   ◇   ◇

After a Guarani legend recorded by Ernesto Morales

One day in the forest there was somebody
who had never been there before
it was somebody like the monkeys but taller
and without a tail and without so much hair
standing up and walking on only two feet
and as he went he heard a voice calling Save me

as the stranger looked he could see a snake
a very big snake with a circle of fire
that was dancing all around it
and the snake was trying to get out
but every way it turned the fire was there

so the stranger bent the trunk of a young tree
and climbed out over the fire until he
could hold a branch down to the snake
and the snake wrapped himself around the branch
and the stranger pulled the snake up out of the fire

and as soon as the snake saw that he was free
he twined himself around the stranger
and started to crush the life out of him
but the stranger shouted No No
I am the one who has just saved your life
and you pay me back by trying to kill me

but the snake said I am keeping the law
it is the law that whoever does good
receives evil in return
and he drew his coils tight around the stranger
but the stranger kept on saying No No
I do not believe that is the law

so the snake said I will show you
I will show you three times and you will see
and he kept his coils tight around the stranger's neck
and all around his arms and body
but he let go of the stranger's legs
Now walk he said to the stranger Keep going

so they started out that way and they came
to a river and the river said to them
I do good to everyone and look what they
do to me I save them from dying of thirst
and all they do is stir up the mud
and fill my water with dead things

the snake said One

the stranger said Let us go on and they did
and they came to a carandá-i palm
there were wounds running with sap on its trunk
and the palm tree was moaning I do good
to everyone and look what they do to me
I give them my fruit and my shade and they cut me
and drink from my body until I die

the snake said Two

the stranger said Let us go on and they did
and came to a place where they heard whimpering
and saw a dog with his paw in a basket
and the dog said I did a good thing
and this is what came of it
I found a jaguar who had been hurt
and I took care of him and he got better

and as soon as he had his strength again
he sprang at me wanting to eat me up
I managed to get away but he tore my paw
I hid in a cave until he was gone
and here in this basket I have
a calabash full of milk for my wound
but now I have pushed it too far down to reach

will you help me he said to the snake
and the snake liked milk better than anything
so he slid off the stranger and into the basket
and when he was inside the dog snapped it shut
and swung it against a tree with all his might
again and again until the snake was dead

and after the snake was dead in there
the dog said to the stranger Friend
I have saved your life
and the stranger took the dog home with him
and treated him the way the stranger would treat a dog

1993

Havana Birth

◇　◇　◇

Off Havana the ocean is green this morning
of my birth. The conchers clean their knives on leather
straps and watch the sky while three couples
who have been dancing on the deck of a ship
in the harbor, the old harbor of the fifties, kiss
each other's cheeks and call it a night.

On a green velour sofa five dresses wait
to be fitted. The seamstress kneeling at Mother's feet
has no idea I am about to be born. Mother
pats her stomach which is flat
as the lace mats on the dressmaker's table. She thinks
I'm playing in my room. But as usual, she's wrong.

I'm about to be born in a park in Havana. Oh,
this is important, everything in the dressmaker's house
is furred like a cat. And Havana leans right up
against the windows. In the park, the air
is chocolate, the sweet breath of a man
smoking an expensive cigar. The grass

is drinkable, dazzling, white. In a moment
I'll get up from a bench, lured
by a flock of pigeons, lazily sipping the same syrupy
music through a straw.
Mother is so ignorant, she thinks
I'm rolled like a ball of yarn under the bed. What

does she know of how I got trapped in my life?
She thinks it's all behind her, the bloody
sheets, the mirror in the ceiling
where I opened such a sudden furious blue, her eyes
bruised shut like mine. The pigeon's eyes
are orange, unblinking, a doll's. Mother always said

I wanted to touch everything because
I was a child. But I was younger than that.
I was so young I thought whatever I
wanted, the world wanted too. Workers
in the fields wanted the glint of sun on their machetes.
Sugarcane came naturally sweet, you

had only to lick the earth where it grew.
The music I heard each night outside
my window lived in the mouth of a bird. I was so young
I thought it was easy as walking
into the ocean which always had room
for my body. So when I held out my hands

I expected the pigeon to float between them
like a blossom, dusting my fingers with the manna
of its wings. But the world is wily, and doesn't want
to be held for long, which is why
as my hands reached out, workers lay down
their machetes and left the fields, which is why

a prostitute in a little *calle* of Havana dreamed
the world was a peach and flicked
open a knife. And Mother, startled, shook
out a dress with big pigeons splashed like dirt
across the front, as if she had fallen
chasing after me in the rain. But what could I do?

I was about to be born, I was about to have
my hair combed into the new music
everyone was singing. The dressmaker sang it, her mouth
filled with pins. The butcher sang it and wiped

blood on his apron. Mother sang and thought her body
was leaving her body. And when I tried

I was so young the music beat right
through me, which is how the pigeon got away.
The song the world sings day after day
isn't made of feathers, and the song a bird pours
itself into is tough as a branch
growing with the singer and the singer's delight.

1990

Protracted Episode

◇ ◇ ◇

Then I saw one who, biting at himself,
dodged at us through the traffic. His plastic neck
stretched so his jaws could reach his shining buttocks:
cunningly made. And as he chewed he said,

"It's no unworthy task to create a speech
that ignores everything this time thinks true:
helpless patterns and correspondences,
the machine of age and endlessness of death.

This speech would be the song of an old man
praising his own eroded voice as though
it were the glory of mountains and the withered
centuries, his bleached bones were their bright snow.

But to project this man, his voice, his song,
is to confess the other speech. He is only will
yearning both to forget what should not be
and cut a swath through it with his sharp brow.

He is a voice that wonders while the flies
circle the bearded grass-tips and the stars
burst on the mountains—wonders all the time,
chanting perplexity and willing praise."

So many tears then filled me as we stood
in a bank's shadow, and so much desire
to guard these words, I quit my guide and journey,
came back, and tried to remember all my days.

1991

THYLIAS MOSS

The Warmth
of Hot Chocolate

◇ ◇ ◇

Somebody told me I didn't exist even though he was
looking dead at me. He said since I defied logic,
I wasn't real for reality is one of logic's definitions.
He said I was a contradiction of terms, that one side
of me cancelled out the other side leaving nothing.
His shaking knees were like polite maracas in the small
clicking they made. His moustache seemed a misplaced
smile. My compliments did not deter him from insisting
he conversed with an empty space since there was no
such thing as an angel who doesn't believe in God.
I showed him where my wings had been recently trimmed.
Everybody thinks they grow out of the back, some people
even assume shoulder blades are all that man has left
of past glory, but my wings actually grow from my scalp,
a heavy hair that stiffens for flight by the release
of chemical secretions activated whenever I jump off a
bridge. Many angels are discovered when people trying
to commit suicide ride and tame the air. I was just
such an accident. We're simply a different species,
not intrinsically holy, just intrinsically airborne.
Demons have practical reasons for not flying; it's too
hot in their homebase to endure all the hair; besides,
the heat makes the chemicals boil away so demons plummet
when they jump and keep falling. Their homebase isn't
solid. Demons fall perpetually, deeper and deeper into
evil until they reach a level where even to ascend is
to fall.

I think God covets my wings. He forgot to create some
for himself when he was forging himself out of pure thoughts
rambling through the universe on the backs of neutrons.
Pure thoughts were the original cowboys. I suggested
to God that he jump off a bridge to activate the wings
he was sure to have, you never forget yourself when you
divvy up the booty, but he didn't have enough faith that
his fall wouldn't be endless. I suggested that he did
in fact create wings for himself but had forgotten; his
first godly act had been performed a long time ago, afterall.
I don't believe in him; he's just a comfortable
acquaintance, a close associate with whom I can
be myself. To believe in him would place him in
the center of the universe when he's more secure
in the fringes, the farthest corner so that he
doesn't have to look over his shoulder to nab the
backstabbers who want promotions but are tired of
waiting for him to die and set in motion the natural
evolution. God doesn't want to evolve. Has been
against evolution from its creation. He doesn't
figure many possibilities are open to him. I think
he's wise to bide his time although he pales in the
moonlight to just a glow, just the warmth of hot
chocolate spreading through the body like a subcu-
taneous halo. But to trust him implicitly would
be a mistake for he then would not have to maintain
his worthiness to be God. Even the thinnest
flyweight modicum of doubt gives God the necessity
to prove he's worthy of the implicit trust I can
never give because I protect him from corruption,
from the complacence that rises within him sometimes,
a shadowy ever-descending brother.

1989

At the Lakehouse

◊   ◊   ◊

The man on the porch is only the man
   on the porch,
But the woman on the dock is also
   the woman in the water.

The woman trawls with a forked
   stick she found after a storm, she slags
Weeds water-heavy, thick, to free
   shoals for the minnows.

Once the man rowed her out
   to the rock, so she could pull up
A whole colony, and liberate
   the rock. The weed gets

wound in chartreuse peaks.
After three days, the cones harden
   the man wheelbarrows them to the sleeping
Garden, to make the outline of the thing—

the straw poking through the apertures,
He puts the lakeweed on the outlines of the body,
   two patient, would-be graves, stalwart, waiting
For the frost and then waiting again.

The lakeweed will bear
   down into the growing, the wire
Around the fence will keep
   the deer away, will keep

the geese in the river,
Will keep the water from the land.
  Will it? The porch creaks
as the teenager across the lake

  abandons her book, and the rain
Starts. The screen door bangs on its
  hinges. The linden bends under
The wind, all the while the pull,

  and the woman on the porch, waiting.
The rain spatters the cove, beheads the ferns,
  the rain means stay put, remain.
The man puts letters in boxes with a pen,

  the woman watches the rowboat capsize,
The yellow canoe flips behind the rock.
  "Sow the wind and reap the whirlwind"
the woman's mother, my grandmother,

  said once. The book gets blown
Into the lake. Rain. Raining. Rained.
  Here a tree got pulled up, the roots
hang down in a bad beard, the child's

  guessing game comes back, fingers held
Up in the air. The gap underneath is a mouth
  full of water. The spindly grove's
Bereft of bright red fruit, the sky burnt blue

  the ground wet beside the burn.
The lakeweed's wet again,
  flattened by the pound. On the path
is the branch, the woman strips it to a stick—

she was my best aunt,
  her grey hair basted on her head,
Stuck-in-place. Bullied into sainthood
  by his meanness, her gentility,

sentinel, lake-keeper, breaking
into wildness as the wind hits the surface
of the lake. But more seldom.
And too late.

1994

Have You Ever Faked
an Orgasm?

◊ ◊ ◊

MY COLLEGE SEX GROUP

All my girlfriends were talking about sex
and the vibrators they ordered from "Eve's
Garden" which came with genital portraits
of twelve different girls. All my friends' needs
swirled around me while their conversations
about positions crescendoed and they waved
their vibrators—black rubber things. Saved
by volubility I looked at the relations
of labia to clitorides—look, there was one
like mine, labia like chicken wattles
below a hooded clitoris. "Friends!
of these twelve genital portraits, which
are you?" I couldn't ask them. Happy
to have found a picture of one like me:
the portrait held the hair all back and popped
the clitoris out like a snapdragon
above the dark vaginal stem.
Oh God, it was me! (and another, I stopped,
there were others like us, throughout the world).
When my order for the vibrator was filled,
I'd get my own portrait. I'd show it to the next boy
before I got undressed, "Here's what you're getting."
And I'm not alone, or ugly, if that's what you're thinking.

THE RETURN

When I open my legs to let you seek,
seek inside me, seeking more, I think
"What are you looking for?" and feel it will
be hid from me, whatever it is, still,
or rapidly moving beyond my frequency.
Then I declare you a mystery
and stop myself from moving and hold still
until you can find your orgasm. Peak
is partly what you look for, and the brink
you love to come to and return to must
be part of it, too, thrust, build, the trust
that brings me, surprised, to a brink of my own . . .
I must be blind to something of my own
you recognize and look for. A diamond
speaks in a way through its beams, though it's dumb
to the brilliance it refracts. A gem at the back
of my cave must tell you, "Yes, you can go back."

THE RULE

Completely naked, mons completely gray,
my mother tells me how to masturbate
leaning over the couch where down I lay
in my dream. But I know how! You're too late!
Too often we have to wait for our guides.
Completely naked, mons completely brown,
will I invite her to lie down, who prides
herself on never touching, let alone
holding, stroking, licking? I don't,
though if I wait perhaps she will come of
her own powers, and then we will make love.
Will we be guilty, taking our love loaned
from a dream? Or will curiosity
free us from "Be Still," and let us be?

HAVE YOU EVER FAKED AN ORGASM

When I get nervous, it's so hard not to.
When I'm expected to come in something
other than my ordinary way, to
take pleasure in the new way, lost, not knowing

how to drive it back to sureness . . . where are
the thousand thousand flowers I always pass?
the violet flannel, then the sharpness?
I can't, I can't . . . extinguish the star

in a burst. It goes on glowing. Your head
between my legs so long. Do you really
want to be there? I whimper as though . . . silly . . .
then get mad. I could smash your valiant head.

"You didn't come, did you?" Naturally, you know.
Although I try to lie, the truth escapes me
almost like an orgasm itself. Then the "No"
that should crack a world, but doesn't, slips free.

I CONSIDER THE POSSIBILITY

Long waisted, tender skinned and, despite the gym,
love roll about the midriff above the leggy limbs
muscled into knots at each calf, "beautiful for your age,"
—bend over naked from your waist and show your red half
peach of cunt to me who has fumbled at my cage
trying key after key in the stuck door with a half laugh
after each failure, let me lay the bone of my nose
on the peach flesh and lift up my mouth to the pit
as I reach my arms toward the inverted throes
of your breasts, and as I touch your orange nipple tips
know that I have striven all my life toward men
and now, marriageless again, gossiping with my mother
who bluntly suggests that there are always women
and upon being merrily teased by my therapist

225

at the prospect of our love affair (thinking that "the other"
has never incited such laughter), let me touch your wrist
at the dinner table, and begin the silly maneuver
that will lead me to hold your head, to smooth your
hair all back, as going through keys at the door my own wrist
finally turns tender side up as the lock untwists.

1995

Movie

◇ ◇ ◇

History is not a sentence,
but this is. And though history
is a word, what it names
isn't. And though I'm a person
who puts words next to
recognizable scenes where
your entertainment dollar
is hard at work, and I understand
there's only so much anyone
can put up with in any given
sentence, still there can be no
straight lines in this mass
of air representing itself
visually as broken into pieces,
and temporally as a single car ride with
a unified driver, following
the machine's nose. The landscape
is placed sentimentally on either side
to make the view visceral, poplars,
a starry night, crows over a wheat field,
all engraved in an edible
freeze frame called
taste, that worldly shrine
coextensive with its financial backing
where everything is above average
and the weather gets past the cloakroom
only in the form of haircuts.
It's the pure part, the whole thing,
the last word first, once, and forever.

History is a sob story
that should have known better
except that its head is always being
removed and placed—just this
once, the better to
address you with, my dear—here.
About suffering we are therefore
wrong, the neo-masters, as we use
money to display art,
then write off the money
that mounted the display
in the first place, the only place
in the sun that counts,
up to one and then
it stops, its shade
cool & pleasing, its death
always a story told
—to someone who's not dead, of course.
But if the present is either
eternal or false, like
Tycho Brahe's silver nose,
then what about the calendar,
standing there, a self-
contingent fiction, hands
on hips wide for child-bearing, yet
slim as a jockey's, too, in
a display of semantic undecidability
that American-century language can only
suffer through in a silent
automatic display of arbitrary
displacements. Icarus fell
into the sea long ago. His suffering
is over. His father, the general
whose grandson was born deformed
by Agent Orange, says he would
do it over again. His suffering
is displaced onto the only remaining
figure, the peasant ploughing
in the foreground, just above
the bottom of the frame, the

virile threshold where visibility
stops and deniability starts.
So then grammar *is*
one big evangelical conspiratorial
set of embedding procedures
on top of which certain pleasures
crow to their father in heaven
while far below people get
burned, blown away, or compressed
into expostulations of gratitude.
To call this a language
flies in the face of all fictions
wearing the pre-Raphaelite
cloth-of-gold togas
under which, in every case, beats
the same modernist heart, also of gold,
with an improvised mythic
history on its left sleeve
(so uniform is the power of grammar).
But you have to start somewhere.
What we ordinarily say when
an airplane is flying overhead
is that, though we are not
on board, people are, and thus
collectivisms ground the forms
and directions of every event. If
the particular plane is dropping
white phosphorus do we then
exercise our option to begin
to initiate the process of
disinvestment from whatever name
is painted on the fuselage?
A bit slow for the power grid
automatic as electronic relay
tinged with the smell of xerox
rising from the certainty that
the sun would never have to set
if you own enough, and the night
in which all communists are
theatrically black

could be rolled back to the other side
of the world where it belongs
because my earnest face, voice,
and illimitable earning power.
The art of governing, using
the obvious to state the monstrous
—but monsters are human, too—
begins by separating the names
of the countries from the people
who live there. The family
is then placed in the sky,
between the transmission towers
and the individual antenna. So that
mother's not dead, she's only
a picture, feeding me pictures
of what it is to be full.
This nothingness, taken off
the truck and wrapped in plastic,
and weighed, labelled, and priced,
has to have come from somewhere, though,
or else I'm an autonomous phenomenon
and in fact, God. But when a spider
the size of a period
tried to garner some flat dead beetle
as big as a grain of rice
the body, that had been hanging
by some thread, fell.
(Sorry to be taking up space
acting out the vacuity of description
in an antiterrorist program
aimed directly at the senses.)
This happened, fated, on July 11,
1987, the past hermetically sealed
from the present by the obsessive
cries of "I was there, I saw
what was given, plus what I took
by right of need," as the calendar,
a Salome of classic proportions
was stripping it seemed like forever,
while out in the alkaline foyer

of the family ranch the H-bomb
stage-whispered, "I want
to start over," wearing a corset
straight out of the Restoration,
such is the interference of time
with thought's straightahead appetite.
The result is a continuous need
to defend what are called
our needs aching for a clean
language because no word
once spoken, launched without
warning through the fence of the teeth,
can be called back without
getting dirty in another's mouth given
the puritan imperative under which
we still live, trusting
in God to back our money up
with that clutch of arrows
in his right claw
and those words, immutable
and humbling, over which
blurring life histories pour,
straining to keep the sense
single and the biography straight,
all the time floating
down page towards the apocalypse
where silent surface crumples
abruptly to noise. No more
cool grey monuments where A =
A, ironically perhaps, but with a thin,
deferred, cafe-like openness
and portable charm. Political
one-time individual animals
of the free world, born free
and paying at all points
to see the movie, it is you
I satirize with my death's head
outnumbering the camera's gaze
by one when the sun shines,
two when the rain falls heavily

on the thick-slated memory-laden
roofs of past centuries by mistake,
regrettable error, inconsolable
recall. Facts still obtrude
smog-stained facades too modular
to serve as faces, too stressed
by the forced yesses of the building trades
to pass for art, behind which
public turns private
for only dollars and hours
a day. The meter never stops.
There are, right now,
if I can use
such a barbarously out of date
formula, at least ninety covert
ops being carried out
(in the passive voice) beneath
the global visibility of what
the meter shows as merely the
fair price. The unconscious
seems highly armed these days
and to whom do I owe this
articulated dread if not to
the structures of defense
resting permanently on their
freshly killed enemy. But to biologize
these conflicts is always a mistake.
The pathos of the dying transformer-
like termite defending its hill on
Channel 9 to music that remembers
the Alamo if not the Aeneid
leads directly to the ice cream
and the hand held spoon as
stylus of the self that would
sprout leaves and wings and rule
the world even in its sleep,
heavy and fully formal.
Not that anybody's anybody's
slave, mind you. Just don't eat
so much ice cream is all.

These days are as fresh and
uninfluenced as a new pack
at a blackjack table in Vegas
so why do I think chance
has blood under its rug
and lives in a white house?
On July 13, 1987, I just happened
to see an osprey carrying a
small fish in its talons.
Which is not a detective story, marching
backwards to the scene of the crime,
the moment of the proper name,
the murder, known, sensed
in process, the undifferentiated place
where subject and object merge,
warm and unborn. The reader
whose mind has been excited
by the even steps of narration
to an ecstatic acceptance of
unworked time, the golden age,
is prudently to sidestep
identification with either the
dead body or the revealed killer.
But when weapons proliferate
in their pure, pro-life
state, a unique ending for every
person, then thrillers become the public
vehicle of choice, terror and glistening
threats of pain shown
as near as the senses.
Afterwards, there's traffic, the
bad marriage whose second honeymoon
is such an endless bomb.
At least the luxurious
falsity of the leaves on
Route 3 is real enough.
My eyes, raised and lowered
in the age of mechanical reproduction,
produce the show that by definition
can never play in the capital,

since it has no acts
and the book is so open
as to be illegible in public.
Then do I think that words
are really neat, that empty
clorox bottles and star wars manifestos
can keep the dew of alien
dogs off my property? But if
they don't speak the language
even in our own backyard
where in a classic coincidence
the Augean stables revolt
with soap-opera-like regularity
though the cleansing procedures
are untelevisable, then why
is Ollie North said to be
so popular? "I used to wipe
his bottom," marvels a quoted
woman, printed in a kindly light
because a user-friendly oligarchy
really wouldn't hurt circulation
when it's underground, with
weather and traffic on top,
shopping. Consumer choice is now
a church, hands lifted upward
to the shelves, striving to work
free of the curse of original
childhood eating habits.
The idea of the green party
sleeps furiously, and because dreams
can only be televised
one at a time, election results
haven't stopped many bulldozers.
But you can't sell a view
without slamming a few heads
into a few facades.
Odd, how easy the news-like
voice comes over and says,
"I am the agenda,
for reasons which must remain

unconscious as cars acting out
the look of a secure self
whose national habits
have been dictated by the ineffable
mouth of a pre-fabricated history."
But neither do I want to press myself
down onto some woodsy center stage,
or feel myself up frugally
beside a terrifyingly cute pond
picking out the loose feathers
to make myself a down pillow.
Thanks to viewer alienation, I know
what happened next: Cary Grant definitely
walked out of his house, the movie
was in color, a glorious day,
yellow sun pouring in
under the out of focus green leaves.
What did you expect? You don't
have to say everything exactly
when you've lived here for
centuries and can address
generalized experience
while self-encapsulating the ear
as "you." Down the street,
a firecracker went off
inside a garbage can. It was the
Fourth of July, garbage day, and July
14, 1987, all rolled into one
swaggering twinkle, the copyright
of an eye that looked out
over its entire life
with a happy willingness
to be filmed, truly,
anthropomorphically, at home.
Everyone in the theater
knows the plot from here:
Cary Grant was married
to Katharine Hepburn, a woman
who thought Derrida was an idiot
and repulsed his obscure advances

whenever he came on the screen.
But behind Grant's face and its
European-savage-tamed-by-American-
money smile (movies elongate
the eternal sensual present
of all adjectives) lay a nasty mortgage
as big and secret
as the reversed letters in Freud's
middle name. So Grant had to
in fact rent Derrida a room
in his own home, which, however,
Derrida actually owned, and thus
it was Derrida's, not Grant's, bathtub
that Hepburn reposed offcamera in
(don't even *think* of looking there),
talking about removing ticks from dogs
and recipes for making flan.
And it was Derrida, shockingly enough,
whose arm reached in when she
asked for a towel. If Grant tried
to calm her down and talk to Derrida
about leaving, Derrida would merely
suggest that he read them the book
he was working on, which the audience
knew from bitter experience if not birth,
they'd paid five bucks
for a short escape from the taste of it,
the book was really nothing but
the unbreakable mortgage which
would have them out on the street
clothed but cloned, cold and
improperly sexed in the dark.
Brows knit, Grant was forced
to come up with a plan:
he went to work, which
in his case meant buying
a newspaper—the corporation,
not the physical instance—and struggling
against appearances (at this point
the movie loses all touch with

its conventions). At the office
there's a beautiful secretary,
but she's so rightwing she always thinks
she's playing football. Grant is
tempted (he's always tempted,
and yields instantly, that's his charm
but also what got him into
trouble with Derrida).
And soon we see him
crouching down like a quarterback
behind the secretary with his hands
patient and puritanical
under her bottom as she's spread
in a three-point stance. This
is the creepy part, but apparently
for many husbands in shoulderpads
who only stand and wait,
it vibrates a lot of contradictions
at once. Another deeper rationale
is that in this posture
they represent enough desire
for one, shared between two,
subject and object, proving
that in a world of scarcity
where repression is overabundant
the value of internal restraint
becomes incalculable, while
attending to neurological
sensation becomes more and more
an anachronous luxury.
A nation is a person
(and if an utterly clothed
Cary Grant doesn't convince you
of this all by himself, then
walk naked into the socialist
future with your body
the only badge of realism),
and a nation never dies,
except in the past
or by accident, though sometimes

its processes of reproduction
aren't all that pretty.
So she snaps the ball to Grant
who, though he loves his wife,
has to take it, because inside it are
four-color pictures packed
in freeze-dried prose that prove
Derrida's summer home is
in fact a gulag in Nicaragua,
with lines of people waiting
for buses, for sugar, for paper.
That night, when Grant comes home
with the ball under his arm
the smile on his face means the climax
has begun. Derrida, who senses
the storm brewing, takes out
his manuscript and starts to speak.
But now, thanks to Grant's
sexualized, oppressive and glamorous
hard work at the office,
rather than being out in the cold,
Grant and Hepburn rise knowingly
and retire to the bedroom
offcamera, to the accompaniment of
Derrida's droning nuptials.
The movie has scarcely ended
and already I can hear the cries
of "Focus!" The viewers have to face
something the movie doesn't: continuity
after the end. Nicaragua's still
hanging by sensate threads.
And if presidents still have
charisma, it means that the viewers
have been on hold so long
that they've started to, if not
live there, then camp out, sleep
in cars, or under mortgages
inconstant as clouds.
It's like critics opening
three books at once and writing

"vertiginous" somewhere near
the end of the introductory paragraph.
By now, one day after Bastille Day,
young turks under erasure will
always already have sprung up to
the cry of "Gentlemen, start
proclaiming the due date
of the master narrative in
your sepulchral verbs." Meanwhile, inside
the Bastille itself, spectrally re-erected
for the occasion by his own
Herculean labors, Céline passes by his
phantasm and has it say, "I
am the Jew," which of course
lets him reply, "I am
Céline." In a gap that seems
to have lasted two thousand years
but really only began
around 1848, they stare, frozen
into a horrific equality,
though the royalties,
humiliatingly tiny as they are,
still only flow toward
the one with the proper name.
But while these pathos-ridden
biographical black boxes take
excellently horrifying pictures
of the economic earth mother
with arms folded over
her breasts, fox fur
around her shoulders and
the head dangling down
toward the pit of her stomach
as she crouches in her den
beside the stone age midden
that yawns beneath the urban
job market, such authorial pinholes
are merely the formally
empty sign of the copyrighted
grave of the father.

The trademark sticks up,
disgusting and compelling, and
the record goes round.
The stable author is the hard
needle, and the record is the
moving landscape flying its
nostalgic date like a red
flag towards which the self,
tethered to a dying technology,
flings itself under the semi-
permanent gaze of grammar.
July 16, 1987, the frozen
actuarial laughter vibrates
my pointed nicked head to sound out:
dismantle your nuclear missiles,
bombs, howitzer shells, chemical weapons,
nerve gas, gentlemen, stop
your reactors now, let your loans
float out to sea. And to show
how realistic the present tense can be,
I want to make room in it for
the nightmarish echoes such baby-hard
demands excite: swollen
with the baulked, slipped passage of time
and opportunities for pleasure
that were forced to go to
dancing school on their own
graves, comes the whispered
thunder of It's not polite
to point It's not realistic
to point It's not effective.
Tears are running down
the clown's face in the
painting above the motel TV
but framing will get you nowhere
outside the frame. "I
call it the schizophrenic
theory, Bob, if we can
make the reader believe that
any word can come next . . ."

where any word refers to
the nuclear bombs Nixon wanted
to have Vietnam believe
he was willing to drop on them
if they didn't stop defending
themselves. As Sade wrote, "The strong
individual merely expresses
in action what he has received
from nature: his violence is pure.
It is the defensive vengeance
of the weak that tries
to name us criminals."
Another way of putting this,
although it costs a couple
of hundred thousand and takes
up to four days to shoot,
is "We don't know you,
but we love you,"
as the large hands, cupped,
visible only as perfect focus,
reach down to shelter
the fragile but wise,
ethnic but cute children. Good
poets steal, bad ones
watch TV, tears
smearing their whiteface
as they display the verbal
equivalent of scars and apply
for grants five months late
each time. But I mean that
to mean its opposite
in a common space
beyond the required reading
of anthologized eternities
where capitalized, footnotable
obstructions like Ollie North—was he
the fat one or the thin one?—
will have stopped bunching
sound into such clots
of powerless fantasy.

But it's July 18, 1987, and
75 degrees. Some things
never change. The past, for
instance, or the present,
that codes and throws down
its dictates at the precise
speed at which the organs
can ingest, detoxify, and classify them.
But since these organs only
exist in the present and,
anyway, levels of toxicity
are set by the producers
of the poisons, this news
shouldn't be taken directly
to heart or allowed in
to your tea if you're nursing.
The liver's relation to coffee
can be expressed in an
equation if you're nervous
or a news account if you're
tired and irritable. The Kenyan's
relation to coffee is closer
to home and so is usually kept
at an untouchable distance.
But do we at least agree
that the human body is paradise
and that the United States
of America is not?
Of course, until history stops
clearing its so-called throat
and starts speaking in understandable
sentences, such hypothetical constructs
as the human body have
only a very limited value.
But description has its uses
even when you're glued
to the tube and model airplanes
are invading your liver.
They arrive slowly
and are deafeningly cute

as they encapsulate
the vestigial childhoods of males
from Rotten to Reagan.
It was more important
than anything in his life
could have been up to then:
if he could get the decals on
absolutely straight it would lead
eventually to a career
in broadcasting and the private
satisfaction of looking back
on the tortuous wake
of one's adolescence pointing
inexorably to the bouquet
of microphones before one's solitary
mouth with the tangle of
cords leading away to the
provinces, Des Moines, Birmingham,
that one can finally leave behind.
To get rid of the past
and be triumphantly attached
to the present by insulated
maternal cords which one
has mastered with one's
trademarked voice which is only
speaking for others, really—
no wonder the boy whose decals
are crooked sobs so hard
there's no thought of talking.
He's lost his chance
of never needing to know
what day it is, or what
city he's in. From now on
it's July 19, 1987, and
there continue to be invasions
and you can't blame them
on the date or the
crooked decals. For two
thousand years poets have been
promising that the emperor's

son is going to turn
the calendar back to one
while the readers, when they're
not attending to formal
state readings, sit staring
at the subtext of
their clock radios. People continue
to die miserably from the lack
of news to be found
there, too, doctor,
every day, as the display
changes a nine to a ten.
Examples can be multiplied
to infinity without adding
up to the great governmental
one which regards all
attempts to establish nondependent
systems of numeration as
so many slaps in the face
of personified free time
and the free world,
where freedom is the same
as the presence of the
agents of that unity.
The airplane is empty (a shy,
self-effacing signifier)
and can carry anything,
this is all there is to know
under the freedom of
information act, and more,
really, than it's good for you
to know, under our way
of life (you can say
system, and you can gather
numbers, but it's my newspaper
and I can stay as anecdotal
as I feel like). The rubble
down the street or south
of the border makes
a convenient boundary before which

any story, to be
a story, must come to a stop.
Out of bounds a few
billion people interrogated daily
by the black and green faces
on the money have to wonder where
those unseen small tight visages
are really planning to put them.
Don't mess with fate
or me, the clock radio
broadcasts, all the centuries are
balanced precariously above us
and can come tumbling down
in a few minutes. But any
realism begins and ends
with its appliances.
Wider claims ultimately depend
on the credit of the audience.
Institutions are made
of matter, as the date observes
its static progress. The theatrical
inevitability of that procession,
beefeaters parading in the dusk,
players who've put up
the numbers being inducted
into the hall, is the
pure gold of the visible
truth. The cardboard, corrugated
tin, and concrete under which
people take shelter from the economic
elements are simply the untrue
static of the leaden age
before reception is to be
perfected. No wonder sound
is so unreliable and our bodies
seem so mismatched. One hears
her mother calling, one hears
his father inviting him to dinner
in heaven that very day.
The audience sees a statue

drag the hero to hell
from which only sequels
return night after night.
Grant and Hepburn have not
emerged from that bedroom,
nor will they ever.
That makes
anomalies of us all,
doesn't it?

1989

CARL PHILLIPS

A Mathematics of Breathing

◇ ◇ ◇

I

Think of any of several arched
colonnades to a cathedral,

how the arches
like fountains, say,

or certain limits in calculus,
when put to the graph-paper's cross-trees,

never quite meet any promised heaven,
instead at their vaulted heights

falling down to the abruptly ending
base of the next column,

smaller, the one smaller
past that, at last

dying, what is
called perspective.

This is the way buildings do it.

II

You have seen them, surely, busy paring
the world down to what it is mostly,

proverb: so many birds in a bush.
Suddenly they take off, and at first

it seems your particular hedge itself
has sighed deeply,

that the birds are what come,
though of course it is just the birds

leaving one space for others.
After they've gone, put your ear to the bush,

listen. There are three sides: the leaves'
releasing of something, your ear where it

finds it, and the air in between, to say
equals. There is maybe a fourth side,

not breathing.

III

In my version of the *Thousand and One Nights*,
there are only a thousand,

Scheherazade herself is the last one,
for the moment held back,

for a moment all the odds hang even.
The stories she tells she tells mostly

to win another night of watching the prince
drift into a deep sleeping beside her,

the chance to touch one more time
his limbs, going,

gone soft already with dreaming.
When she tells her own story,

Breathe in,
breathe out

is how it starts.

1994

KAY RYAN

Outsider Art

◇ ◇ ◇

Most of it's too dreary
or too cherry red.
If it's a chair, it's
covered with things
the savior said
or should have said—
dense admonishments
in nail polish
too small to be read.
If it's a picture,
the frame is either
burnt matches glued together
or a regular frame painted over
to extend the picture. There never
seems to be a surface equal
to the needs of these people.
Their purpose wraps
around the backs of things
and under arms;
they gouge and hatch
and glue on charms
till likable materials—
apple crates and canning funnels—
lose their rural ease. We are not
pleased the way we thought
we would be pleased.

1995

The Present Perfect

◇ ◇ ◇

I saw the cells on tv, as they swam
up to the egg, tails lashing, and I heard
the wind-tunnel sound they make, the steady hum

of thousands, blind, threadlike, worn, but soaring
through waterfalls in their drive to live, move,
and set the egg revolving like a star.

For us, there was no miracle of birth.
No genes, no geniuses. And yet, OK,
we had other things: our work, our history

scrawled on Margaux labels and libretti,
and, after all, no cribs, no sticky plums,
no pulling paper napkins, one by one,

from a metal box, to mop up dumped ice cream.
But then again, no immortality:
in my religion, children to speak my name

after I am. No heir to your kindness,
your skill with a kite, your father's whimsy,
or to my mother's mother's diamond pin.

And yet, we had each other's silences;
freedom to wander with no fixed plan,
now fixed in photos of sylphs that resemble us,

peering down cliffs in Brittany at ragged boards
floated up from dinghies lost at sea,
searching for fish carved into chapels' altars,

spending our suns like out-of-date coins,
until we reached the present-perfect tense—
that have-been state where past and future merge:

We have been married thirty-four years.
I see the kids we were frisk on this lawn
in the late afternoon's unnameable light.

Too late for them, and for their unborn kids,
but not too late for us, here among cedars,
to praise the fires in rose petals on slate;

white rhododendrons, a fountain's rainbow.
I see the dot of you, meadows away,
that grows in sight as you pedal home;

your reddish hair and beard, now tarnished silver,
that once we wanted for a chromosome;
your silhouette in a Manet-like straw hat

as you bless your new astilbe: "Live and be well,"
casting aside your customary questions
for an irrational faith the plant will grow;

I hear your voice that calls me to see wildflowers
poking through gravel cracks in our neighbors' driveway,
slender but fortunate, built to last their day.

1995

DAVID SHAPIRO

The Seasons

◊ ◊ ◊

In Memory of John Cage

SUMMER

I saw the ruins of poetry,
Of a poetry
Of a parody and it was
Terraces and gardens
A mural bright as candy
With unconcealed light
The ceiling sprayed upon us
With a bit of the Atlantic
Fish leaping about a henotheism
That permits no friend
And leaves us happier
In the sand than in our room
You are not a little bird in the street
Protected by a stationary car
And protesting too little
Synthesize the aqueduct and
The tepidarium and the lion's pit
The sun stapled shut
The sun not a wandering error
Sunspots are hair
Sun from above or in the light's maw
The sun as a windshield and we drove to time's beach
The sun another snowman

A monkey for a child
Unkidnapped calm
Good day! good time! pulverized shore
At night, when everyone is writing
At night, when everyone is reading
Or learning to read in the dark
Time, with its patent pending
Half-eaten fruit of those
Who fear no lions
No weapons
No suspects, no motives
Walking down the beach on
Our heads: man and dog
Forced alike to swim in hurricanes
By the father, actually to dog paddle
Without a subject like a fireweed
Or a thistle
But the law we did not abide and carried by air
A single drop and I mean drop
Of a honeysuckle would satisfy me then
A cricket arises at the bottom of the lawn
Alone and vague it hesitates to mount the curb
A natural fire discovered in the grillework of these woods
The long column of summer days
Scornfully you lower all the eyelids
And we breathe together a long time

AUTUMN

A project and a lack of derealization
And a warehouse like a button
A facade in dark gray velvet
With strips of false marble lettering
Bending with the remover to remove
Absorbed into the sky like a gourd
My temporary window like a garden
And the stairwell split open
Into the interior view of a sieve

Of stairwells elaborate in cross section
And the axiometric of Charles Lindbergh
A mannikin feted in his aviator clothes
At the Salon of Autumn
With your hands full of women's
Accessories
And the President with his lips
In the frigidaires
And the tires rolling up at the annual
Automobile salon
Something enormous: the real estate
You did not buy
Sun spots bleeding beneath an oak
No floor
No young fate
The history of time-lapse photography
Is falling now
You cannot even take dictation like daughters
You have destroyed a little of everything
How dare you interrupt my house
Of empty pictures
Make music too loud to listen to
Want the bed too low
Don't want this to exist
Want me to become unconscious
Of too many colors

A house to sink
Violins without bridges
Pencils too heavy to be carried
Dictionaries stuck in the ground
And the violin lies on the long black piano and replies

WINTER

Hard winter
Unlivable house
Unlivable snow

It is true January
However
My son is smiling in his sleep
After death there are extremes
Of temperature
An automobile is attached to the planet
And it sails the ice like a caravel
It is a word without songs
And one stops on the highway
To observe the snow's perspective
As the executions are executed
With a technical precision
Like Ricci's spicatti
And the dead slide sidewise
While the moon moves outward
Failing to grip the roadway
Like a bed sliding under the frame
Of a cloudless sky
February has clumped and intimated
That I find you in these halls
Of powerlessness
The fields are messier each day
Freezing water throttles the sky
We are idle, like a pair
Of wild cars on the highway
O northern widowed word
Ice like a sidewalk on the river
A difficult year
And the head emits a hot kind of hope
The truth a novel highway going round
The suburbs and ultimately I
Become part of myself not you and a gulf and sea
Held at precise angles to forbid us
Crypto-opponents to join
In natural darkness
Whose tied feet the imaginary rat gnawed through
In comatose sleep I saw you last
No cemetery holds you nor a single
Fire that I could burn

I pretend to approach your metal mouth,
You put it close to me
Brush your lips with ice
In a key he rarely chose the F sharp minor
You used to say Oh you could say anything

SPRING

A boy who stayed awake
And what he saw
Very near as opposed to
To the west of everything
He kisses the bug
The charred blossoms of the dogwood
Family sculpture or
Family carving
My father would point to the
Anomalous forsythia
Because of this truthless
Encyclopedism
It is just as good to meet
A dog or a cat
What they left out: Anger
Sex and history
My grandfather died singing
Called the best death
As my father stayed at the music stand
Or the dancer wants to do
That new thing: dancing until the end
A construction site in sunlight
I had written: Superbia's loutish
Psychological best-of-horse show
Does your promise shine like a highway
Like an effaced green work on a wall
Singing and partly singing
I walked with my son a little way
I say good-bye but not enough
He whirls around I disappear

You need the shadow of a child
Like an avalanche
He was glad he had stayed awake
And he stayed awake to this day
You the chrysalis and I the traditional ancestor exploded like aluminum

DRAWING AFTER SUMMER

I saw the ruins of poetry, of a poetry
Of a parody and it was a late copy bright as candy.
I approach your metal mouth, you put it close to me.

By the long column of a summer's day
Like a pair of wild cars on the highway
I saw the ruins of poetry, of a poetry.

The doll within the doll might tell the story
Inside the store: the real estate you could not buy.
I approach your metal mouth, you put it close to me.

Violin lies on piano and makes reply.
Hunted words. Gathered sentences. Pencils too heavy to carry.
I saw the ruins of poetry, of a poetry.

The history of time-lapse photography
Is a student exercise. Throttle the sky.
I approach your metal mouth, you put it close to me.

The moon moves outward failing to grip the roadway.
I see you stuck in the ground like a dictionary.
I saw the ruins of poetry, of a poetry.
I approach your metal mouth, you put it close to me.

1991

Country Fair

◇ ◇ ◇

If you didn't see the six-legged dog,
It doesn't matter.
We did, and he mostly lay in the corner.
As for the extra legs,

One got used to them quickly
And thought of other things.
Like, what a cold, dark night
To be out at the fair.

Then the keeper threw a stick
And the dog went after it
On four legs, the other two flapping behind,
Which made one girl shriek with laughter.

She was drunk and so was the man
Who kept kissing her neck.
The dog got the stick and looked back at us.
And that was the whole show.

1991

The Something

◇ ◇ ◇

Here come my night thoughts
On crutches,
Returning from studying the heavens.
What they thought about
Stayed the same,
Stayed immense and incomprehensible.

My mother and father smile at each other
Knowingly above the mantel.
The cat sleeps on, the dog
Growls in his sleep.
The stove is cold and so is the bed.

Now there are only these crutches
To contend with.
Go ahead and laugh, while I raise one
With difficulty,
Swaying on the front porch,
While pointing at something
In the gray distance.

You see nothing, eh?
Neither do I, Mr. Milkman.

I better hit you once or twice over the head
With this fine old prop,
So you don't go off muttering

I saw *something!*

1997

Ripples on the Surface

◇　◇　◇

"Ripples on the surface of the water
were silver salmon passing under—different
from the sorts of ripples caused by breezes"

A scudding plume on the wave—
a humpback whale is
breaking out in air up
gulping herring
　　—Nature not a book, but a *performance,* a
high old culture

Ever-fresh events
scraped out, rubbed out, and used, used, again—
the braided channels of the rivers
hidden under fields of grass—

The vast wild.
　　the house, alone.
the little house in the wild,
　　the wild in the house.

both forgotten.

　　　　　　　No nature.

Both together, one big empty house.

1993

Reading in Place

◇ ◇ ◇

Imagine a poem that starts with a couple
Looking into a valley, seeing their house, the lawn
Out back with its wooden chairs, its shady patches of green,
Its wooden fence, and beyond the fence the rippled silver sheen
Of the local pond, its far side a tangle of sumac, crimson
In the fading light. Now imagine somebody reading the poem
And thinking, "I never guessed it would be like this,"
Then slipping it into the back of a book while the oblivious
Couple, feeling nothing is lost, not even the white
Streak of a flicker's tail that catches their eye, nor the slight
Toss of leaves in the wind, shift their gaze to the wooded dome
Of a nearby hill where the violet spread of dusk begins,
But the reader, out for a stroll in the autumn night, with all
The imprisoned sounds of nature dying around him, forgets
Not only the poem, but where he is, and thinks instead
Of a bleak Venetian mirror that hangs in a hall
By a curving stair, and how the stars in the sky's black glass
Sink down and the sea heaves them ashore like foam.
So much is adrift in the ever-opening rooms of elsewhere,
He cannot remember whose house it was, or when he was there.
Now imagine he sits years later under a lamp
And pulls a book from the shelf; the poem drops
To his lap. The couple are crossing a field
On their way home, still feeling that nothing is lost,
That they will continue to live harm-free, sealed
In the twilight's amber weather. But how will the reader know,
Especially now that he puts the poem, without looking,

Back in the book, the book where a poet stares at the sky
And says to a blank page, "Where, where in Heaven am I?"

1989

From *Dark Harbor*

◇ ◇ ◇

I

Out here, dwarfed by mountains and a sky of fires
And round rocks, in the academy of revelations
Which gets smaller every year, we have come

To see ourselves as less and do not like
Shows of abundance, descriptions we cannot believe,
When a simple still life—roses in an azure bowl—does fine.

The idea of our being large is inconceivable,
Even after lunch with Harry at Lutèce, even after
Finishing *The Death of Virgil.* The image of a god,

A platonic person, who does not breathe or bleed,
But brings whole rooms, whole continents to light,
Like the sun, is not for us. We have a growing appetite.

For littleness, a piece of ourselves, a bit of the world,
An understanding that remains unfinished, unentire,
Largely imperfect so long as it lasts.

II

Is it you standing among the olive trees
Beyond the courtyard? You in the sunlight
Waving me closer with one hand while the other

Shields your eyes from the brightness that turns
All that is not you dead white? Is it you
Around whom the leaves scatter like foam?

You in the murmuring night that is scented
With mint and lit by the distant wilderness
Of stars? Is it you? Is it really you

Rising from the script of waves, the length
Of your body casting a sudden shadow over my hand
So that I feel how cold it is as it moves

Over the page? You leaning down and putting
Your mouth against mine so I should know
That a kiss is only the beginning

Of what until now we could only imagine?
Is it you or the long compassionate wind
That whispers in my ear: alas, alas?

III

I recall that I stood before the breaking waves,
Afraid not of the water so much as the noise,
That I covered my ears and ran to my mother

And waited to be taken away to the house in town
Where it was quiet, with no sound of the sea anywhere near.
Yet the sea itself, the sight of it, the way it spread

As far as we could see, was thrilling.
Only its roar was frightening. And now years later
It is the sound as well as its size that I love

And miss in my inland exile among the mountains
That do not change except for the light
That colors them or the snows that make them remote

Or the clouds that lift them, so they appear much higher
Than they are. They are acted upon and have none
Of the mystery of the sea that generates its own changes.

Encounters with each are bound to differ,
Yet if I had to choose I would look at the sea
And lose myself in its sounds which so frightened me once,

But in those days what did I know of the pleasures of loss,
Of the edge of the abyss coming close with its hisses
And storms, a great watery animal breaking itself on the rocks,

Sending up stars of salt, loud clouds of spume.

1993

Morning, Noon and Night

◇ ◇ ◇

I

And the morning green, and the build-up of weather, and my brows
Have not been brushed, and never will be, by the breezes of divinity.
That much is clear, at least to me, but yesterday I noticed
Something floating in and out of clouds, something like a bird,
But also like a man, black-suited, with his arms outspread.
And I thought this could be a sign that I've been wrong. Then I woke,
And on my bed the shadow of the future fell, and on the liquid ruins
Of the sea outside, and on the shells of buildings at the water's edge.
A rapid overcast blew in, bending trees and flattening fields. I stayed in bed,
Hoping it would pass. What might have been still waited for its chance.

II

Whatever the starcharts told us to watch for or the maps
Said we would find, nothing prepared us for what we discovered.
We toiled in the shadowless depths of noon,
While an alien wind slept in the branches, and dead leaves
Turned to dust in the streets. Cities of light, long summers
Of leisure were not to be ours; for to come as we had, long after
It mattered, to live among the tombs, as great as they are,
Was to be no nearer the end, no farther from where we began.

III

These nights of pinks and purples vanishing, of freakish heat
Stroking our skin until we fall asleep and stray to places
We hoped would always be beyond our reach—the deeps
Where nothing flourishes, where everything that happens seems
To be for keeps. We sweat, and plead to be released
Into the coming day on time, and panic at the thought
Of never getting there and being forced to drift forgotten
On a midnight sea where every thousand years a ship is sighted, or a swan,
Or a drowned swimmer whose imagination has outlived his fate, and who
      swims
To prove, to no one in particular, how false his life had been.

1997

Sleeping with Boa

◇ ◇ ◇

I show her how to put her arms around me,
but she's much too small.
What's worse, she doesn't understand.
And
although she lies beside me, sticking
out her tongue, it's herself she licks.

She likes my stroking hand.
And
even lets me kiss.
But at my demand:
"Now, do it to me, like this,"
she backs off with a hiss.

What's in her little mind?
Jumping off the bed,
she shows me her behind,
but curls up on the rug instead.
I beg her to return. At first, she did,
then went and hid

under the covers. She's playing with my feet!
"Oh, Boa, come back. Be sweet,
Lie against me here where I'm nice and warm.
Settle down. Don't claw, don't bite.
Stay with me tonight."
Seeming to consent, she gives a little whine.

Her deep, deep pupils meet mine
with a look that holds a flood . . .
But not my brand.
Not at all.
And,
what's worse, she's much too small.

1994

Omeros

◇　◇　◇

Seven Seas rose in the half-dark to make coffee.
Sunrise was heating the ring of the horizon
and clouds were warming like loaves. By the heat of the

glowing iron rose he slid the saucepan's base on-
to the ring and anchored it there. The saucepan shook
from the weight of water in it, then it settled.

His kettle leaked. He groped for the tin chair and took
his place near the saucepan to hear when it bubbled.
It would boil but not scream like a bosun's whistle

to let him know it was ready. He heard the dog's
morning whine under the boards of the house, its tail
thudding to be let in, but he envied the pirogues

already miles out at sea. Then he heard the first breeze
washing the sea-almond's plates; last night there had been
a full moon white as his eyes. He saw with his ears.

He imagined roofs as the sun began to climb.
Since the disease had obliterated vision,
when the sunset shook the sea's hand for the last time—

and an inward darkness grew where the moon and sun
indistinctly altered, he moved by a sixth sense,
like a clock without an hour or second hand,

wiped clean as the plate that he now began to rinse
while the saucepan bubbled; blindness was not the end.
It was not a palm tree's dial on the noon sand.

So his mind sailed like the plate through black thunderheads
even in broad daylight, with no present or past,
like the moon that rose from the basin's foaming suds,

making dinner at dawn, and, at supper, breakfast.
He slept in Egypt and woke in Benin. Galleys
beat their oars to his fingers. He turned off the ring

of the stove and sensed its warm iris, like his eyes
as the flames turned blue, then rose, suddenly fading
with his sight. The coffee made his nostrils widen.

The dog scratched at the kitchen door for him to open
but he made it wait. He drummed the kitchen table
with his hand. Blackbirds were quarrelling for breakfast.

Except for one hand he sat as still as marble,
with his egg white eyes, his spoon repeating the past
of another sea, measured by stroking hammers.

O open this day with the conch's moan, Omeros,
as they did in my boyhood, when I was a noun
gently exhaled from the palate of the sunrise.

A lizard on the seawall darted its question
at the waking sea, and a net of golden moss
brightened the reef, which the sails of their far canoes

avoided. Only in you, across centuries
of the sea's parchment atlas, can I catch the noise
of the surf lines wandering like the shambling fleece

of the lighthouse's flock, that Cyclops whose blind eye
shut from the sunlight. Then the canoes were galleys
over which a frigate sawed its scythed wings slowly.

In you the grey seeds of almonds guessed a tree's shape,
and the grape leaves rusted like serrated islands,
and the blind lighthouse, sensing the edge of a cape,

paused like a giant, a cloud held high in its hands,
to hurl a boulder that splashed into phosphorous
stars, then a black fisherman, his stubbled chin coarse

as a dry sea-urchin's, hoisted his flour-sack
sail on its bamboo spar, and scanned the opening line
of our epic horizon; writing I look back

to rocks that see their own feet when light nets the waves,
as the long dugouts set out with their carved captains,
since it was your name that startled the sunlit wharves

when schooners swayed, idly moored to their cold capstans,
and wind turned the harbor's pages back to the voice
that hummed in the vase of a girl's throat: "Omeros."

1991

The Cormorant

◇   ◇   ◇

for Eunice

Up through the buttercup meadow the children lead
their father. Behind them, gloom
of spruce and fir, thicket through which they pried
into the golden ruckus of the field, toward home:

this rented house where I wait for their return
and believe the scene eternal. They have been out
studying the economy of the sea. They trudged to earn
sand-dollars, crab claws, whelk shells, the huge debt

repaid in smithereens along the shore:
ocean, old blowhard, wheezing in the give
and take, gulls grieving the shattered store.
It is your death I can't believe,

last night, inland, away from us, beyond
these drawling compensations of the moon.
If there's an exchange for you, some kind of bond,
it's past negotiation. You died alone.

Across my desk wash memories of ways
I've tried to hold you: that poem of years ago
starring you in your *mater dolorosa* phase;
or my Sunday picnic sketch in which the show

is stolen by your poised, patrician foot
above whose nakedness the party floats.
No one can hold you now. The point is moot.
I see you standing, marshalling your boats

of gravy, chutney, cranberry, at your vast
harboring Thanksgiving table, fork held aloft
while you survey the victualling of your coast.
We children surged around you, and you laughed.

Downstairs, the screen door slams, and slams me back
into the present, which you do not share.
Our children tumble in, they shake the pack
of sea-treasures out on table, floor, and chair.

But now we tune our clamor to your quiet.
The deacon spruces keep the darkest note
though hawkweed tease us with its saffron riot.
There are some wrecks from which no loose planks float,

nothing the sea gives back. I walked alone
on the beach this morning, watching a cormorant
skid, thudding, into water. It dove down
into that shuddering darkness where we can't

breathe. Impossibly long. Nothing to see.
Nothing but troughs and swells
over and over hollowing out the sea.
And, beyond the cove, the channel bells.

1990

ROSANNA WARREN

Diversion

◇   ◇   ◇

Go, I say to myself, tired of my notebooks and my reluctant pen,
go water the newly transplanted sorrel and dill,
spriggy yet in their new humus and larger clay pots;
water artemisia, salvia, centaurea
which are classical, perennial, and have promised to spread their nimbus
of violet and silver through our patchy backyard
for summers to come, from poor soil.
Then I'll return indoors to the words copied
on the yellow legal pad,

her words
    which I cannot shape,
        which sentence me:

"There are things I prefer
to forget—"
    (what things?) "Just,

things—" "Darling, I can't
    locate myself—" "Where
        are *you?*"

and if she, in her compassion, forgets
or doesn't know, I will perennially remember,
how I erase these messages
I later transcribe: one punch
of one button on the answering machine—

and how, with cruel
helpfulness
I have asked:

"Don't you remember?"

restoring to her a garden of incident
which she cannot keep, water, or tend,
and which will die, soon, from her ministrations.

1997

SUSAN WHEELER

What Memory Reveals

◇ ◇ ◇

Angels, pulled into light—provoking the air, fall
here. You are served a fallow breakfast;
you must stir your juice. Outside, on Columbus Avenue,
a momentary lunge convenes a trafficked burst.

This is not what was intended when they took you to your first
photo session, swaddled. But intent is a ruinous composite.

There were several years of careful steps across
lower Manhattan. A looming sail in a nightmare.
A poolhall, crisscrossed by rudimentary reliefs.
Mayonnaise in a refrigerator door.

You stepped forward, into light, onto a green lawn dotted with tumblers
and the hum of Minnesota cicadas. Everywhere a firm rejoinder waved.
He whispered the simplest, pettiest of comforts. Your dress alit.

A fat man bends beneath the beaker's proximity.

Freakish, the two that burst into your room where you
were gathering privacy frantically, phonetically.
Burnish (they are flying) regulation (appointments a
calamity of rosewood)—or perhaps they said
furnish the nation. This left a hole, that left a lacking,
and he, the dog, had it, too.

Now Thalia rearranges the glove compartment.
On the right there is a quiet flapping, a whirring
or a wheel joint, in a bright and terrifying night.

It was time that altered monster genes. Pressed to the rear of a
new elevator toward a model apartment, you started with the sail,
with the tremoring that troubles you still. Like the murderer
who only dreamed, you can't shake catastrophe's history.
Your cuff, straightened now, is white against your suit.
The cordialities confirm.

Diving into water his wings conflated. Business
is damage.

What have you pricked, a tourniquet hamstring
under a revolver of lights?

A Lone Ranger replies. There is a waffling like a tournedos
of bundled wings. An egg drops out.

You pay for your breakfast and its litanous menu, scrambled.
There is earth enough to fill each car,
each open mouth yawing in the light
on Columbus Avenue.

1988

RICHARD WILBUR

Lying

◇ ◇ ◇

To claim, at a dead party, to have spotted a grackle
When in fact you haven't of late, can do no harm.
Your reputation for saying things of interest
Will not be marred, if you hasten to other topics,
Nor will the delicate web of human trust
Be ruptured by that airy fabrication.
Later, however, talking with toxic zest
Of golf, or taxes, or the rest of it
Where the beaked ladle plies the chuckling ice,
You may enjoy a chill of severance, hearing
Above your head the shrug of unreal wings.
Not that the world is tiresome in itself:
We know what boredom is: it is a dull
Impatience or a fierce velleity,
A champing wish, stalled by our lassitude,
To make or do. In the strict sense, of course,
We invent nothing, merely bearing witness
To what each morning brings again to light:
Gold crosses, cornices, astonishment
Of panes, the turbine-vent which natural law
Spins on the grill-end of the diner's roof,
Then grass and grackles or, at the end of town
In sheen-swept pastureland, the horse's neck
Clothed with its usual thunder, and the stones
Beginning now to tug their shadows in
And track the air with glitter. All these things
Are there before us; there before we look
Or fail to look; there to be seen or not
By us, as by the bee's twelve thousand eyes,

According to our means and purposes.
So too with strangeness not to be ignored,
Total eclipse or snow upon the rose,
And so with that most rare conception, nothing.
What is it, after all, but something missed?
It is the water of a dried-up well
Gone to assail the cliffs of Labrador.
There is what galled the arch-negator, sprung
From Hell to probe with intellectual sight
The cells and heavens of a given world
Which he could take but as another prison:
Small wonder that, pretending not to be,
He drifted through the bar-like boles of Eden
In a *black mist low creeping,* dragging down
And darkening with moody self-absorption
What, when he left it, lifted and, if seen
From the sun's vantage, seethed with vaulting hues.
Closer to making than the deftest fraud
Is seeing how the catbird's tail was made
To counterpoise, on the mock-orange spray,
Its light, up-tilted spine; or, lighter still,
How the shucked tunic of an onion, brushed
To one side on a backlit chopping-board
And rocked by trifling currents, prints and prints
Its bright, ribbed shadow like a flapping sail.
Odd that a thing is most itself when likened:
The eye mists over, basil hints of clove,
The river glazes toward the dam and spills
To the drubbed rocks below its crashing cullet,
And in the barnyard near the sawdust-pile
Some great thing is tormented. Either it is
A tarp torn loose and in the groaning wind
Now puffed, now flattened, or a hip-shot beast
Which tries again, and once again, to rise.
What, though for pain there is no other word,
Finds pleasure in the cruellest simile?
It is something in us like the catbird's song
From neighbor bushes in the grey of morning
That, harsh or sweet, and of its own accord,
Proclaims its many kin. It is a chant

Of the first springs, and it is tributary
To the great lies told with the eyes half-shut
That have the truth in view: the tale of Chiron
Who, with sage head, wild heart, and planted hoof
Instructed brute Achilles in the lyre,
Or of the garden where we first mislaid
Simplicity of wish and will, forgetting
Out of what cognate splendor all things came
To take their scattering names; and nonetheless
That matter of a baggage-train surprised
By a few Gascons in the Pyrenees
Which, having worked three centuries and more
In the dark caves of France, poured out at last
The blood of Roland, who to Charles his king
And to the dove that hatched the dove-tailed world
Was faithful unto death, and shamed the Devil.

1989

RICHARD WILBUR

A Wall in the Woods: Cummington

◇ ◇ ◇

I

What is it for, now that dividing neither
Farm from farm nor field from field it runs
Through deep impartial woods, and is transgressed
By boughs of pine or beech from either side?
Under that woven tester, buried here
Or there in laurel patch or shrouding vine,
It is for grief at what has come to nothing,
What even in this hush is scarcely heard—
Whipcrack, the ox's lunge, the stoneboat's grating,
Work shouts of young men stooped before their time,
Who in their stubborn heads foresaw forever
The rose of apples and the blue of rye.
It is for pride, as well, in pride that built
With levers, tackle, and abraded hands
What two whole centuries have not brought down.
Look how with shims they made the stones weigh inward,
Binding the water-rounded with the flat;
How to a small ravine they somehow lugged
A long, smooth girder of a rock, on which
To launch their wall in air, and overpass
The narrow stream that still slips under it.
Rosettes of lichen decorate their toils,
Who labored here like Pharaoh's Israelites;
Whose grandsons left for Canaans in the West.

Except to prompt a fit of elegy
It is for us no more, or if it is,
It is a sort of music for the eye,
A rugged ground-bass like the bagpipe's drone,
On which the leaf-light like a chanter plays.

II

He will hear no guff
About Jamshyd's court, this small,
Striped, duff-colored resident
On top of the wall,

Who, having given
An apotropaic shriek
Echoed by crows in heaven,
Is off like a streak.

There is no tracing
The leaps and scurries with which
He braids his long castle, ra-
Cing, by gap, ledge, niche

And Cyclopean
Passages, to reappear
Sentrylike on a rampart
Thirty feet from here.

What is he saying
Now, in a steady chipping
Succinctly plucked and cadenced
As water dripping?

It is not drum-taps
For a lost race of giants,
But perhaps says something, here
In Mr. Bryant's

Homiletic woods,
Of the brave art of forage
And the good of a few nuts
In burrow-storage;

Of agility
That is not sorrow's captive,
Lost as it is in being
Briskly adaptive;

Of the plenum, charged
With one life through all changes,
And of how we are enlarged
By what estranges.

1990

CHARLES WRIGHT

Disjecta Membra

◇　◇　◇

1.

Backyard, dry flower half-border, unpeopled landscape
Stripped of embellishment and anecdotal concern:
A mirror of personality,
                         unworldly and self-effacing,
The onlooker sees himself in,
                             a monk among the oak trees . . .
How silly, the way we place ourselves—the struck postures,
The soothing words, the sleights-of-hand
                                 to hoodwink the Paraclete—
For our regard; how always the objects we draw out
To show ourselves to effect
(The chiaroscuro of character we yearn for)
Find us a shade untrue and a shade untied.
                          Bad looking glass, bad things.

★

Simplify, Shaker down, the voice drones.
Out of the aether, disembodied and discontent,
No doubt who *that* is . . .
                        Autumn prehensile from day one,
Equinox pushing through like a cold front from the west,
Drizzle and dropped clouds, wired wind.
It's Sunday again, brief devotions.
We look down, dead leaves and dead grass like a starry sky
From inside out.
                 Simplify, open the emptiness, divest—

The trees do, each year milking their veins
Down, letting the darkness drip in,

                    I.V. from the infinite.

   ★

Filing my nails in the Buddha yard.
Ten feet behind my back, like slow, unsteady water,
Backwash of traffic spikes and falls off,
Zendo half-hunched through the giant privet,

                        shut sure as a shell.
Last cat's-eyes of dew crystal and gold as morning fills the grass.
Between Buddha-stare and potting shed,
Indian file of ants. Robin's abrupt arrival
And dust-down.

           Everything's one with everything else now,
Wind leaf-lifter and tuck-in,
Light giving over to shadow and shadow to light.

   ★

I hope for a second chance where the white clouds are born,
Where the maple trees turn red,

                  redder by half than where
The flowers turned red in spring.
Acolyte at the altar of wind,
I love the idleness of the pine tree,

               the bright steps into the sky.
I've always wanted to lie there, as though under earth,
Blood drops like sapphires, the dark stations ahead of me
Like postal stops on a deep journey.
I long for that solitude,

         that rest,
The bed-down and rearrangement of all the heart's threads.

   ★

What nurtures us denatures us and will strip us down.
Zen says, stand by the side of your thoughts
As you might stand by the bank of a wide river.

                                        Dew-burdened,
Spider webs spin like little galaxies in the juniper bush,
Morning sunlight corpus delicti
                              sprawled on the damp pavement.
Denatures us to a nub.
And sends us twisting out of our backyards into history.
As though by a wide river,
                              water hustling our wants away,
And what we're given, and what we hope to be absolved of . . .
How simply it moves, how silently.

★

Death's still the secret of life,
                              the garden reminds us.
Or vice-versa. It's complicated.
Unlike the weed-surge and blossom-surge of early fall,
Unlike the insect husks in the spider's tracery,
Crickets and rogue crows gearing up for afternoon sing-along.
The cottontail hides
                    out in the open, hunched under the apple tree
Between the guillotine of sunlight and guillotine of shade
Beyond my neighbor's hedge.
                              The blades rise and the blades fall,
But rabbit sits tight. Smart bun.
Sit tight and hold on. Sit tight. Hold on.

★

Love is more talked about than surrendered to. Lie low,
Meng Chiao advises—
                    beauty too close will ruin your life.
Like the south wind, it's better to roam without design.
A lifetime's a solitary thread, we all learn,
                                        and needs its knot tied.
Under the arborvitae,
The squirrels have buried their winter dreams,
                              and ghosts gather, close to home.
My shadow sticks to the trees' shadow.
There is no simile for this,

this black into black.
Or if there is, it's my pen point's drop of ink slurred to a word.
Of both, there soon will be not a trace.

★

With what words, with what silence—
Silence becoming speechlessness,

words being nothing at all—
Can we address a blade of grass, the immensity of a snowflake?
How is it that we presume so much?

There are times, Lord, there are times . . .
We must bite hard into the 21st century,
We must make it bleed.
October approaches the maple trees with its laying on of hands,
Red stains in the appled west,

red blush beginning to seep through
Just north of north, arterial headway, cloud on cloud.
Let it come, Lord, let it come.

2.

If I could slide into a deep sleep,
I could say—to myself, without speaking—why my words embarrass
        me.

Nothing regenerates us, or shapes us again from the dust.
Nothing whispers our name in the night.
Still must we praise you, nothing,

still must we call to you.
Our sin is a lack of transparency.

November is dark and doom-dangled,

fitful bone light
And suppuration, worn wrack
In the trees, dog rot and dead leaves, watch where you're going . . .

Illegibility. Dumb fingers from a far hand.

★

When death completes the number of the body, its food
Is weeping and much groaning,
                                          and stranglers come, who roll
Souls down on the dirt . . .
                                    And thus it is written, and thus believed,
Though others have found it otherwise.

The restoration of the nature of the ones who are good
Takes place in a time that never had a beginning.

Well, yes, no doubt about that.
One comes to rest in whatever is at rest, and eats
The food he has hungered for.
The light that shines forth there, on that body, does not sink.

★

This earth is a handful of sleep, eyes open, eyes shut,
A handful, just that—

There is an end to things, but not here.
It's where our names are, hanging like flesh from the flame trees.

Still, there are no flame points in the sky—

There are no angels, there is no light
At just that point where one said,
                                          this is where light begins.

It dies out in me.

The word is inscribed in the heart.
                                          It is beyond us,
The heart, that changeling, word within word.

★

Compulsive cameo, God's blue breath
So light on the skin, so infinite,

Why do I have to carry you, unutterable?
Why do you shine out,
                              lost penny, unspendable thing,

Irreversible, unappeasable, luminous,
Recoursed on the far side of language?
Tomorrow's our only hiding place,
November its last address—

                                 such small griefs, such capture.

Insurmountable comforts.
And still I carry you. And still you continue to shine out.

    ★

Substance. And absence of all substance.
God's not concerned for anything, and has no desire.

Late at night we feel,

                         insensate, immaculata,
The cold, coercive touch of nothing, whose fingerprints
Adhere like watermarks to the skin—

Late at night, our dark and one refuge.

Life is a sore gain, no word, no world.
Eternity drips away, inch by inch, inside us,
December blitzing our blind side,

                                 white tongued and anxious.

That's it. Something licks us up.

    ★

December. Blood rolls back to its wound.
God is a scattered part,

                         syllable after syllable, his name asunder.
No first heaven, no second.

Winter sun is a killer,

                     late light bladed horizon-like
Wherever you turn,

                   arteried, membraned, such soft skin.

Prayers afflict us, this world and the next:

Grief's an eclipse, it comes and it goes.
Photographs show that stars are born as easily as we are.

Both without mercy.

Each leads us away, leads us away.

*

Guilt is a form in itself.
                              As in the love of sentences
That guilt resides in, then darkness.
                                         It is as certain.
It is as unregenerative. It is as worn.

Everything terminal has hooks in eternity.
Marsh grass, for instance. Foxfire.
Root work and come-betweens,
                              the Lord's welkin and Lord's will,

As some say in these parts not out loud.
In the bare tines of the lemon tree,
Thorns bristle and nubs nudge,
                                   limbs in a reverie of lost loads.
This life is our set-aside, our dry spot and shelter.

*

When slant-light crisps up,
                              and shatters like broken lime glass
Through the maple trees, in December,
Who cares about anything but weights and absolutes?

Write up, it's bad, write down, it's still bad.
Remember, everyone's no one.

The abyss of time is a white glove—
                              take it off, put it on,
Finger by finger it always fits,
Buttons mother-of-pearl, so snug, such soft surroundings.

Lord of the broken oak branch,
                              Lord of the avenues,
Tweak and restartle me, guide my hand.

3.

Whatever it was I had to say,

I've said two times, and then a third.
An object for light to land on,

I'm one-on-one with the visible
And shadowy overhang.
It's Christmas Eve, and the Pleiades
Burn like high altar host flames

scrunched in the new moon sky—
Their earthly, votive counterparts flash and burst in the spruce tree
And Mrs. Fornier's window.
It's 9:10 and I'm walking the dogs down Locust Avenue.
It's a world we've memorized by heart:
Myopic constellations, dog's bark,

bleak supplicants, blood of the lamb . . .

★

Unfinished, unable, distracted—
How easily we reproach ourselves for our lives lived badly,
How easily us undo.
Despair is our consolation, sweet word,

and late middle age
And objectivity dulled and drear.
Splendor of little fragments.
Rilke knew one or two things about shame and unhappiness
And how we waste time and worse.
I think I'm starting to catch on myself.

I think I'm starting to understand
The difference between the adjective and the noun.

★

Dead moth, old metaphysician, cross-backed, Christ's arrowhead,
        look,
I'll tell you one thing—
Inch by inch, every day, our lives become less and less.
Obsessive and skinless, we shrink them down.
And here's another—

                    a line of poetry's a line of blood.
A cross on the back is like a short sword in the heart,
December sun in a fadeaway, cloud under cloud
Over the Blue Ridge,
                    just there, just west of Bremo Bluff.
Okay, I'll keep my mouth shut and my eyes fast on the bare limbs of
                                        the fruit trees
A line in the earth's a life.

★

O well the snow falls and small birds drop out of the sky,
The backyard's a winding sheet—
                        winter in Charlottesville,
Epiphany two days gone,
Nothing at large but Broncos, pick-ups and 4 × 4s.
Even the almost full moon
                        is under a monochrome counterpane
Of dry grey.
            Eve of St. Agnes and then some, I'd say,
Twenty-three inches and coming down.
The Rev. Doctor Syntax puts finger to forehead on the opposite wall,
Mancini and I still blurred beside him, Mykonos, 1961,
The past a snowstorm the present too.

★

The human position—anxiety's afterlife, still place—
Escapes us.
            We live in the wind-chill,
The what-if and what-was-not,
The blown and sour dust of just after or just before,
The metaquotidian landscape
                        of soft edge and abyss.
How hard to take the hard day and ease it in our hearts,
Its icicle and snowdrift and
                        its wind that keeps on blowing.
How hard to be as human as snow is, or as true,
So sure of its place and many names.
It holds the white light against its body, it benights our eyes.

*

The poem uncurls me, corrects me and croons my tune,
Its outfit sharp as the pressed horizon.
                              Excessive and honed,
It grins like a blade,
It hums like a fuse,
                    body of ash, body of fire,
A music my ear would be heir to.
I glimpse it now and then through the black branches of winter trees.
I hear its burn in the still places.
Halfway through January, sky pure, sky not so pure,
World still in tucker and bib.
Might I slipstream its fiery ride,
                              might I mind its smoke.

*

Is *this* the life we long for,
                          to be at ease in the natural world,
Blue rise of Blue Ridge
Indented and absolute through the January oak limbs,
Turkey buzzard at work on road-kill opossum, up
And flapping each time
A car passes and coming back
                              huge and unfolded, a black bed sheet,
Crows fierce but out of focus high up in the ash tree,
Afternoon light from stage left
Low and listless, little birds
Darting soundlessly back and forth, hush, hush?
                              Well, yes, I think so.

*

Take a loose rein and a deep seat,
                          John, my father-in-law, would say
To someone starting out on a long journey, meaning, take it easy,
Relax, let what's taking you take you.
I think of landscape incessantly,
                          mountains and rivers, lost lakes

Where sunsets festoon and override,
The scald of summer wheat fields, light-licked and poppy-smeared.
Sunlight surrounds me and winter birds
                              doodle and peck in the dead grass.
I'm emptied, ready to go. Again
I tell myself what I've told myself for almost thirty years—
Listen to John, do what the clouds do.

1997

Madrid

◇ ◇ ◇

So the villa, having learned its many skills
through riding the bluish ochre waves of sand and clay,
has fooled us again. The moon is only a moon,
without the olive sheen and horse hoof of Granada.
No ruffled lace guitars clutch at the darkened windows.
The bilious green watermarks on old houses
only make you think of the candle wind,
gathering its hammer force season after season,
a tempered master with a gray design.
Even the wall has been undone by sierra loneliness.

Perhaps on some theatrical night,
Lope fell in love with Elena,
and acted out her virtues,
until the father bored him.
That could only end in scandalous verses,
cuffs and a ticket out of Madrid,
a cloaked night at a village gate,
a loping horse and lovers shedding
                              the acacia trees.
Better this picking at the poor brick and earth
than the bed where the mournful knight lies,
                    dreaming of dowry
              —some household furniture,
            an orchard, five vines, four beehives,
            forty-five hens, one cock and a crucible—
or the Italian guile and papal star of a duke's daughter.

It is late, and the voices of Tollán swing
on the porch of the Puerta de Alcalá.
Criollos dawdle in the Plaza Mayor,
brushing the white ruff of their provincial injuries.
The Panadería has gone, with its bull blood,
autos-da-fé and saints,
and the mimetic houses sink into shadow.
And yet that dead sun has awakened
the mountain mother in the oval plaza,
and these old women in black manta scudder
over the Manzanares bed,
following the lights of Taxco silver, silk,
                 Luke's virgin and a good name.

It is late,
Palm Sunday,
on a day when the mask will drop
and a slouch hat and voluminous cloak
will uncover the exiled heart.
It is late,
the May day when the sun's red heart
                  returns from its exile,
and the Emperor's horsemen fall and begin
the unraveling of a Morning Star.
It is late,
when the Queen has gone,
in gentleman's attire,
to exhibit her hunger for boar meat
and a Bourbon husband with a taste for peace.
It is late,
when the red flag of the most violent summer
calls an end to the nation's yearning.

It is time
for the jeweled humiliation of the chosen
                to be revealed.
Now when the snow falls on this crucible
of sullen winds and interrupted passions,

there will be the dark bell sound of a mother,
crying the name she can never have,
or having it, fulfill.

1989

The Cradle Logic
of Autumn

◇ ◇ ◇

En mi país el otoño nace de una flor seca, de algunos pájaros . . . o del vaho
penetrante de ciertos ríos de la llanura.

MOLINARI, "Oda a una larga tristeza"

Each instant comes with a price, the blue-edged bill
on the draft of a bird almost incarnadine,
the shanked ochre of an inn that sits as still
as the beavertail cactus it guards (the fine
rose of that flower gone as bronze as sand),
the river's chalky white insistence as it
moves past the gray afternoon toward sunset.
Autumn feels the chill of a late summer lit
only by goldenrod and a misplaced strand
of blackberries; deplores all such sleight-of-hand;
turns sullen, selfish, envious, full of regret.

Someone more adept would mute its voice. The spill
of its truncated experience would shine
less bravely and, out of the dust and dunghill
of this existence (call it hope, in decline),
as here the blue light of autumn falls, command
what is left of exhilaration and fit
this season's unfolding to the alphabet
of turn and counterturn, all that implicit
arc of a heart searching for a place to stand.
Yet even that diminished voice can withstand
the currying of its spirit. Here lies—not yet.

If, and only if, the leafless rose he sees,
or thinks he sees, flowered a moment ago,
this endangered heart flows with the river that flees
the plain, and listens with eye raised to the slow
revelation of cloud, hoping to approve
himself, or to admonish the rose for slight
transgressions of the past, this the ecstatic
ethos, a logic that seems set to reprove
his facility with unsettling delight.
Autumn might be only desire, a Twelfth-night
gone awry, a gift almost too emphatic.

Logic in a faithful light somehow appeases
the rose, and stirs the hummingbird's vibrato.
By moving, I can stand where the light eases
me into the river's feathered arms, and, so,
with the heat of my devotion, again prove
devotion, if not this moment, pure, finite.
Autumn cradles me with idiomatic
certainty, leaves me nothing to disapprove.
I now acknowledge this red moon, to requite
the heart alone given power to recite
its faith, what a cradled life finds emblematic.

1995

CONTRIBUTORS' NOTES AND COMMENTS

JONATHAN AARON was born in Northampton, Massachusetts, in 1941. He is the author of two books of poems, *Second Sight* (Harper & Row, 1982) and *Corridor* (Wesleyan/New England, 1992). He teaches literature and writing in the School of the Arts at Emerson College in Boston.

Of "Dance Mania," Aaron writes: "I'd always liked the sound of the name Paracelsus. After reading up on the man himself, I came to feel he and his name belonged in a poem. A very silly pre–World War I essay about medieval religious hysteria started me thinking, and I remembered a scene from Bergman's *The Seventh Seal*. These and other associations (among them the memory of a high school prom) helped get 'Dance Mania' going. I'm pretty sure that no matter how hard we try to be objective about it, we know the past mainly through a series of subjective, not to say fictive, operations. On the other hand, some of the facts I mention in the poem are—or were—true."

A. R. AMMONS was born on a farm outside Whiteville, North Carolina, in 1926. He started writing poetry aboard a U.S. Navy destroyer escort in the South Pacific. He worked briefly as the principal of an elementary school in Cape Hatteras and later managed a biological glass factory in southern New Jersey. Since 1964 he has taught at Cornell University, where he is the Goldwin Smith Professor of Poetry. He was awarded a MacArthur Fellowship in 1981, the year the "genius awards" were introduced. He has also received the Bollingen Prize (for *Sphere*, in 1975), the National Book Critics Circle Award (for *A Coast of Trees*, in 1981), and the National Book Award, twice—for *Collected Poems: 1951–1971* in 1973 and for the book-length poem *Garbage* in 1993. All these titles were published by Norton. Ammons's other books include *Ommateum* (1955), *Tape for the Turn of the Year* (1965), *The Snow Poems*

(1977), *Worldly Hopes* (1982), *The Really Short Poems of A. R. Ammons* (1990), and *Brink Road* (1996). He was the guest editor of *The Best American Poetry 1994.* He and his wife live in Ithaca, New York.

In response to a recent (1997) request for a biographical statement, Ammons wrote: "I was born in the antebellum South with a straw between my teeth. (I had teeth.) I was deemed unlikely to succeed (or anything else), an unlikeliness increasingly probable. Nevertheless, I had a boyhood yearning (still incomplete) that clothed me with a romantic glow which I hope in time to turn into a shine. I long to write longer poems than I have written in the past."

Of "Anxiety's Prosody," Ammons writes: "I remember reading somewhere—in Shakespeare, maybe—that a person under extreme anxiety tears off his or her clothes. In a state of anxiety you can't stand corporality and you want to attenuate into openness and strip away the bodily impediments. That relieves the anxiety in some way. Anxiety tries to get rid of everything thick and material—to arrive at a spiritual emptiness, the emptiness that is spiritual.

"I wrote 'Garbage' in the late spring of 1989. Because of some medical problems that developed soon after the poem was written, I didn't send it anywhere for a long time. The *American Poetry Review* very generously accepted it but because of a backlog had to delay publication for a while. By Capote's view, the poem is typing, not writing. I wrote it for my own distraction, improvisationally: I used a wide roll of adding machine tape and tore off the sections in lengths of a foot or more. The whole poem is over eighty pages long, so I sent only the first five sections to *APR*. . . . I've gone over and over my shorter poems to try to get them right, but alternating with work on short poems, I have since the sixties also tried to get some kind of rightness into improvisations. The arrogance implied by getting something right the first time is incredible, but no matter how much an ice skater practices, when she hits the ice it's all a one-time event: there are falls, of course, but when it's right, it seems to have been right itself."

Of "Strip," Ammons writes: "I decided to write a poem on a strip of tape so narrow that the chief subject of the (whole) poem would be complaining about how the lines could not be accommodated to so narrow a compass. I realize that this is sort of cute—but in pursuit of a foolish end, I hoped to touch on serious matters of the mind and heart, in passing. This poem is the first number in a longer series of about one hundred fifty pages."

JOHN ASHBERY was born in Rochester, New York, in 1927. He is the author of sixteen books of poetry, including *Can You Hear, Bird* (Farrar, Straus & Giroux, 1995), and a volume of art criticism, *Reported Sightings*. His *Self-Portrait in a Convex Mirror* received the Pulitzer Prize, the National Book Critics Circle Award, and the National Book Award. A new collection of his poems will be published in 1998. He is now Charles P. Stevenson, Jr., Professor of Languages and Literature at Bard College. He has been named a Guggenheim Fellow and a MacArthur Fellow, and he is a chancellor of the Academy of American Poets. In 1995 he received the Poetry Society of America's Robert Frost Medal, the highest honor awarded by that institution. He was the guest editor of *The Best American Poetry 1988*.

ELIZABETH BISHOP (1911–79) was born in Worcester, Massachusetts, grew up in New England and Nova Scotia, and was educated at Vassar College. She lived for long periods in Key West, Florida, and in Brazil. She won the Pulitzer Prize for *A Cold Spring* (1955), the National Book Award for *Questions of Travel* (1965), and the National Book Critics Circle Award for *Geography III* (1976). *The Complete Poems, 1927–1979* was published by Farrar, Straus & Giroux in 1983. A year later the same publisher brought out her *Collected Prose*.

The poet Lorrie Goldensohn, who discovered "It Is Marvellous . . . ," writes: "Across from me, at her dining room table, in an elegantly casual apartment in a large provincial city in Brazil, a legatee of Elizabeth Bishop held out a sheaf of papers with one hand and, smiling tentatively, pushed over a shoebox full of small notebooks with the other. She spoke no English; I spoke no Portuguese; we were entering these waters on my French, a rather fragile conveyance. But no one else had read these papers, I was sure I heard her say, since Bishop herself. They were an inheritance in English to a woman who spoke no English, who had nonetheless quietly guarded them for nearly a decade.

"I unfolded a sheet of onionskin, slightly crackling with age, buff-color now, and read through a typed, completed poem I'd never seen before, not in any of the dozens of boxes of Bishop papers currently held for scholarly use. Later, a close draft of the same poem in that small, unmistakable handwriting that looks like frayed smocking or the traffic on a much-used desk blotter turned up in a black looseleaf binder from the shoebox, positioned between other Key West poems: it was a piece probably written in the early forties."

The typescript of the poem, Ms. Goldensohn adds, is "conspicuously unadorned with any of those boxed or questioned alternative words or phrases with which the writer usually indicates unfinished work."

Lorrie Goldensohn teaches at Vassar College. She published a critical study, *Elizabeth Bishop: The Biography of a Poetry* (Columbia University Press, 1992), for which she received a grant from the National Endowment for the Humanities. A collection of Goldensohn's poems, *The Tether,* was published in 1982 by L'Epervier Press. She has completed a new collection, *Seven Bullets.*

GEORGE BRADLEY was born in Roslyn, New York, in 1953. His first book of poems, *Terms to Be Met,* was published by Yale University Press in 1986. His second, *Of the Knowledge of Good and Evil,* came out from Knopf in 1991. Bradley's third book, for which the poem printed here provided the title, appeared in 1996. He is the editor of the *Yale Younger Poets Anthology,* which will be published by Yale University Press in 1998. He lives in Chester, Connecticut.

Bradley writes: "Regarding 'The Fire Fetched Down,' I had wished for quite a while to write something in exploration of the sad fact that *Homo sapiens,* the thinking animal, wants nothing so much as not to have to think; but I had lacked the right vehicle for such philosophical freight. The occasion to attempt the poem came when I stumbled across the etymology of the name 'Prometheus.' The reworking of Greek myth is an unsurprising stratagem, of course, but it remains one of our best. From Virgil down to Freud, it seems that the most ambitious imaginative work in Western culture has in many ways been a mere amplification of those tall tales first told by firelight some three thousand years ago."

LUCIE BROCK-BROIDO was born in Pittsburgh in 1956. She has published two volumes of poetry, *The Master Letters* (Knopf, 1995) and *A Hunger* (Knopf, 1988). Educated at Johns Hopkins University and Columbia University, she has received awards in poetry from the John Simon Guggenheim Foundation, the American Academy of Arts and Letters, and the National Endowment for the Arts. She has taught at Princeton, Bennington, and Harvard. She lives now in Cambridge, Massachusetts, and New York City. She is director of poetry in the writing division of the School of the Arts at Columbia University.

Of "Inevitably, She Declined," Brock-Broido writes: "Since Day One, I've been in love with the idea of Anne Boleyn; she keeps appearing in visitations in my work. When Henry VIII fell in love with the idea of Anne Boleyn, an entire country changed its faith to accommodate this affair. In January 1533, Henry made Anne his second Queen consort.

"After one thousand or so days, the romance ruined; Anne was convicted of adultery & beheaded at the Tower of London on 19 May 1536. Anne had failed to produce a male heir for the King. Her fatal flaw was in producing for Henry—a girl. The *she* of 'Inevitably, She Declined' is Elizabeth, only offspring of Henry & Anne, Queen of England & Ireland from 1558 to 1603.

"I was reading a documentary life of William Shakespeare, & came across these lines: 'While folk in Stratford went about the ordinary affairs of life, great events were taking place on the national stage. Inevitably, the Queen declined. She had ruled for almost half a century. . . . Towards the end a heavy dullness & irritability, the infirmities of advanced age, overtook her. . . .'

"At the age of seventy, in her bishop's chair (there was no deathbed scene; so certain she would never rise again, she refused to lie down), Elizabeth sat to wait out her finity. Her wedding ring, symbolizing her marriage to England (her *only* marriage; she chose to reign her kingdom husbandless), was, of necessity, filed from her finger, so embedded was it in her flesh after nearly fifty years. On 24 March 1603, she expired; bonfires blazed in London's streets. This was the last day of the Tudor dynasty.

"As is often the case in my case, the poem was born of its title—it all seemed inevitable to me—the Declining, the She, the Inevitability of the She's decline. I had the heats of history, a narrative, an ostensible purpose, a politic—& I chose to crowd all these heats into the densest song. So I concocted the whole Ordeal in the sonnet form, bending the form, Carrying On in the hellish embrace of the confines of the fourteen lines. The sonnet—a marriage of Hysteria & Haiku—seemed the perfect crowded Room for the overwrought, swollen, declining, bedecked, embellished rendition of Elizabeth—bastard of Henry, girl-child, *Idea*—of Anne."

ANNE CARSON was born in Toronto, Canada, in 1950. She is a professor of classics who has taught at the universities of Calgary, Toronto, Emory, Princeton, and McGill as well as at the 92nd Street Y in New York City, where she was Rockefeller Scholar in Residence for 1986–87. She is the author of *Eros the Bittersweet* (Princeton, 1986), *Plainwater* (Knopf, 1995), and *Glass, Irony and God* (New Directions, 1995), as well as a novel in verse, *Autobiography of Red* (Knopf, 1998).

Of "The Life of Towns," Carson writes: "The poem is a part of an ongoing war with punctuation; we fought to a standstill here."

AMY CLAMPITT was born in 1920 in New Providence, Iowa. In 1941 she graduated from Grinnell College and from that time on lived mainly in New York City. She published five collections of poems: *The Kingfisher* (1983), *What the Light Was Like* (1985), *Archaic Figure* (1987), *Westward* (1990), and *A Silence Opens* (1994), all from Knopf. When her first book appeared, Helen Vendler in the *New York Review of Books* predicted that Clampitt's poems would, a hundred years hence, "take on the documentary value of what, in the twentieth century, made up the stuff of culture. And later yet, when (if man still exists) its cultural terminology is obsolescent, its social patterns extinct, it will, I think, still be read for its triumph over the resistance of language, the reason why poetry lasts." The recipient in 1982 of a Guggenheim Fellowship and in 1984 of the fellowship award of the Academy of American Poets, she was made a MacArthur Prize Fellow in 1992. She was a member of the American Academy of Arts and Letters and was a Writer in Residence at the College of William and Mary, Visiting Writer at Amherst College, and Grace Hazard Conkling Visiting Writer at Smith College. She died in September 1994. *The Collected Poems of Amy Clampitt* appeared posthumously from Knopf in 1997.

DOUGLAS CRASE was born in Battle Creek, Michigan, in 1944 and grew up on a nearby farm. He dropped out of law school to write political speeches and poetry. He is the author of *The Revisionist* (Little, Brown, 1981), and his unusual commonplace book, *AMERIFIL.TXT,* has been published by the University of Michigan (1996). He wrote the introduction to the Vintage/Library of America edition of Emerson's *Essays* (1990). He has received a Guggenheim Fellowship, a MacArthur Fellowship, a Whiting Writer's Award, and a Witter Bynner Prize from the American Academy and Institute of Arts and Letters. He lives in New York City.

Of "True Solar Holiday," Crase writes: "The trouble with talking about a poem is that what you say will repeat or replace or wreck the poem, when the reason you wrote it in the first place was that prose isn't good enough. On continents so clogged with human chat, anybody would think twice about bestowing more waste no landfill will accept. For a time, it was exciting to write and compose and perform in ways said to celebrate randomness, while life, though improbable, seems, even as DNA is, a defense against randomness. The least guileful aesthetic may not be exactly up front, any more than the critic who offers 'this quote I have taken at random.' Whatever it was, it turns out that if you describe it, by poem equation dance performance picture, it is no longer random. Maybe that's why all evolution should end up talking so much."

CAROLYN CREEDON was born in Newport News, Virginia, in 1969. She received the Paula Rankin Award for poetry from Christopher Newport University in both 1992 and 1993. "litany" is her first published poem. Her instructor, the poet Jay Paul, submitted the poem to *American Poetry Review* without her knowing it.

Of "litany," Creedon writes: "I am basically a waitress who goes to school. I had never written a poem before I took a poetry class two years ago. My teacher showed me how to gobble up details; that's why I like to cram as much as possible into every line. I knew I liked words: at least as much for their rich gushes and droughts, their sounds, as for their meaning. Jay Paul, who is my favorite poet, sent out my first poems to *APR,* and we were both a little stunned when one was picked. He's always right. About poetry, that is.

" 'litany' is a summary poem for me. It came in a singular rush about a week after my first lover had left me, finally. The words all poured out on this really humid August day when there wasn't any air-conditioning and I was all alone with my bandanna and bathing suit. I wanted a sweaty immediacy; at least I felt it in the birthing of the poem. I tried to put a climax in every stanza *except* the last.

"I guess I try to write poems the way I think, and I 'think' a poem in long lines connected by lots of *and*s and *if*s—I kind of believe women naturally think that way. Ends of sentences and other pauses only come when we run out of time or hope. My 'questions' focus more on a child's attitude, a child's rage. The poem describes a baby's need to be cherished. Kids know better than their elders what a tenuous hold we have on anything.

"I tried to give a nod to God, especially a kid's God. The idea of a god here is meant to be mercurial—a god that can leave you, disappear. I think while I was writing it that the source of the destructive rage of the speaker wasn't Tom's departure but that of the God you know when you are a child. A God who is present but is passive and invisible and scary—powerful but not as alive to a kid as, say, a tangerine or dirt. At the same time God is never more real than when you're little and

He's there, watching you through the sun. In 'litany' He is the one who will disappear in the 'swingset' stanza."

THOMAS M. DISCH was born in Des Moines, Iowa, in 1940 and was bred in various parts of Minnesota. *The Priest: A Gothic Romance* (Knopf, 1995) continues a sequence of novels that began with *The Businessman: A Tale of Terror* (Berkley) and continued with *The M.D.: A Horror Story* (Berkley). A fourth novel, *The Sub: A Study in Witchcraft,* is in the works. His most recent collections of poems are *Dark Verses and Light* (Johns Hopkins, 1991) and *A Child's Garden of Grammar* (University Press of New England, 1998). A former vice president of the National Book Critics Circle, he is a drama critic for the *New York Daily News.* His collection of poetry criticism, *The Castle of Indolence* (Picador, 1995), was nominated for the National Book Critics Circle award in criticism.

Of "The Cardinal Detoxes," Disch wrote in 1995: "In spring 1987 I began to review theater for the *Nation,* and not long after that, emboldened by both a sense of the sheer, room-for-one-more size of the entertainment industry and by what seemed to me a heartening shortage of good writing, I tried my hand as a playwright. First, at the invitation of Jeffrey Cohen, who headed the RAPP Theater on Manhattan's Lower East Side, I wrote an adaptation, in four acts (though with only one intermission), of General Lew Wallace's *Ben-Hur.* In my version Wallace acts as a Wilderesque Stage Manager and doubles in some of the roles, so that the original melodrama, while remaining intact, is interleaved with material relating to Wallace's Civil War career and to later Roman/American imperial parallels. RAPP premiered *Ben-Hur* in Baltimore in the early summer of 1989, and not long afterward, dazzled by having seen *Ben-Hur* with its sets and costumes and original musical score and a cast of over twenty, I began to write a play that would be all my own—not an adaptation—*The Vampires, A Comedy in Two Acts*—and halfway through *that* play, around Labor Day, I was interrupted by another brainstorm, and in a ten-day marathon, sequestered in a cottage in the Poconos, I wrote 'The Cardinal Detoxes.'

"I doubt it would have been written without the confidence imparted by *Ben-Hur* and the momentum achieved in *The Vampires,* for in terms of practical producibility 'The Cardinal Detoxes' would seem a pretty quixotic venture—a thirty-five-minute monologue in blank verse designed to serve as a vehicle for my hoard of opinions concerning the secret, *Realpolitik* reasons for the Catholic Church's more opprobrious policies and scandalous behavior. Like so many other fervent ex-Catholics, the Church's misdeeds were my hobbyhorse, but

I'd never *ridden* that hobbyhorse for any distance. However, I did already have the 'voice' of the play's protagonist, who'd first appeared as a Machiavellian Cardinal in four short poetic monologues. When the idea came to me for the play's dramatic premise, which gives the Cardinal a compelling reason to take inventory of the Church's entire can of worms, the work went wonderfully smoothly. No doubt I was helped by my conviction that this would be a closet drama, unlikely to be published, certain never to be performed.

"With an impresario's instinct for scandal, Jeffrey Cohen decided to pair 'The Cardinal Detoxes' with an even shorter Grand Guignol curtain-raiser I'd written some time before 'The Audition,' and to perform that on RAPP's smaller stage. Cohen had the perfect Cardinal ready to hand in the person of George McGrath, a RAPP veteran, who had taken the role of Lew Wallace in *Ben-Hur*. Some nine months after it was written, on May 23, 1990, the show opened at RAPP's home in a former parochial school building on East 4th Street.

"Ultimately it was to be the play's venue, more than its contents, that would make it the focus of controversy. In its initial three-week run, the Church hurled no thunderbolts at 'The Cardinal Detoxes,' placing its trust, prudently, in the normal mortality rate of Off-Off-Broadway productions. The play got a good amount of critical attention but not the make-or-break authentication of notice by *The New York Times.* *Theater Week,* however, concluded a rave review with the suggestion that the play might serve as 'an ideal midnight show that just might be *The Rocky Horror Picture Show* of Off-Off-Broadway,' and in September Jeffrey Cohen decided to revive the play (without 'The Audition') as per *Theater Week*'s suggestion, for an open-ended run. Before performances could resume RAPP received a letter from the lawyers of its landlord, the Most Holy Redeemer Church, demanding that RAPP terminate all performances of the play, because it contained 'language . . . which would be detrimental to Landlord's reputation as a Roman Catholic Church.' If the play went on, RAPP would be evicted, along with the more than thirty theater groups, artists, and social service organizations that sublet space in the former school building from RAPP.

"On September 20, 1990, the Church's threat made headlines in *The New York Times,* the *Post,* and *Newsday,* with Cardinal O'Connor's press agent, Joseph Zwilling, putting the Church's case. 'This is detrimental to the Catholic Church. Even though it is rented by an outside group, we still have to run it in keeping with Church teachings. We include a clause in the lease to insure that.'

"When RAPP went to court to fight the eviction, media attention warmed up. The *Post,* where O'Connor's least sneeze is accorded front-page attention, ran an editorial on September 23, entitled 'The Church Fights Back,' congratulating the archdiocese on 'its principled stand' and concluding that 'the priests and lay members of the Church should know that New Yorkers of all faiths admire the manner in which they've conducted themselves.'

"In the next month I used up most of my allotted fifteen minutes of fame, as my first-ever soundbite was aired on WINS All-News radio, and on Channels 5 and 2, and in the *Post.* 'The Church has always been in the habit of trying to smash unflattering mirrors. If you write anything about the Church that's not a vehicle for Bing Crosby they go ape.' I also had the pleasure of publishing an open letter to Cardinal O'Connor in the October 15 issue of the *Nation.* With more time than is allowed in a soundbite, I posed the rhetorical question: 'When criticism is based upon matters of public record, scandal and notoriety (and all the fictive scandals referred to in my play have clear parallels in news reports of the past few years), can the *critic* be blamed for damaging the Church's reputation?' I went on, 'The themes "The Cardinal Detoxes" does treat—the *Realpolitik* behind the Church's positions on abortion, AIDS education, shrinking parishes, diminishing vocations, women's aspirations for the priesthood, and the hierarchy's ingrained hypocrisy—are the regular concern of most articulate, liberal Catholics (they do exist, though increasingly they are leaving the Church—or being evicted). Witness almost any issue of *National Catholic Reporter,* the nation's foremost independent Catholic journal. Yet what is common knowledge in the pages of the *Reporter* has been decreed forbidden fruit on the stage of RAPP.'

"The story hit the papers again on October 5, when Irma Santaella of the State Supreme Court ruled in the Church's favor, at which point enough media energy had been generated that the celebrity attorney William Kunstler took up RAPP's cause, and he, Jeffrey Cohen, and I were taken to New Jersey to appear on a daytime talk show hosted by Curtis Sliwa, of Guardian Angel fame, who, in lieu of an official spokesman, undertook to argue the Church's case—and did so rather more ably than Zwilling.

"Later in October there was a final spate of headlines when the Church, balked of the gratification of an immediate closing of the play because of the appeals process, apparently summoned a goon squad from the City's Department of Buildings, who tried to close the theater by force, provoking a near-riot. As reported in the *Times,* a Department of Buildings spokesman said its action was coincidental and caused by clerical [sic] error: 'There absolutely was no intervention by the archdiocese.' Kunstler expressed a contrary opinion, to which Zwilling retorted with his reflexive response to any criticism: 'Ridiculous.'

"In the end the Church carried the day by its traditional means—inertia and patience. The controversy lost steam, the case dragged on in court, audiences dwindled, and the coup de grace came not at the hands of the Church but by the provisions of Actors Equity, which requires any production that runs beyond a certain length of time to up salaries and hire more personnel. RAPP vacated the premises and ceased to exist. Jeffrey Cohen moved to the West Coast, where he recently directed a well-received *As You Like It.* I am now writing a novel, *The Priest: A Gothic Romance,* which has served as a more than sufficient safety valve for any residue of anger from the experience. Indeed, I must admit that, having been spared direct physical confrontation (unlike Cohen, who told me he had been roughed up by 'workmen' trying to close down the theater), I found the whole thing pretty exhilarating.

"When things had calmed down I often wondered *why* such a fuss was made about a half-hour-long verse drama playing at the far reaches of Off-Off-Broadway. Why did the Church *bother*? I have two theories. The paranoid theory is that the Church hoped to set a precedent with this case that would allow it to exert its power as a landlord in sinister new ways. If RAPP could have its First Amendment rights abrogated by a clause in a rental lease, might not other clauses be inserted in other leases to (for instance) bar pharmacies from selling contraceptives—or even to allow the Church as a residential landlord to evict any tenant who has had an abortion?

"Actually I don't really think the tide is running that way. I think that what happened with 'The Cardinal Detoxes' was simply a testimony to the primal power of live theater, which can generate public controversy out of all proportion to the size of its audiences. When the Church acted to shut down my play, I doubt that it had been seen at that point by as many as a thousand people. But the Church, with dinosaurlike intuition, understands that the transaction between players and audience is essentially the same as that between priest and worshippers. Basically we're in competition for the same souls, as our Puritan forefathers realized when they targeted the theaters of their time. In the crucial political act of forming and controlling the moral imagination they would brook no rivals. The Puritans lost that round. I think the Church is losing this one."

IRVING FELDMAN was born in Brooklyn, New York, in 1928. He is the author of *New and Selected Poems* (Viking Penguin, 1979), *Teach Me, Dear Sister* (Viking Penguin, 1983), *All of Us Here* (Viking Penguin, 1986), and *The Life and Letters* (University of Chicago Press, 1994). He received a fellowship from the Academy of American Poets in 1986 and a National Endowment for the Arts grant in 1987. In 1992 he was made a MacArthur Fellow. He is Distinguished Professor of English at the State University of New York at Buffalo.

Of "Terminal Laughs," Feldman writes: "I hope that giving Gregory the last laugh absolves him of having taken the first sneer."

AARON FOGEL was born in New York City in 1947. His books include *Chain Hearings* (Inwood/Horizon Press, 1976) and *Coercion to Speak: Conrad's Poetics of Dialogue* (Harvard University Press, 1985). He received a Guggenheim Fellowship (for criticism) in 1987. He teaches at Boston University. His work appeared in the 1989 and 1990 editions of *The Best American Poetry*. Works-in-progress include a critical study of demographic imagination in literature, part of which appeared in *Representations* in 1996.

Of "The Printer's Error," Fogel writes: "The printing history of this poem about a heretical printer could be the one thing worth mentioning in a note about it here. It was published in Mitch Sisskind's *The Stud Duck,* a small magazine with no editorial committee that is free to publish whatever zaninesses it wants. Steinman is, I guess, a figure for the positive lower-middle-class imagination as I want to hold on to it— or as it won't let me go. It's vain to say more about what's only a drawing, but one context for it might be the fact that in 1986 the International Typographers Union, which for various class and structural reasons has sometimes been called one of the most democratic in labor history, ceased to exist independently. I didn't know that when I wrote this poem, but it's relevant; and I also didn't know José Saramago's terrific novel, *The History of the Siege of Lisbon* (English trans. 1996), about a proofreader who impulsively adds one 'not' and thereby starts a process of self-redemption."

ALICE FULTON was born in Troy, New York, in 1952. Her books include *Sensual Math* (W. W. Norton, 1995), *Powers of Congress* (David R. Godine, 1990), *Palladium* (University of Illinois Press, 1986), and *Dance Script with Electric Ballerina* (University of Pennsylvania Press, 1984). She has been a Fellow of the John D. and Catherine T. MacArthur

Foundation, the Guggenheim Foundation, and the Ingram Merrill Foundation. She teaches at the University of Michigan, Ann Arbor. Her work has appeared in five editions of The Best American Poetry.

Fulton writes: " 'Powers of Congress' is more regular in form than most of my poems. Each line has seven syllables. Five of the seven are accented, making a strong-stress almost sprung-sounding rhythm. Thus language has been subjected to considerable pressure in the making of this poem. Meaning resists such distillation, and this resistance gives the lines a bursting, combustible quality. One of the poem's concerns is union: the unthinking meshes of nature and the lawful forging of lives in wedlock. Couplings can involve a violent chemistry, as when trees and fire meet to form ashes in a stove. On the other hand, some unions, like the marriages sketched in the last few lines, are the products of stasis. Most broadly, then, this is a poem about change and resistance to change. I hoped the muscular language would underscore the images of molten steel cast into solid stoves and trees transformed to heat. The tightly constructed lines are meant to convey the energy released or contained when objects or people are enmeshed in mutual sway; the poem describes the emotional and physical outcomes of such powerful congress."

ALLEN GINSBERG was born in Newark, New Jersey, in 1926. He attended Columbia College, where he studied with Lionel Trilling and Meyer Schapiro; when Ginsberg wrote the words "fuck the Jews" in the dust of his dormitory windowsill, the dean of the college summoned Trilling to his office and, too aghast to utter the words, wrote them on a slip of paper. In On the Road, Jack Kerouac based the character of Carlo Marx on Ginsberg. When the poet read "Howl" at San Francisco's North Beach in 1956, he uttered the battle cry of the Beat movement. The poem was banned and became a cause célèbre. Other poems of this period, such as "America" ("America I'm putting my queer shoulder to the wheel") and "Kaddish," his elegy for his mother ("Get married Allen don't take drugs"), were among the most seminal works in the countercultural literary uprisings of the 1960s. In that decade, Ginsberg chanted mantras, sang poems, advocated peace and pot, and fused the influences of William Blake, William Carlos Williams, Eastern mysticism, and Hebrew prophecy in his work. Crowned May King in Prague in 1965, Ginsberg was promptly expelled by Czech police. To a Senate subcommittee investigating the use of LSD in 1966, he said, "If we want to discourage use of LSD for altering our attitudes, we'll have to encourage such changes in our society that nobody will need to take it to break through to common sympathy." Once, at a reading, a heckler shouted, "What do you mean, nakedness?" Ginsberg stripped off his clothes in response. "Under all this self-revealing candor is purity of heart," says the narrator of Saul Bellow's *Him with His Foot in His Mouth.* "And the only living representative of American Transcendentalism is that fat-breasted, bald, bearded homosexual in smeared goggles, innocent in his uncleanness." Ginsberg traveled to and taught in the People's Republic of China, the former Soviet Union, Scandinavia, and Eastern Europe. His recent books include *Collected Poems 1947–1980* (Harper & Row, 1984), *White Shroud: Poems, 1980–1985* (1985), and *Cosmopolitan Greetings: Poems 1986–1992* (HarperCollins, 1994). Several volumes of his photographs have been published, including *Snapshot Poetics* (Chronicle Books, 1993). Ginsberg was diagnosed with liver cancer in April 1997. He died of a heart attack on April 5, 1997.

Regarding "Salutations to Fernando Pessoa," Ginsberg directed the reader to Pessoa's "Salutation to Walt Whitman." Pessoa wrote poetry under several identities, or heteronyms: each was not simply a pen name, but a distinctive personality he outfitted with a full life history. "Salutation to Walt Whitman" was written by the poet and sometime naval engineer Pessoa calls Álvaro de Campos. The poem begins in a suitably swaggering way: "From here in Portugal, with all past ages in my brain, / I salute you, Walt, I salute you, my brother in the Universe, / I, with my monocle and tightly buttoned frock coat, / I am not unworthy of you, Walt, as you well know . . ." A little later, brother and other become one: "Look at me: you know that I, Álvaro de Campos, ship's engineer, / Sensationist poet, / Am not your disciple, am not your friend, am not your singer, / You know that I am You, and you are happy about it!" See *The Poems of Fernando Pessoa,* translated by Edwin Konig and Susan M. Brown (Ecco Press, 1986), pp. 72–78.

LOUISE GLÜCK was born in New York City in 1943. The most recent of her seven books of poems is *Meadowlands* (Ecco Press). She received the Pulitzer Prize for *The Wild Iris* and the National Book Critics Circle Award for *The Triumph of Achilles.* Currently she teaches at Williams College and divides her time between Vermont and Cambridge, Massachusetts. She was the guest editor of *The Best American Poetry 1993.* "Celestial Music" was delivered as the Phi Beta Kappa Poem at Harvard University in 1990.

Of "Celestial Music," Glück writes: "Of all fantasies, the dream of

being out of the reach of time has always been, for me, the most per-
sistently seductive. At the same time it seems impossible to deny the
resemblance between unchanging and inert: Art that aspires to be
immutable, perfected music may unfortunately prove lifeless. 'Celestial
Music' was an experiment, an attempt to find a more casual language, to
use a more common occasion—I hoped these changes of manner would
disrupt old patterns of thought. What's continuous is the obsession;
what's changed is its function. Hunger for the eternal is present here as
thematic issue rather than embodied aesthetic. I hope the debate feels
unresolved; the poem, in any case, seemed a great adventure to write.

" 'Vespers' was one of eight poems written in the summer of 1990,
the first poems I'd done in nearly two years. It didn't please me much;
nothing in that group pleased me much. The poems were an argument
with the divine; they seemed simultaneously incomplete and a dead
end—too pat, too expert, a little warmed over, limited by cleverness.

"Context has modified my assessment: 'Vespers' has become part of
a book, its facility sabotaged (I hope) by the poems around it, poems
written, in the summer of 1991, with a kind of wild ease for which my
life affords no precedent. The risk of the unchecked ecstatic is tedium:
'Vespers' borrows the depth it lacks from the poems around it and, for
its part, grounds those poems in something recognizable.

"My reservations about this poem as a single thing remain intact."

JORIE GRAHAM was born in New York City in 1950. She grew up in
Italy, studied in French schools, and attended the Sorbonne, New York
University, Columbia University, and the University of Iowa. She has
published seven books of poetry: *Hybrids of Plants and of Ghosts* (1980)
and *Erosion* (1983) from Princeton University Press; *The End of Beauty*
(1987), *Region of Unlikeness* (1991), *Materialism* (1993), *The Dream of the
Unified Field: Selected Poems 1974–1994* (1995), and *The Errancy* (1997)
from the Ecco Press. She has received a MacArthur Fellowship and the
Morton Dauwen Zabel Award from the American Academy of Arts
and Letters. She lives in Iowa City with her husband and daughter and
teaches at the University of Iowa Writers' Workshop. She was the guest
editor of *The Best American Poetry 1990*. She received the Pulitzer Prize
in poetry in 1996.

Of "Manifest Destiny," Jorie Graham writes: "I don't know if this has
much to do with the poem as it stands, but Fabrice Helion was my first
lover, and when I received news of his death (an apparent suicide) by
drug overdose, I happened to be unpacking books I'd kept in storage for

twenty-two years—many of them inscribed to me by him—tattered Gallimard editions of German and French philosophers. Notes in my fifteen-year-old hand (in French) all over Marx and Engels and Spinoza and Schopenhauer and Kierkegaard and Nietzsche took me aback—especially the earnestness and seriousness of them and the great, helplessly imperial desire to *know* inscribed in them tonally. As I was holding these books in my hand—reading the notes in his eighteen-year-old hand alongside mine (corrective, instructive)—the phone rang with the news of his death. All of our time together had been in Rome during my early and mid-teens. He was shooting heroin on and off then. In case anyone should care, the restaurant and bar in question are Il Bolognese and Rosati—then rather inexpensive. The opening scene takes place on a dirt road in Wyoming where, driving to town, I recalled the rest. As far as I can tell, it's all, though layered over time, true."

ALLEN GROSSMAN was born in Minneapolis in 1932. He works at the Johns Hopkins University as Mellon Professor in the Humanities. His most recent books are *The Ether Dome and Other Poems* and *The Philosopher's Window* (both from New Directions, 1991, 1995) and *The Long Schoolroom: Lessons in the Bitter Logic of the Poetic Principle* (University of Michigan Press, 1997).

Of "The Piano Player Explains Himself" Grossman writes: "God may create everything (alas!), but persons must not. To 'play the piano' is to reduce the splendor of the music (His music) in accord with the imperfect powers of the human maker—as to *write* a poem is to reduce the inhuman forces of which it is the trace to the human form of their saying, in accord with the blessed laws of our imperfection which the poet knows. We have in *mind* an unplayed instrument which defines our nature by exhausting it. That instrument must be taken in hand because it can only be taken in hand for what the hand can do.

"Thus 'The Piano Player Explains Himself' is about the purpose for which the poet (the piano player in the poem) takes in hand his instrument. The purpose for which the poet must, despite all, keep on saying his say is the regulation of the forces of mind and world—not in themselves human, as we see everywhere about us. The instrument of the poet is no other than the great Laws of his practice. In the reality of the poem (which is the world in which we live) the instrument is unplayed and yet remains to be played, like the piano in a middle-class living room which no one alive can play and no one can remove—or like a power of mind capable of overcoming the violence of mind, to which the poet (perhaps the poet alone) has access by reason of his knowledge of the poetic instrument.

"As for the Lady, she is the sign of the force (in all its dark and numinous beauty) for which the music of the Law secures the human form—the *fashion* of the person. The wind is from the direction of fair weather (North, and North by West). Through death after death her lover grows more powerful in her service, as the formal courtesy of the poem intends to exemplify."

DONALD HALL was born in Connecticut in 1928, and in 1942 decided to write poetry for the rest of his life. Afternoons, coming home from a suburban high school, he worked on poems; summers on the farm in New Hampshire, he wrote in the morning. In 1975 Hall and his wife, Jane Kenyon, moved from Michigan to New Hampshire, where he writes in the room where he wrote in the 1940s. *The Old Life* appeared from Houghton Mifflin in 1996, and in 1998 he published his fourteenth book of poems, *Without,* concerning the illness and death of Jane Kenyon. He was the guest editor of *The Best American Poetry 1989.*

In 1988 Hall wrote: " 'Prophecy' is one of 'Four Classic Texts' (together with 'Pastoral,' 'History,' and 'Eclogue') that make the middle of a long poem, *The One Day,* which Ticknor & Fields published in September 1988. The whole poem began in the fall of 1971, when I was subject to long and frequent attacks of language. I wrote as rapidly as I could write, page after page, loose free verse characterized by abundance and strangeness rather than by anything else, certainly not by art. After a month or two the onslaught stopped. Every now and then over the next few years, lines would occur that announced themselves as part of this work. In 1979 and 1980 I tried to find a form. In 1981 the poem began to shape itself.

"Not that I knew what I was doing. If *The One Day* (or 'Prophecy') is intended, it is intended by not being crossed out. I wrote with excitement but without judgment; afterward I concentrated to decide whether to keep what I wrote down. If it succeeds, this poem is impulse validated by attention."

Of "The Porcelain Couple," Hall writes: "My wife, Jane, was diagnosed with leukemia 31 January 1994. Seven weeks later my mother died at ninety, and I had to empty her house in Connecticut. Under ordinary circumstances Jane and I would have spent a week making choices about the disposition of my mother's things—but Jane was too sick, at our house in New Hampshire, and I could not bear to be away from her too long. On 23 April I drove four hours to empty my mother's house, a week before the new family moved in; I drove back the same day.

"People who dismantle parental houses dread the dismantling of their own. Jane's illness exacerbated this dread. The day after my trip I took notes toward this poem, and worked it over during the next twelve months as I sat beside Jane's bed in the hospital or at home. 'The Porcelain Couple' began at four or five times its present length, sunken under detail and circumstance. I wrote about the drive from New Hampshire to Connecticut, and about help from my children and a neighbor. I listed the contents of drawers and closets and table-tops—the multitudinous relics of a long life, bound for the dump like everything and everyone. At one point I listed forty-odd objects or categories of objects; maybe I still list too many, but in revision I omitted the names of most things—as well as mention of my helpers.

"As I worked on this poem during the last year of Jane's life, I read it aloud to her from time to time, and she helped me. Among more important matters, she changed the title. First I had called it 'The Ceramic Couple.' "

VICKI HEARNE was born in Austin, Texas, in 1946. She lives in Westbrook, Connecticut, trains dogs for a living, and is a visiting Fellow at the Yale Institution for Social and Policy Studies. Her books of verse are *Nervous Horses* (University of Texas, 1980), *In the Absence of Horses* (Princeton, 1984), and *The Parts of Light* (Johns Hopkins University Press, 1994). She has written a novel, *The White German Shepherd* (Atlantic Monthly Press, 1988). Her nonfiction includes *Adam's Task: Calling Animals by Name* (Knopf, 1986; Vintage, 1987), *Bandit, Dossier of a Dangerous Dog* (HarperCollins, 1991), and *Animal Happiness* (Harper-Collins, 1994). She is married to the philosopher Robert Tragesser.

Of "St. Luke Painting the Virgin," Hearne writes: "Being mostly a denizen of the deserts of the Southwest, I discovered museums at a fairly advanced age, and so was bowled over when I came across this painting in the Boston Museum of Fine Arts. The hazards it meditates on, of being dangerously entranced by divine light, were real to me the two days I spent visiting the painting. I visited it over and over. I would go look at it, then escape across the way to a dim coffee shop, write bits of the poem, and then return and look at the painting again, to find that the hazards continued to be real.

"For some reason I am now unclear about, I ended up paying admission every time I went back in, which seemed only right and natural, though my friends tell me it was idiotic, since you are given a button when you enter and you just have to show your button to get back in."

ANTHONY HECHT was born in New York City in 1923. His B.A. from Bard College was granted in absentia (1944) while he was overseas with the army; he later earned his M.A. from Columbia University. After forty years of teaching at Bard College, Kenyon College, Smith College, the University of Rochester, Iowa State University, and Georgetown University, he retired in 1993. Most of his poetry has been assembled in *The Collected Earlier Poetry of Anthony Hecht* and *The Transparent Man,* both published by Knopf. His other works include *Obligatti: Essays in Criticism* (Atheneum); a critical study of W. H. Auden's poetry, *The Hidden Law* (Harvard University Press, 1994); *On the Laws of the Poetic Art: The Andrew Mellon Lectures, 1992* (Princeton, 1995); and *The Presumptions of Death* (Gehenna Press, 1995). His latest publications include a collection of poems, *Flight Among the Tombs* (1996), and the Introduction to the New Cambridge Shakespeare edition of the sonnets (1996). "Just as Hecht's indispensable method is what used to be known as *brevitas,* or concise verbal expression, so his compulsive subject is the brevity of life," Stephen Yenser observed in reviewing *Flight Among the Tombs,* "a consummate example of a long-practicing artificer's work." Hecht has received the Pulitzer Prize, the Bollingen Prize, and the Eugenio Montale Award. He and his wife live in Washington, D.C.

Of "Prospects," Hecht writes: "The villanelle form is truly challenging, and I avoided it for a long time, while admiring the successes of such practitioners as Elizabeth Bishop, William Empson, Dylan Thomas, James Merrill, Mark Strand, and W. H. Auden. Mine is a little pilgrimage or quest poem, as perhaps the industrial by-product of a set of poems written (in the paradisal setting of the Rockefellers' Villa Serbelloni at Bellagio) to accompany woodcuts by Leonard Baskin, and called 'The Presumptions of Death.' The poem's title is meant to convey our very ambivalent feelings about the future, since 'prospects' can be hopeful, referring to financial profits, to favorable expectations in mining operations, but also can be fearful or troubled, and can neutrally refer to panoramic overviews and remote landscapes. The 'theme' to be heard in the 'pale paradigm of birdsong' at the end of the poem is meant to be the very faint echo, almost undetectable, of something hinted at in the opening lines: 'He maketh me to lie down in green pastures: he leadeth me beside the still waters.' If mountain streams are not, strictly speaking, 'still,' the lines in the psalm refer to 'the waters of quietude.' Implied, perhaps, but unstated: 'He restoreth my soul.' "

EDWARD HIRSCH was born in Chicago in 1950 and educated at Grinnell College and the University of Pennsylvania. He has published four books of poems: *For the Sleepwalkers* (Knopf, 1981), *Wild Gratitude* (Knopf, 1986), *The Night Parade* (Knopf, 1989), and *Earthly Measures* (Knopf, 1994). He teaches at the University of Houston.

Of "Man on a Fire Escape," Hirsch writes: "This poem is an attempt to explore the literal and metaphorical possibilities of its dramatic situation: a man on a fire escape on a late day in the empire. There are a couple of things I had it in mind to do. To send a man out of his empty room onto iron stairs overlooking a city, and then to reel him back in. To describe a moment that is both ordinary and extraordinary, inside and outside of time. To invoke dusk, the hour of changes, as vividly as possible. To imagine and dwell upon an extended apocalyptic moment, the world being destroyed, and then to see that visionary moment transfigured and withdrawn, the twilight seeping into evening, the world continuing on as before. What has the man seen and what has he envisioned? Nothing. That resonating answer bears the full burden of meaning in the poem."

JOHN HOLLANDER was born in New York City in 1929. He has published seventeen books of poetry here and abroad, the most recent being *Tesserae and Other Poems* and *Selected Poetry,* both from Knopf in 1993. He is the author of several books of criticism and theory, including *Melodious Guile* (Yale University Press, 1988). Among the awards he has received for his work are the Bollingen Prize, the Levinson Prize, and a MacArthur Fellowship. He lives in Connecticut and is A. Bartlett Giamatti Professor of English at Yale University.

Of "The See-Saw," Hollander writes: "This 'mad song' grew out of two germs. The first was the note of Hegel's now preserved in the epigraph, which seemed to me the silliest thing I'd read in months. I'd jotted it down, together with a reminder of the old nursery rhyme 'See-saw, / Margery Daw, / Jack shall have a new master,' etc. The idea of confounding it with an idée fixe of see-sawing itself seemed inevitable. The other was the *dah-di-di-dah* rhythm of the words 'Margery Daw,' which I'd scrawled right under Hegel's note; being that of a sort of sapphic-stanza short line (with the final unstressed syllable missing), it seemed to belong at the end of a stanza of three longer lines. But I started out with it in 'Margery Daw,' and then it wandered crazily through subsequent stanzas, even as the name metamorphosed. I hadn't planned for the speaker to break out into German, but he suddenly did, perhaps because of Hegel, perhaps because I was remembering the voices of German refugee nannies in Central Park playgrounds in my early childhood.

" 'An Old-Fashioned Song' was written in response to a request for some verse for adults who had recently learned to read; it was to have short lines and syntax that wasn't too demanding. I started out with a version of the first line of Théodore de Banville's well-known *'Nous n'irons plus au bois, / Les lauriers sont coupés,'* and simply let the resonance of that line, and its desire to return as a refrain, take it from there. The turn on 'they are gone for good, and you for ill' may in fact have been elusive for some of the intended readers, but perhaps not."

Of "Kinneret," Hollander writes that the title derives from *"Yam Kinneret,* the Sea of Galilee, whose name may be related to the word *kinnor,* or *harp."* He adds: "The disjunct form of these quatrains is borrowed from the Malay *pantun* (not from its fussy, refrain-plagued French derivative, the *pantoum*), in which the first and second lines frame one sentence, and the next two another, apparently unrelated one. These two are superficially connected only by the cross-rhyming in the quatrain and by some common construction, scheme, pun, assonance, or the like. But below the surface, they are united in some deeper parable. A self-descriptive example of the form shows this most clearly:

Catamaran

> Pantuns in the original Malay
> > Are quatrains of two thoughts, but of one mind,
> Athwart my two pontoons I sail away,
> > Yet touching neither; land lies far behind.

The expository disjunctive in these stanzas extends even to the personages referred to by pronouns, and 'he' or 'she' are quite different in the first and last two lines. But the groups of four quatrains are rhythmically paced: there is a refrainlike return, in every fourth stanza, of some allusion to the lake over whose tranquillity and beauty, remembered from early spring evenings, I was brooding over during the rather personally agitated weeks during which this poem was composed."

RICHARD HOWARD was born in Cleveland, Ohio, in 1929. He was educated at Columbia University and the Sorbonne. The most recent of his ten books of poetry is *Like Most Revelations,* and he is at work on an eleventh, *Trappings;* for his third, *Untitled Subjects,* he received the Pulitzer Prize in 1970. He has translated more than 150 works from the French and received the American Book Award for his translation of Baudelaire's *Les Fleurs du mal.* He is a member of the American Academy and Institute of Arts and Letters and a chancellor of the Academy of American Poets, and in 1994–95 he served as the Poet Laureate of New York State. In 1996 he was named a MacArthur Fellow. He is poetry editor of both the *Paris Review* and *Western Humanities Review,* and he teaches in the writing division of the School of the Arts at Columbia University. He is currently completing a new translation of Stendhal's *Charterhouse of Parma* for the Modern Library. He was the guest editor of *The Best American Poetry 1995.*

Of "Like Most Revelations," Howard writes: "The paintings of Morris Louis were created, for the most part, by tilting the canvas so that the paint could slide across the surface, staining it according to the artist's determination. The poem attempts to respond to the exigencies of this novel fashion of producing an image."

DONALD JUSTICE was born in Miami, Florida, in 1925. He currently resides in Iowa. For his poetry he has received both the Pulitzer Prize and the Bollingen Prize. His recent books include *A Donald Justice Reader* (University Press of New England, 1992) and *New and Selected Poems* (Knopf, 1995), the latter of which contains the two poems represented in this volume. In 1996 he received the Lannan Literary Award.

Of "Nostalgia of the Lakefronts," Justice writes: "I had in mind Auden's 'Canzone' and the Dante on which it was modeled, but settled for something much simpler. The lake I thought of as like the Lake George of such painters as Kensett, Heade, and O'Keeffe, but my own childhood was spent a long way from any such demiparadise. The childhood of the poem is entirely fictive. I would argue, nevertheless, that one is entitled to a certain nostalgia for what one never knew or had."

Of "Invitation to a Ghost," Justice writes: "Henri Coulette was a very fine poet and a dear friend. His death was an occasion I could not in conscience refuse."

BRIGIT PEGEEN KELLY was born in Palo Alto, California, in 1951. She has received the *Nation*/Discovery Award, the Yale Younger Poets Prize, and a National Endowment for the Arts Fellowship. *To the Place of Trumpets,* her first book, was published by Yale University Press in 1988. Her second book, *Song,* published in 1995 by BOA Editions, Ltd., was awarded the Lamont Poetry Prize by the Academy of American Poets. She teaches creative writing at the University of Illinois at Champaign-Urbana.

Of "The White Pilgrim: Old Christian Cemetery," Kelly writes: "In a number of poems I've been using multiple narrative lines, interweaving narratives separate in time and space but related in theme, incident, feeling, etc. I'm trying to suggest a world of circular time in which seemingly disparate events are seen as part of larger patterns within a constantly recurring whole."

JANE KENYON was born in Ann Arbor, Michigan, in May 1947. She died of leukemia in New Hampshire on April 22, 1995. She had published four books of poems and a book of translations. Her poetry books, all from Graywolf, are *The Boat of Quiet Hours* (1986), *Let Evening Come* (1990), *Constance* (1993), and *Otherwise: New and Selected Poems* (1996). She had received fellowship grants from the National Endowment for the Arts and the Guggenheim Foundation. She lived with her husband, Donald Hall, on Eagle Pond Farm.

Of "Three Songs at the End of Summer," Kenyon wrote: "This poem is personal, and painful, and it is the kind of poetry I'd like to turn away from. There's very little invention in it. It is memory and reportage."

GALWAY KINNELL teaches in the creative writing program at New York University. He is a former state poet of Vermont. His most recent book is *Imperfect Thirst* (Houghton Mifflin, 1994).

KARL KIRCHWEY was born in Boston in 1956 and grew up in the United States and abroad. Educated at Yale and Columbia, he is the author of three books of poems, *A Wandering Island* (Princeton, 1990; recipient of the Norma Farber First Book Award from the Poetry Society of America), *Those I Guard* (Harcourt Brace, 1993), and *The Engrafted Word,* forthcoming from Holt in the spring of 1998. Since 1987 he has been director of the Unterberg Poetry Center of the 92nd Street YM-YWHA in New York City. The recipient of fellowships from the Ingram Merrill and Guggenheim Foundations and the NEA, he received the Rome Prize in Literature in 1994. He has taught at Smith College and in

Columbia University's writing division. Mr. Kirchwey lives in New York with his wife and two children.

Of "Sonogram," Kirchwey writes: "The immediate occasion of this poem is evident from the title. In April 1992, my wife and I received a glimpse *in utero* of our first child, a boy named Tobias, who was born in September of that year. My emotions at witnessing this procedure were twofold. On the one hand, the medical sophistication of it, and the audacity of being able to view such hidden things, seemed so astounding that the only adequate response was through the imagination—the metaphors by which the parts of the body are described—in the form of a prayer. My other emotion, which also justified prayer, was anxiety, since the chief purpose of a sonogram is to detect birth defects in the fetus.

"Traveling in Sicily years ago, I had walked through the deep ancient quarries at Syracuse, now full of citrus trees but once an open-air prison in which thousands of Athenian soldiers died of exposure and disease during the Peloponnesian War in September 413 B.C. The cultural critic and historian George Steiner has written, 'The quarries of Syracuse have long signaled that in the lotteries of the unpredictable it is disaster that has all the luck.' And it was the image of these quarries, and their shadowed promise, which suggested itself last in the little catalogue of images I offered my then unborn son as I contemplated the life that lay ahead of him."

KENNETH KOCH was born in Cincinnati, Ohio, in 1925. He lives in New York City and teaches at Columbia University. His recent books include *On the Great Atlantic Rainway* (selected poems) and *One Train*—both published by Knopf in 1994—for which he was awarded the Bollingen Prize in American Poetry (in 1995) and the Bobbitt National Poetry Prize from the Library of Congress (in 1996). In 1997 Knopf published *The Gold Standard,* a collection of plays; and a collection of writings—parodies, poems, essays—about poetry, *The Art of Poetry,* was published by the University of Michigan Press. Scheduled for 1998 is *Straits,* a new book of poems (Knopf), and *Making Your Own Days,* a book about reading and writing poetry (Scribner).

Of "One Train May Hide Another," Koch writes: "I saw the railway-crossing sign 'One Train May Hide Another' when I was traveling in Africa in 1982. I wrote it down in a journal I was keeping and thought about it from time to time till a few years ago, when I finally wrote a poem about it. Apparently, there are quite a few signs of this kind, in

Kenya, England, and elsewhere. In France, too, where what they say is *'Un Train Peut en Cacher un Autre.'* "

YUSEF KOMUNYAKAA was born in Bogalusa, Louisiana, in 1947. He served with the United States Army in Vietnam and was a correspondent and editor of the *Southern Cross.* He has taught at Indiana University and at Washington University in St. Louis. His books include *Copacetic* (1984), *I Apologize for the Eyes in My Head* (1986), *Dien Cai Dau* (1988), *Magic City* (1992), and *Neon Vernacular* (Wesleyan, 1993). *Neon Vernacular* was awarded the Kingsley Tufts Award in addition to the 1994 Pulitzer Prize. His new collection, *Thieves of Paradise,* has been published by Wesleyan, and in 1997 he received the Hanes Poetry Prize. He is a professor of creative writing at Princeton University.

Of "Facing It," Komunyakaa writes: "Now, as I think back to 1984 when I wrote 'Facing It,' with the humidity hanging over New Orleans (a place raised by the French out of the swampy marshes) in early summer, I remember that it seemed several lifetimes from those fiery years in Vietnam. I lived at 818 Piety Street, and was in the midst of renovating the place: trekking up and down a twelve-foot ladder, scribbling notes on a yellow pad. I had meditated on the Vietnam Veterans Memorial as if the century's blues songs had been solidified into something monumental and concrete. Our wailing, our ranting, our singing of spirituals and kaddish and rock anthems, it was all captured and refined into a shaped density that attempted to portray personal and public feelings about war and human loss. It became a shrine overnight: a blackness that plays with light—a reflected motion in the stone that balances a dance between the grass and sky. Whoever faces the granite becomes a part of it. The reflections move into and through each other. A dance between the dead and the living. Even in its heft and weight, emotionally and physically, it still seems to defy immediate description, constantly incorporating into its shape all the new reflections and shapes brought to it: one of the poignant shrines of the twentieth century.

"Today, I have attempted to journey from that blues moment of retrospection that produced 'Facing It' to this moment, now, when I am a member of the advisory council for the My Lai Peace Park Project in Vietnam. This project is also connected to the reflective power of that granite memorial in D.C. Joined in some mysterious and abiding way, we can hope that the two can grow into a plumb line or spirit level etched with names and dates that suggest where we are and the distance we have journeyed—something instructive that we can measure ourselves against."

ANN LAUTERBACH was born and grew up in Manhattan. She majored in painting at the High School of Music and Art and then went to the University of Wisconsin at Madison, where she majored in English. She received a Woodrow Wilson Fellowship to Columbia University (contemporary literature) but left after one year of graduate work. In the fall of 1967 she embarked on a three-week trip to Dublin, London, and Paris, which she extended to seven years, settling in London, where she worked in publishing and for the Institute of Contemporary Arts. After returning to New York in the early 1970s, she worked at a number of art galleries before taking up teaching, first at Brooklyn College and subsequently in the graduate writing programs at Columbia, Princeton, Iowa, Bard, and City College. She received a Guggenheim Fellowship in 1986 and a MacArthur Fellowship in 1993. She is the author of thirteen books, including several collaborations with artists and five poetry collections: *Many Times, But Then* (University of Texas, 1979), *Before Recollection* (Princeton University Press, 1987), *Clamor* (Viking Penguin, 1991), *And for Example* (Viking Penguin, 1994), and *On a Stair* (Viking Penguin, 1997). She currently is Theodore Goodman Professor of Creative Writing and Modern Poetry at City College and the Graduate Center in New York City.

Lauterbach writes: " 'Psyche's Dream' is representative of much of my earlier work, in which I was investigating the possibilities of an extended syntax and the problem of reference in poems; that is, the distinction between a direct visual image (as in a landscape, a painting, or a photograph) and a verbal (sound) image. In this poem, the landscape and its house belonged to my grandmother (and was where my mother grew up), and it had just been sold, so that it was about to become a permanent memory. The image of Psyche toward the end of the poem is based on a French painting of Psyche and Cupid (the image of which can be found, upside-down, on the jacket of *Before Recollection,* the book in which this poem appears, as part of a collage by photographer Jan Groover). I was interested in Psyche also because of a remarkable essay I had read by Hans Neumann. The 'dream within the dream' has to do with the impossibility of conveying an experience other than through the mediating agency of form, where both 'event' and 'response' are transfigured. In later work, I have become increasingly interested in making poems with the status of an event."

PHILIP LEVINE was born in Detroit in 1928. He describes his coming into poetry in his book *The Bread of Time: Toward an Autobiography*

(Knopf, 1994). His most recent collection is *The Simple Truth*, which won the Pulitzer Prize in 1995. "Scouting" appeared in *What Work Is*, winner of the National Book Award in 1991, which he had previously won in 1980 with *Ashes*. Two of his books have won the National Book Critics Circle Award, one the Lenore Marshall Award. In 1987 he received the Ruth Lilly Award "for outstanding poetic achievement." He now divides his time between Fresno, California, where he taught for many years, and New York City. In 1997 he was inducted into the American Academy of Arts and Letters.

Of "Scouting," Levine writes: "In 1954 I went to Boone, North Carolina, to marry Frances Artley (who is still—thank God—my wife). She had a job there costuming a summer play called *Horn in the West*, & I had just given up my last grease-shop job in Detroit, so I had time to walk among the hills and fields and mountainsides. For much of a summer I lived close to nature, and I discovered the rural poor of the South on their own turf. I'd known many of them as fellow students & fellow workers in Detroit, & now I saw the world they'd fled because it has failed to feed them. Except for their hideous racism, they were the most considerate and generous people I had ever met. I remember them often, and one morning in the fall of '87 while living in Somerville, Massachusetts, I felt welling up in me the old hatred for what America has done to its good people, for I was seeing the human cost of Reaganomics every day on the streets of Somerville, Medford, and Boston. I wanted to feel otherwise about my country, so once again I took an imaginative voyage back in time to try to rediscover the people who helped make my life worth living."

HARRY MATHEWS was born in New York City in 1930. He has lived primarily in France since graduating from Harvard in 1952. He is the only American member of the Oulipo (Ouvroir de Littérature Potentielle, or Workshop for Potential Literature), a Paris-based association of mathematicians and writers committed to the development of ingenious new forms and methods of composition. With John Ashbery, Kenneth Koch, and James Schuyler, he founded the literary magazine *Locus Solus* in 1960. *The Conversions* (1962), his first novel, is a picaresque adventure based on a rich man's capricious will. He has published four novels since, most recently *Cigarettes* (1987) and *The Journalist* (1994). The centerpiece of *Armenian Papers: Poems 1954–1984* (Princeton, 1987) is "Trial Impressions," a sequence of thirty versions of the text of an Elizabethan song.

Mathews writes: "Written in 1982, 'Histoire' no doubt harks back to the enthusiastic and edgy days of the late 1960s and early '70s when, more obviously than usual, sex and politics bubbled in a single pot."

J. D. MCCLATCHY lives in New York City and in Stonington, Connecticut. He is editor of *The Yale Review* and has taught at Yale, Princeton, UCLA, and Columbia. He has written four books of poems, *Scenes from Another Life* (Braziller, 1981), *Stars Principal* (Macmillan, 1986), *The Rest of the Way* (Knopf, 1990), and *Ten Commandments* (Knopf, 1998). Two collections of his essays have appeared, *White Paper* (Columbia University Press, 1989) and *Twenty Questions* (Columbia University Press, 1998). In addition, he has written four opera libretti and edited many books, including *The Vintage Book of Contemporary American Poetry* (Vintage, 1990) and *The Vintage Book of Contemporary World Poetry* (Vintage, 1996). He is a chancellor of the Academy of American Poets.

Of "An Essay on Friendship," McClatchy writes: "I had wanted to take a break from the knotty lyric and write a poem in a more relaxed, discursive style, so I assumed an Augustan model and settled on a French film as my lead-in. Renoir's *Règle du jeu,* always my favorite, is a Mozartian drawing-room tragedy about adultery, about romantic love and practical loyalties. (A few sections of the poem depend on a reader's remembering bits of the film. No one who has seen the film is likely to have forgotten them, and the reader who *hasn't* seen it—well, I envy him that first magical encounter!) The purpose of my own poem is to explore differences between love and friendship, the former viewed as half farce, half soulwork, the latter as compromised, life-saving, and enduring. Throughout, I've wanted to make my points as much by little fictions as by larger generalizations; and my format is rather strict, to inhibit any drift toward merely loose talk."

JAMES MERRILL (1926–1995) was born in New York City. He was the son of the financier Charles Merrill, the founder of the giant brokerage firm Merrill Lynch, and his second wife, Hellen Ingram. He interrupted his studies at Amherst College to serve in the infantry for a year during World War II. Returning to Amherst, he impressed his professor, Reuben Brower, with his analysis of the relation of rhetoric to emotion in the writings of Marcel Proust. He graduated summa cum laude, spent a year teaching at Bard College, then went to Europe, to Paris and Venice mostly, for a two-and-a-half-year journey of self-discovery. This is the subject of Merrill's memoir, *A Different Person*

(1993). *First Poems* came out in 1951, *The Country of a Thousand Years of Peace* eight years later. Already in these elegantly crafted poems, Merrill pursued visions of angelic transcendence. "There are moments when speech is but a mouth pressed / Lightly and humbly against the angel's hand," he wrote in "A Dedication." He used sonnets as narrative building blocks in poems determined "to make some kind of house / Out of the life lived, out of the love spent," as he put it in *Water Street* (1962), his watershed volume. In such poems as "A Tenancy" and "An Urban Convalescence," he developed the relaxed conversational style that he perfected in *Nights and Days* (1966), *The Fire Screen* (1969), and *Braving the Elements* (1972). Sometimes dismissed as an opera-loving aesthete, Merrill was able to identify himself with history and could handle subjects that defeat most poets (the anarchist's bomb, the space traveler's capsule, the shopping mall, and the alcoholic's recovery program). He had grown up in a Manhattan brownstone blown up by a radical fringe group in 1970. In "18 West 11th Street" he writes about that incident, as if his own life were passing before him in the slow-motion replay of the blast. His books received two National Book Awards, the Pulitzer Prize, and the Bollingen Prize. The epic poem begun in *Divine Comedies* (1976) and extended in two subsequent volumes was published in its entirety as *The Changing Light at Sandover* (1982), which won the National Book Critics Circle Award. His most recent books of poetry are *Late Settings* (Atheneum, 1985), *The Inner Room* (Knopf, 1988), and *A Scattering of Salts* (Knopf, 1995). *Recitative,* a collection of Merrill's critical prose edited by J. D. McClatchy, appeared from North Point Press in 1986. Merrill owned homes in Stonington, Connecticut, and New York City, and spent many winters in Key West, Florida. He died Monday, February 6, 1995, while on holiday in Tucson, Arizona.

On four consecutive weekday evenings in May 1990, the Metropolitan Opera in New York City staged the four operas that constitute "The 'Ring' Cycle," thus providing the occasion for James Merrill's poem of that title.

Merrill wrote that "Family Week at Oracle Ranch" is "all fairly straightforward, although the name of the institution has been changed."

W. S. MERWIN was born in New York City in 1927 and grew up in Union City, New Jersey, and in Scranton, Pennsylvania. From 1949 to 1951 he worked as a tutor in France, Portugal, and Majorca and later earned his living by translating from French, Spanish, Latin, and Portuguese. He has also lived in England and in Mexico. *A Mask for Janus,* his first book of poems, was chosen by W. H. Auden as the 1952 volume in the Yale Series of Younger Poets. Subsequent volumes include *The Moving Target* (1963), *The Compass Flower* (1977), and *The Rain in the Trees* (Knopf, 1988). *The Carrier of Ladders* (1970) won the Pulitzer Prize. He has translated *The Poem of the Cid* and *The Song of Roland,* and his *Selected Translations 1948–1968* won the PEN Translation Prize for 1968. In 1987 he received the Governor's Award for Literature of the State of Hawaii. *The Vixen,* his latest collection of poems, appeared from Knopf in 1996. Other recent books are *The Lost Upland* (Knopf, 1992), about France, and *The Second Four Books* (Copper Canyon Press, 1996), poems. Copper Canyon Press brought out *Flower & Hand* in 1997, and a poem of book length, *The Folding Cliffs,* a narrative, is scheduled for publication by Knopf. He was the first recipient of the Dorothy Tanning Prize from the Academy of American Poets in 1994. Later that year he won a three-year writer's award from the Lila Wallace–Reader's Digest Fund. He lives in Hawaii—in a place called Haiku, on the island of Maui.

Of "The Stranger," Merwin notes that he found a prose summary of the legend in question "and tried to tell it as the Guarani would tell it." The Guarani are rainforest Indians from the central section of South America, where Paraguay, Brazil, and Bolivia meet. "They are to South America what the Hopi are to the American Southwest: the museum, compendium, and storehouse for the spiritual life of that region."

SUSAN MITCHELL grew up in New York City and was educated at Wellesley College. Her most recent book of poems, *Rapture* (Harper-Collins, 1992), was a National Book Award finalist and winner of the 1993 Kingsley Tufts Poetry Award. Her honors include fellowships from the Guggenheim Foundation, the Lannan Foundation, and the National Endowment for the Arts. She is the Mary Blossom Lee Professor of Poetry at Florida Atlantic University.

Of "Havana Birth," Mitchell writes: "I really did spend an entire winter trying to catch a pigeon on a beach in Florida. I must have been five or six. When I finally caught the bird, I was thrilled, but also terrified—by the reality of the pigeon, by a desire utterly separate from my own, the pigeon's heart pulsing against my fingers, the wings pushing up against my hands. I let the bird go. Through most of my adult life, I was haunted by that experience and kept trying to write about it. It was not until I started to think of what at first seemed a very different subject—the number of times we are born in our lives, those experiences so crucial to us that we tumble out of them glistening and wet and new—

that I began to think of my catching the pigeon as a birth. With that realization, the first five stanzas came very easily. I knew what my stanzaic unit would be almost at once, something that is important to me since I have to visualize a poem, its masses and weights, in order to write it. I also knew early on I would be using rhyme within, rather than at the end of lines. When I had almost finished the fifth stanza, the poem suddenly sealed itself off, like a vein that shuts down sometimes when you give blood. It wasn't until thirteen months later that I was able to continue. Perhaps the fact that I had left New England for Florida, where the experience with the pigeon had occurred, helped get the poem going again. When it did start up, the subject had moved out from the personal to include the social and the political. Though the specific event the poem dramatizes is the Cuban revolution, I imagine the speaker as someone who, on entering adolescence, detaches herself from the narrow interests of her own socioeconomic group to identify with the larger interests of humanity. So the poem found its own definition of birth, not only as freeing oneself from the mother, but more important, as the struggle to enter the world."

A. F. MORITZ was born in Niles, Ohio, in 1947 and educated at Marquette University. Since 1974 he has lived in Toronto. His books of poems include *The Tradition* (Princeton, 1986) and several published in Canada, including *Mahoning* (Brick Books, 1994). He is coauthor, with Theresa Moritz, of *The Oxford Literary Guide to Canada* (1987) and *Stephen Leacock: A Biography* (Stoddart, 1985) and has translated books of poems by Ludwig Zeller, Benjamin Peret, and Gilberto Meza. His poetry has received Guggenheim, Ingram Merrill, and Canada Council Fellowships and the Award in Literature of the American Academy and Institute of Arts and Letters. From 1986 to 1990 he was assistant professor of English at the University of Toronto and in 1994–95 was Northrop Frye Visiting Lecturer in poetry at Victoria College. He works as a writer and occasional teacher.

Moritz writes: " 'Protracted Episode' uses a frame to dramatize the effect of an encounter, and to suggest effects the encounter might have on the reader, who sees it from a more inclusive viewpoint. This reflects, of course, a love of Dante and 'The Rime of the Ancient Mariner.' The four interior stanzas express a typical movement in human culture that I'm often concerned to satirize: the voice starts out strongly for affirmation and then, succumbing to its own self-experience, subsides to a vision of perpetual sameness and defeat—which is put in bitter yet beautiful, consoling terms. The frame stanzas represent a traveler, apparently embarked for some brave goal, who upon hearing this voice goes back and gives himself over to memory. Enlightened? Discouraged?"

THYLIAS MOSS was born in Cleveland, Ohio, in 1954. Her sixth collection of poems, *Last Chance for the Tarzan Holler,* was published by Persea Books in 1997 and an autobiography, *Tale of a Sky-Blue Dress,* is forthcoming from Avon Books in 1998. *Small Congregations,* a volume of new and selected poems, was published by Ecco Press in 1993. *Pyramid of Bone* (Callaloo/University of Virginia Press, 1989) was short-listed for the National Book Critics Circle Award. She has also written two books for children, *I Want to Be* (1993) and *Somewhere It's Tomorrow* (1998), both from Dial Books for Young Readers. A 1996 MacArthur Fellow, she is also the recipient of a Guggenheim Fellowship, a Whiting Writer's Award, and the Witter Bynner Prize. Married and raising two sons in Ann Arbor, she teaches at the University of Michigan.

Moss writes: " 'The Warmth of Hot Chocolate' is a poem of my reconciliation with God, not the God of my Baptist upbringing, the one keeping tally of my soul's absolute devotion to him and to no other by watching and evaluating my every move; no, not that voyeur God I met in Sunday school before I was old enough for kindergarten, not the one who created weak flesh, then condemned, *damned* it for that very weakness; not him. What began to make sense to me in my childhood, what still made sense when I wrote this poem, was that simple, sometimes trite, even exploited definition of God as love. What made more sense was that a God made of love be subject to all of love's fickleness, paradoxes, all of its blindnesses and inconsistencies as well as its pleasures and powers of cure. All of the complexities that challenge love's, so therefore also God's, existence. He would have to fall just as we do to access love. This was pleasing.

"How inviting then to go the next step of literal interpretation of being made in his image. I assumed that our being created in his image meant that already we were like him; there was no striving necessary to reach that status. If as we are, we are also in his image, then what we image, what he is, is not as idealized as many would prefer. (Maybe he's not so omnipotent, not so omniscient; maybe there's a way to circumvent his knowledge, getting at him through those chinks in his armor.) It further seemed likely that if he is to be any kind of unity or totality at all, then everything must reflect some of that immense image, every fossil, root, burr, that gave rise to Velcro, every fungus, lichen, ugliness, concrete block, feather, snowflake, anvil, and crystal, each diatom, imperfection, and fingerprint, some of whose whorls also give image to magma rising up and a feeling of inhospitality. To everything, though these things need not cooperate as if everything is but one organism, is assigned a small part of him (indeed, some of his parts are thoroughly incompatible). In approaching the poem, days before attempting to write it (perhaps much longer; it could be that I think of nothing else), I thought about the never-ending work of that assigning, for he is so large, so encompassing, that everything, both the known and the presently unknown—also the forever unknowable—must be named before all of him may be represented. He is a fragmented deity—and how relieving this is, for he is far easier to accept (and to swallow) in little seemingly insignificant pieces. All of this meant that there were more options for a relationship with God, if a relationship were desired, than what I was taught. I wasn't told the whole truth: the birds, bees, and the truth about God.

"Through the poem, I sent to God my gratefulness for these options. It is, then, a kind of prayer. I could think of no one else who would willingly take his job of absolute responsibility and unification. And then the consequences. Being on the receiving end of so many well-honed barbs. Knowing in advance (that blasted and incredible omniscience!) both the benevolence and the maliciousness to be perpetrated in his name of holiness. He's got his share of problems. I could imagine his hurt and grief as he is rejected and outgrown, as he faces displacement, loss of youth, obsolescence, and, as so many of his fragments must face, extinction. Within this empathy, I could think of at least two ways to terminate him: First, a universe of believers taking up eternal occupancy in heaven. Once utopia has been achieved, once there is this presently incomprehensible universal harmony, God will no longer be needed as God. With incredible longevity, surely everything will be self-sustaining, instant regeneration of losses in the unlikely event of loss in paradise. Those reasons, especially disease and death, for soliciting God's intervention will no longer exist. No systems of reproduction will be required. Once the masses become as immortal as God is, surely will also come that time, as the active gratitude wanes (it wouldn't need to go on forever), that God and the other immortals become indistinguishable from each other. He will be reduced to but a face in the crowd. No reason to fear him (above anyone else). (I was not constructing simultaneous or parallel eternities; if God is eternal and by extension total, then hell cannot exist—beyond being another name for heaven—and is reduced to a historical scare tactic that won for God more believers. I assumed a single universe—God—that contains everything.) He will be surrounded by those equally (for the sake of harmonious continuance) radiant. Perhaps he will retain the ability to create and alter (and would consider therefore, possibly for sake of diversion, ruining the now trustworthy fabric). Perhaps he will rethink his conferring of immortality upon the rank and file, but if he would reintroduce finite life spans and the systems of demise necessary to finish them, then he would risk loss of adoration and could face mutiny perhaps far uglier than the trouble he once had with errant angels (best not to let this happen to him, and that is where the angel, the speaker in the poem, comes in). The other route to his termination would be a totality of nonbelievers and his loss, in the totality, of definition—a consequence of either positive (heaven) or negative (hell) infinity. Belief sustains him. If he is gluttonous at all, it is for belief. If belief in him earns rewards for the believer, it is because God must maintain a steady supply of belief; his life (certainly his ego) depends on it. Not on love; one may despise him in fact and still supply him with belief. Irreverence supports him as does reverence. But no acknowledgment, no belief at all—that is what destroys him (and a certain measure of doubt keeps him in line, so enter the angel).

"Now, with God being in such a predicament, a little levity is necessary to relieve, if but minimally, some of the stress and burden, so the poem attempts to supply this too, somewhat peripherally to its primary task of preventing the fulfillment of either course of God's termination. The poem offers the perspective of one committed to preserving a need for God's continued existence. An angel, because such an act of commitment could come from only one whose love and devotion to God were large enough. From one whose dependence (but not trust) on him was absolute. This dependence takes the place of arrogance, so this angel is not likely to become a threat. But being an angel, she has some abilities beyond the limits of mortality, abilities that enable her to defend herself from God's problematic omnipotence. He could get way too secure in that omnipotence. It's best not to let him truly get the upper hand, so she resists him a bit, plays hard to get so that he will become so occupied with pursuing her, he isn't corrupted by his power. The possibility for corruption looms large so long as the parts of God do not equal or surpass the whole. The angel is sure of herself so professes to have doubt in order to mask the belief that could corrupt God if he were certain of it. He could just dismiss her then. Have his way with her. She wouldn't be important. It would be on to the next conquest. But never, never must he be allowed to run out of doubt to conquer. It really digs into his nerves that she won't totally submit (and she will not, just in case hers is the last doubt, and also just in case he's something less than what he claims to be—and growing more complacent every day—a form of the wolf of legend himself since he is as creator the wolf's antecedent), so he pursues her endlessly, s-o-o-o determined. She knows better than to reveal everything to him so has learned to tell lies that behave like truth. And this angel knows a little bit about Hollywood too, where she has found in Jimmy Stewart (and the "Wonderful Life" he offers her) God's rival. This rivalry inspires God to clean house and offer a miracle or two every now and then in order to retain the angel's affections. The angel knows that things have come too easily for God, so she keeps him challenged (lest he simply self-destruct and can't be saved from himself). She's someone close enough to him to understand him so is also close enough to criticize and suggest, even demand—someone much as a spouse would be if spouses could be closer than currently possible. There you have it; just another love story. The trials and tribulations of romance."

BRIGHDE MULLINS was born in Camp LeJeune, North Carolina, in 1964, and grew up in Las Vegas. Her play *Topographical Eden* received the 1997 Jane Chambers Award in Playwriting. Her other plays include *The Fire Eater, Increase, Meatless Friday, Baby Hades,* and *Pathological Venus.* Her work has been produced at the Magic (San Francisco) and Off-Broadway at LaMaMa, the Ensemble Studio Theatre, Portland Stage, and through Lincoln Center's Director's Lab. Her plays are published in *Lucky Thirteen* (University of Nevada Press) and the *Alaska Quarterly Review,* and her poems can be found in *Chelsea, Colorado Review,* and *Dominion Review.* Mullins is a graduate of the University of Nevada at Las Vegas, the Yale School of Drama, and the Iowa Writers' Workshop. She has received an NEA Fellowship in Theater and an Achievement Award from the Fund for Poetry. She is an assistant professor at San Francisco State University and the director of poetry at DIA Center for the Arts in New York City.

Of "At the Lakehouse," Mullins writes: " 'At the Lakehouse' is one in a long line of elegies I've been writing for the living and the dead. I wanted the clarification in the tenth stanza to occur in the way that shifts occur in one's visual field, while one is walking and naming objects, or the way realizations occur in the theater, when a relationship or a motive becomes—for a brief instant—intelligible, lucid. I was reading Henry James at the time, and there are some Jamesian constructions in the poem."

MOLLY PEACOCK was born in Buffalo, New York, in 1947 and lives both in London, Ontario, Canada, and New York City. She is the author of four books, including *Original Love* (Norton, 1995) and *Take Heart* (Vintage, 1989). Her poems have appeared in *The New Yorker,* the *Paris Review,* the *Nation,* the *New Republic,* and *Poetry.* She was president of the Poetry Society of America from 1989 until 1994. She is a contributing editor of *House & Garden* and the author of a prose memoir, *Paradise, Piece by Piece* (Riverhead/Penguin-Putnam, 1998).

Of "Have You Ever Faked an Orgasm?" Peacock writes: "One of the pleasures of being a poet at the end of the twentieth century is writing about a subject that has existed in its richness since the beginning of the species but has until now been little found in literature: female sexuality. This sequence of five poems about female sexuality depicts psychological experiences that are dangerously unclassifiable because they are complex and require several different responses at once. (The gamble each poem takes is that there are other women out there who feel as I do.) I wrote these poems after the breakup of a long relationship, when I felt it was possible that I would never again feel sexually comfortable with another person. The awkwardness of my early sexuality and of my fantasies and observations surfaced at this time, and I tapped into them as I wrote. In these five poems I am deliberately on the furthest edge of social acceptability. They all ask, How far should art go? And all answer, I hope, that we must reveal to have the experience of revelation."

BOB PERELMAN was born in Youngstown, Ohio, in 1947. He has published nine books of poetry, including *Virtual Reality* (Roof, 1993), *Captive Audience* (The Figures, 1988), and *Face Value* (Roof, 1988); and two critical books, *The Trouble with Genius: Reading Pound, Joyce, Stein, and Zukofsky* (University of California Press, 1994) and *The Marginalization of Poetry: Language Writing and Literary History* (Princeton University Press, 1996). He has edited two books of talks by writers, *Talks* (*Hills* 6/7, 1980) and *Writing/Talks* (University of Southern Illinois Press, 1985). He is associate professor of English at the University of Pennsylvania.

Perelman writes: "The continual shifting in 'Movie,' line by line, sentence by sentence, came from trying to get the entirety of the American world-hallucination that played so widely during the Reagan years onto the page. The Reagan hallucinations came from the movies; my continual sliding of reference was—metaphorically—movielike: hence, I suppose, the poem's title. But while 'Movie' continually refers to political matters, its tonal register is far from 'political,' populist, or single. Ice cream, the Vietnam War, the literary, the bufferings of media—I wanted all of them and their interconnected workings revealed in lines and sentences.

"There's no more than an allegorical stab at a storyline in the middle—the Grant-Hepburn screwball primal scene, with Derrida making a cameo as stage villain—and there's no point in trying to visualize almost any of the phrases. Conrad said he wrote 'above all to make you *see*'; I write to make you hear, think, reconfigure, and reinhabit the obvious, possibly pushing it back to allow for something new to happen. I may refer to Auden's 'Musée des Beaux Arts'—'About suffering they were never wrong,/ The Old Masters,' but to very different ends. Auden concludes his poem with Brueghel's *Icarus;* we see the 'expensive delicate ship' and Icarus's 'white legs disappearing into the green / Water.' Behind his eloquent, stoic commitment to the wide normative world, Auden posits the unerring Masters, unmoved by the deaths of ambitious inventors' sons; and he puts himself in their company, sacrificing his own Icarus-self. 'Movie,' on the other hand, refuses the museum: 'that worldly shrine / coextensive with its financial backing / where everything is above average / and the weather gets past the cloakroom / only in the form of haircuts.' The outside world (the weather) getting into the museum is one thing the whole poem is about. It refuses mastery: 'About suffering we are therefore / wrong, the neomasters.' And it uses Audenesque normative clarity only for phrases at a time. Clarity, in 1987 and now, is a tad suspect, Grant and Hepburn–like, too often in the service of proving that the obvious is the inevitable. Though I do like Grant and Hepburn, for what that's worth: charm is charming. But Derridean critique of presence seemed useful—although the question remains: Can it deflect Grant and Hepburn's trajectory?

"Pure critique seemed a helpless superciliousness; nor did I want to mime external conditions in equally helpless irony. I wanted to present them, critique them, even—who knows?—change them. So at least I wanted to admit the network news, and point beyond it; that's the message of my homage near the end to William Carlos Williams's touchstone 'It is difficult / to get the news from poems / yet men die miserably every day / for lack / of what is found there.' My lines are, in reference to a clock radio, 'People continue / to die miserably from the lack / of news to be found / *there,* too, doctor.' Meanwhile, ten years have passed. Is Agent Orange still in the language? Oliver North? Fawn Hall, his loyal secretary? What was that Goldie Hawn movie where she's the high school football coach, centering the ball to the nonplussed pimply quarterback? 'Movie' was written in its present, 'July 16, 1987,' etc.; America is still, at least for its literate, an 'expensive delicate ship'; I was, and still am, writing to make history palpable."

CARL PHILLIPS, born in Washington in 1959, is the author of three collections of poetry: *In the Blood* (Northeastern University Press), which won the 1992 Samuel French Morse Poetry Prize; *Cortège* (Graywolf), a finalist for the 1995 National Book Critics Circle Award and the 1995 Lambda Gay Men's Poetry Award; and *From the Devotions* (Graywolf, 1998). The recipient of fellowships and awards from the Guggenheim Foundation, the Massachusetts Artists Foundation, the Academy of American Poets, and the National Endowment for the Humanities, Phillips is associate professor of English and of African and Afro-American studies at Washington University in St. Louis, where he also directs the Writing Program.

Of "A Mathematics of Breathing," Phillips writes: "The poem arose from a rather sudden chain of events, the end result of which was that I knew that my life as I'd known it had passed, along with—perhaps more important—the knowledge of how to live any kind of a life. In the effort to recover this knowledge, it seemed important to examine even the least noticed, most taken-for-granted parts of a life—breathing, for example. To understand human breathing, it became necessary to know what nonhuman breathing, if it existed, might be. I had in mind, too, that if such things as buildings and bushes could be made to breathe, so could the most ruined or seemingly ruined lives. It was in this time of reconstruction that the poem found its own construction."

KAY RYAN was born in California in 1945 and grew up in the small towns of the San Joaquin Valley and the Mojave Desert. She studied at the Los Angeles and Irvine campuses of the University of California. Since 1971 she has lived in Marin County and has made her living teaching basic language skills part-time at the College of Marin. She has published three books of poetry, *Flamingo Watching* (1994) and *Strangely Marked Metal* (1985), both from Copper Beech Press, and *Elephant Rocks* (Grove, 1996). She is a recipient of an Ingram Merrill Award.

Of "Outsider Art," Ryan writes: "I had been looking at a big handsome book of American primitive art, and it dawned gradually and disagreeably upon me that I didn't like it. The work of these isolates felt urgent and obsessed. I almost never describe actual things in poems, and the fact that I have here just goes to show how invaded I felt by this stuff. I don't even want to think about whether they're my spiritual cousins."

GRACE SCHULMAN was born in New York City in 1935. Her poetry collections include *Burn Down the Icons* (Princeton, 1976), *Hemispheres* (Sheep Meadow, 1984), and *For That Day Only* (Sheep Meadow, 1994). She is the recipient of a New York Foundation for the Arts Fellowship in Poetry (1995) and the Delmore Schwartz Award for Poetry (1996). Schulman is also the author of *Marianne Moore: The Poetry of Engagement* (University of Illinois Press). She received her M.A. and Ph.D. from New York University and is a professor of English at Baruch College, City University of New York. She is poetry editor of the *Nation* and for ten years was director of the Poetry Center of the 92nd Street YM-YWHA.

Schulman writes: " 'The Present Perfect' is a meditation on a marriage that survived early trials resulting from childlessness, seen here as a state filled with ironies. Its very freedoms—of travel, privacy, conversation—also could threaten life's vitality. While the great works tell us art transcends life, they also harbor archetypal reminders of progeny: the biblical blessings ('that thou and thy seed may live'); and the Kaddish—in the Jewish tradition, a prayer of mourning once thought of as the reciter's plea to liberate his dead parent's soul.

"Still, my poem turned to praise. I had been reading one of Wyatt's sonnets in which love's changes are presented in heightened moments and cast in the present tense. I wanted instead 'the present perfect tense'—not 'I love' but 'I have loved.' At the same time, I looked to Wyatt's poems for the compelling way he uses ironies that contend with form.

"I wrote 'The Present Perfect' as a love poem to my husband, Jerome, a scientist whose wonder at the mystery of living things expresses a faith beyond the secular. Originally it was titled 'And Yet.' It contradicts itself at every turn except one: 'We have been married thirty-four years,' set in the present perfect, the tense of emotional fixity."

DAVID SHAPIRO was born in Newark, New Jersey, in 1947. Since 1965 he has published many volumes of poetry, art criticism, and translation, including an early monograph on John Ashbery's poetry, the first book on Jasper Johns's drawings, and a pioneering text on Mondrian's flower studies. He graduated from Columbia College in 1968 and spent two years at Clare College, Cambridge, as a Kellett Fellow. He received the 1977 Morton Dauwen Zabel Award from the American Academy of Arts and Letters as well as grants from the National Endowment for the Humanities, the National Endowment for the Arts, and the Ingram Merrill Foundation. He has taught at numerous universities, including Columbia and Princeton, and is currently a professor of art history at William Paterson College and an adjunct visiting professor at the Cooper Union. He is also on the faculty at Bard College's Milton Avery School of Arts. Recent books include *After a Lost Original* (1994) and *House (Blown Apart)* (1988), both from Overlook. In 1971 his book *A Man Holding an Acoustic Panel* was short-listed for the National Book Award in poetry.

Of "The Seasons," Shapiro writes: "Jasper Johns asked to trace my son for a panel of his 'Seasons.' My son was about three and wouldn't sit still during the attempt at tracing his shadow. The painter asked, 'I wonder when a child becomes interested in his shadow.' Later he used an older child, but the image of my son comically crayoning over Jasper Johns's tracing—an attempt at forcing his concentration— remains with me, and my admiration for the whole synoptic painting remains. (I used to paint rabbit-ducks for Jasper and urged him to use the pun in one of his paintings, and one does indeed hang over the child in 'The Seasons,' though I am not sure whether the artist was thinking of Wittgenstein's use, Gombrich's famous commentary, and/or my suggestion, but I wrote a poem about it called 'Realism.') I wrote 'The Seasons' in five parts in part as an homage to this careful master, whose every season has been called autumnal. Because I admire his use of 'recycled' older imagery, I went through unpublished poems searching for 'bits and pieces' of seasonal material. I had once dreamed of sending John Cage a book of my poems in random permutations, and this poem was an attempt to achieve a certain aleatoric music, though my preference for unity in multeity would probably repel the composer. In 'Winter,' a few lines parody Tu Fu in the Hung translations. The man who stops on the highway to observe perspective is Johns himself and comes from an anecdote he recounted. My grandfather was Berele Chagy, one of the 'golden *chazzanim*,' and he died davening, if not singing, in 1954. I recently found an early interview with him (from the 1930s) eerily headlined: 'I Will Die Singing.' The villanelle is an attempt to mimic Johns's aristocratic ink details 'after' his own painting. I tried to think of a way in which a poem could be a tracing of a few details. In my poem, the villanelle functions as an envoi, not really an independent section. The poem of course must live by itself and not be excused by any morbid dependency on the great, melancholy work that inspired it."

CHARLES SIMIC was born in Belgrade, Yugoslavia, in 1939 and emigrated to the United States in 1953. Since 1967 he has published about sixty books in this country and abroad. His latest poetry collections include *Walking the Black Cat, A Wedding in Hell,* and *Hotel Insomnia,* all from Harcourt Brace. He won the Pulitzer Prize in 1990 for his book of prose poems *The World Doesn't End.* Four volumes of his prose have appeared in the University of Michigan Press's Poets on Poetry series, most recently *The Unemployed Fortune-Teller* (1994) and *Orphan Factory* (1998). Awarded a MacArthur Fellowship in 1984, he was the guest editor of *The Best American Poetry 1992.* Since 1973 he has lived in New Hampshire.

Of "Country Fair," Simic writes: "I witnessed this scene in the mid-1970s at the nearby fair in Deerfield, New Hampshire. What a life, I thought at the time. It's not enough to have six legs, they want you to do tricks, too.

"Then it occurred to me. That's what a poet is: a six-legged dog.

" 'The Something' is one of those poems written around a single word. An ordinary, often used word which suddenly became odd, unrecognizable, puzzling, haunting, and so forth. One is always looking for *something,* thinking of *something,* pointing at *something.* What the hell is this *something?* one asks oneself one day. A *something* that doesn't seem to have any other name.

"Well, there was plenty there for me to play with."

GARY SNYDER was born in San Francisco in 1930. In 1956 he traveled to Kyoto and took up residence in the Zen temple of Shokoku-ji. He returned from Japan in 1969 and has been living in the northern Sierra Nevada on the edge of the Tahoe National Forest. Since 1985 he has been a member of the English department faculty at the University of California at Davis. He has published sixteen books of poetry and prose, including *Turtle Island,* winner of the 1975 Pulitzer Prize, and *No Nature* (Pantheon), a finalist for the 1992 National Book Award. In 1996 he received the Bollingen Poetry Prize. His most recent book is *Mountains and Rivers Without End* (Counterpoint, 1997).

Of "Ripples on the Surface," Snyder writes: "I had been out on Sitka Sound learning how to read the water from Richard Nelson (and also, in Juneau, from Nora Marks Dauenhauer). The poem deals with the levels of play between 'nature' and 'culture' or, as the ancient Chinese Buddhists would say, 'host' and 'guest.' "

MARK STRAND was born in Canada of American parents in 1934. After many years of teaching at the University of Utah, he now lives in Baltimore and teaches at Johns Hopkins. He has held a MacArthur Fellowship. His most recent books are *Dark Harbor* (1993) and *The Continuous Life* (1990), both from Knopf, and a monograph on Edward Hopper (Ecco Press, 1994). He has also published short stories and translations from the Spanish and the Portuguese. He was the guest editor of *The Best American Poetry 1991*.

Of "Reading in Place," Strand writes: "I have nothing to say about the poem that the poem doesn't say about itself, except, perhaps, that 'Where, where in Heaven am I?' comes from Robert Frost's poem 'Lost in Heaven.'

"*Dark Harbor* is a long poem in forty-five sections. When I sent out the sections for magazine publication, I sent them out in groups of three, not believing at the time that the single sections could stand on their own. Sometimes they were titled, but most often they were called 'From *Dark Harbor.*' Though grouped together for the purpose of magazine publication, the sections are not necessarily together in the long poem, that is, they are taken from different parts of it. The principle by which I grouped them was simply whether or not they seemed right together."

Of "Morning, Noon and Night," Strand writes: "I don't recall much about the composition of this poem. I worked on it over a long stretch of time, pulling it out of a drawer, looking at it, putting it back in a drawer. That sort of thing. The end, getting it right—if I ever did—took lots of rewriting. A delicate, unpleasant paradox imbedded in few words."

MAY SWENSON (1913–1989) was born in Logan, Utah. Her books include *A Cage of Spines* (1958), *Half Sun Half Sleep* (Scribner, 1967), and *In Other Words* (Knopf, 1987). She translated from the Swedish the selected poems of Tomas Tranströmer, *Windows and Stones* (University of Pittsburgh Press, 1972). She received many honors and awards, including Rockefeller and Guggenheim grants, the Bollingen Prize, and a MacArthur Fellowship. Three books of her poetry have been published posthumously: *The Love Poems of May Swenson* (Houghton Mifflin, 1991), *The Complete Poems to Solve* (Macmillan, 1993), and *Nature* (Houghton Mifflin, 1994). A collection of Swenson's prose, edited by Gardner McFall, will appear in the University of Michigan

Press's Poets on Poetry series in 1998. "Sleeping with Boa" was written on November 28, 1980, and left unpublished at the time of her death on December 4, 1989.

In a letter to Elizabeth Bishop written on June 24, 1958, May Swenson wrote: "From the beginning I came to poetry backwards. I never acquired a background in what had already been done by others. . . . To date I've never followed a pre-determined form, either one of my own or in imitation of others. . . . I try to impose consistency and an inner logic for each poem—but a *total* consistency or a pre-arranged logic or following a strict form, that doesn't work for me—I don't *enjoy* that. . . . The poems I think are worth something (a few) have *come* to me from somewhere—it hardly feels as though I made them."

DEREK WALCOTT was born in Saint Lucia, the West Indies, in 1930. His books of poems include *Another Life* (1973), *The Star-Apple Kingdom* (1979), *The Fortunate Traveller* (1982), *Midsummer* (1984), and *The Arkansas Testament* (1987), all from Farrar, Straus & Giroux. Walcott won a MacArthur Fellowship in 1981 and the Nobel Prize for literature in 1992. His recent works include *Omeros* (1990) and *The Bounty* (1997). He is the founder of the Trinidad Theater Workshop, and his plays have been produced by the New York Shakespeare Festival, the Mark Taper Forum in Los Angeles, and the Negro Ensemble Company. He has published four books of plays with Farrar, Straus & Giroux. He divides his time between Boston, where he teaches at Boston University, and Trinidad.

ROSANNA WARREN was born in Connecticut in 1953. She is an associate professor at Boston University, teaching in the University Professors Program and the Department of English. Her recent publications include a verse translation (with Stephen Scully) of Euripides' *Suppliant Women* (Oxford, 1995), and a collection of poems, *Stained Glass* (Norton, 1993). She has taught poetry to prisoners at the Massachusetts Correctional Institute in Framingham. She has received awards from the Lila Wallace–Reader's Digest Fund and the Guggenheim Foundation and was recently elected to the American Academy of Arts and Sciences.

Of "The Cormorant," Warren writes: "It's difficult, and possibly superfluous, for the poet to comment on a poem that's found at least its provisional form. After all, one wrestled the thing out of the 'comment' stage into rhymed quatrains, in this case, and made them as tight as possible. . . . The problems with this poem involved the multiple perspectives of narrator, husband/father, children, and the overelaborate economic metaphors. The poem grew from the perception of the contrast between the somber 'deacon spruces' and the riotous yellow hawkweed on an island in Maine, a perception that grew intrinsicate with the surprise and sorrow I felt at the death of a beloved aunt, far away. The tight stanzas, I suppose, were an attempt to 'hold' her: an impossible attempt, in any event."

Of "Diversion," she writes: "The poem plays with time and memory of forms: the large memory in which ancient myth still presides and certain cadences hold consecrated place; and the shards of personal memory, our human transience and fragmentation."

SUSAN WHEELER was born in Pittsburgh in 1955 and grew up in Minnesota, Connecticut, and Massachusetts. Her first collection of poetry, *Bag 'o' Diamonds,* published in 1993 by the University of Georgia Press, was selected by James Tate to receive the Norma Farber First Book Award of the Poetry Society of America, and was short-listed for the Los Angeles Times Book Award in poetry. Robert Hass chose her second volume, *Smokes,* for the Four Way Books Award; it will be published in the spring of 1998. Her work has appeared in four editions of The Best American Poetry (1988, 1991, 1993, and 1996). She received a Pushcart Prize in 1994 and two recent fellowships from the New York Foundation for the Arts. She teaches in the graduate creative writing program at the New School for Social Research in New York City.

Of "What Memory Reveals," Wheeler writes: "I had imagined this as a kind of generic biography, which would apply to almost anyone I know."

RICHARD WILBUR was born in New York City in 1921. He was educated at Amherst College and Harvard University and served in the army in World War II as a cryptographer with the 36th Infantry in Africa, southern France, and Italy. In 1957 he received the Pulitzer Prize and the National Book Award for his book *Things of This World.* He received his second Pulitzer Prize for his *New and Collected Poems* (Harcourt Brace Jovanovich, 1988). In 1987–88 he served as the nation's second official poet laureate, succeeding Robert Penn Warren. His translations from Molière and Racine (of which the latest is Molière's *Amphitryon,* 1995) are frequently performed, and the musical show *Candide,* for which he wrote most of the lyrics, was revived on Broadway in 1997. *The Catbird's Song,* a collection of prose pieces, came out in the same year, and a children's book called *The Disappearing Alphabet* is forthcoming. He divides his time between Cummington, Massachusetts, and Key West, Florida.

Of "Lying," Richard Wilbur has written that he chose blank verse ("the most flexible of our meters, and the best in which to build large verse-masses") and that the poem is addressed to "You" ("perhaps because everybody is something of a poet"). He adds: "When I first showed 'Lying' to my wife, who is always the first and best reader of my poems, she said, 'Well, you've finally done it; you've managed to write a poem that's incomprehensible from beginning to end.' Then, reading it again, she came to find it, considered as a statement, quite forthright. It seems that 'Lying' is the sort of poem which ought first to be heard or read without any distracting anxiety to catch all of its connections and local effects, and that it then asks to be absorbed in several readings or hearings. I make no apology for that: some of the poetry written these days has the relaxed transparency of talk, and would not profit by being mulled over, but much is of the concentrated kind which closes with an implicit da capo. Provided it's any good, a poem which took months to write deserves an ungrudging quarter hour from the reader.

"I'm reluctant to expound the obvious, saying for instance that there are 'lies' or fictions which are ways of telling the truth, and that the poem ends with three fictions having one burden. What I would most respond to, in conversation with an interested reader, would be noticings or questionings of details: the use of birds throughout, and of the word *shrug* for the hovering of an unreal grackle; the echo of Job, and its intended evocation of a whole passage; the water-figure, strange but not untrue, in which the idea of 'nothing' is dismissed; the transformation of the *black mist* into a rainbow; the perching of the catbird on a mock-orange spray; the vitrification of a river, beginning with 'glazes' and ending with 'cullet.' But the fact is that the details are too many for me to worry them in this space; what we have here, I figure, is a baroque poem, in the sense that it is a busy and intricate contraption which issues in plainness."

Of "A Wall in the Woods: Cummington," Wilbur writes: "This poem is in two voices, the second opposing whatever there is of elegiac sadness in the first. I suppose that 'A Wall in the Woods' may raise the technical question of whether a two-part poem can effectively shift from blank verse to syllabics. But perhaps not: the rhythms of part 2 are apparently strong enough to have disguised, for some good readers, the 5775 syllabic pattern which I used in hopes of embodying the fluent skittering of the chipmunk. Yes, it is a chipmunk. Two of my correspondents, neither a New Englander, took it to be a bird; but it seems to me that I give sufficient evidence for its being *Tamias striatus*. In any case, there's a certain additional immediacy to be got by not naming what you are talking about."

CHARLES WRIGHT was born in Pickwick Dam, Tennessee, in 1935. Educated at Davidson College, he served in the army for four years, then attended the Writers' Workshop at the University of Iowa. He lectured at the universities of Rome and Padua under the Fulbright program. He has received fellowships from the National Endowment for the Arts and the Guggenheim Foundation and won a PEN award for his translation of Eugenio Montale's *The Storm and Other Things*. He is a professor of English at the University of Virginia at Charlottesville, where he lives with his family. In 1996 he was awarded the Lenore Marshall poetry prize for his book *Chikamauga* (Farrar, Straus & Giroux, 1995). "Disjecta Membra" is the concluding poem in his latest collection, *Black Zodiac* (Farrar, Straus & Giroux, 1997).

Of "Disjecta Membra," Wright notes: "All that's necessary—and all that I really want to say—is that the title of this poem comes from Guido Ceronetti's *The Science of the Body:* 'These fragments are the *disjecta membra* [scattered parts] of an elusive, coveted and vaguely scented knowledge.' "

JAY WRIGHT was born in Albuquerque, New Mexico, in "1934 or 1935." He is a poet and playwright whose publications include *The Homecoming Singer* (Corinth Books, 1971), *Soothsayers and Omens* (Seven Woods Press, 1976), *Dimensions of History* (Kayak Books, 1976), *The Double Invention of Komo* (Texas, 1980), *Explications/Interpretations* (University Press of Virginia, 1984), *Selected Poems* (Princeton, 1987), *Elaine's Book* (University Press of Virginia, 1988), and *Boleros* (Princeton, 1991). He lives in Vermont.

EXCERPTS FROM
THE INTRODUCTIONS
WITH HEADNOTES BY DAVID LEHMAN

John Ashbery was once characterized by his friend the painter Fairfield Porter as "lazy and quick." Ashbery had to be cajoled into editing the first volume in this series but was all alacrity when the work of reading, winnowing, and selecting began in earnest. Like several other guest editors, Ashbery had reservations about the uncompromising title of the anthology. "Couldn't we call it OK Poems of 1988?" *he asked.*

John Ashbery wrote: Reading through the poetry of 1987, I was struck, perhaps for the first time, by the exciting diversity of American poetry *right now,* and by the validity of this diversity, the tremendous power it could have for enriching our lives—I hesitated before using this hoary phrase but am going to let it stand. . . .

I like the light these poets involuntarily shed on each other. I think we read them differently in such mixed company, where they are inflected by the tuning-fork vibrations of their neighbors. Leafing through this anthology one can be reminded that red looks very different when placed next to green; that a D-sharp and an E-flat sound different in different contexts. One doesn't approach an anthology in the same way one approaches a collection of poems by a single poet: in the former case a "rubbing off" happens that can be disorienting but—I hope—also stimulating, and of course we can always return to our favorite poets for more concentrated scrutiny on some other occasion.

In discussing the supposed gulf between abstract and representational art, the late French painter Jean Hélion wrote in his journal: "I wonder . . . whether all the valid painting being done today doesn't bear certain resemblances which escape us at the present time." One could wonder the same thing about poetry, but in the meantime, while we await that uniform utopia, the dissimilarities—the splintering, the impurity—could be those of life itself. Life is what present American poetry gets to seem more like, and the more angles we choose to view it from, the more its amazing accidental abundance imposes itself.

In his introduction to The Best American Poetry 1989, *Donald Hall mounted a spirited defense of poetry and counteracted the mosquito whine of complaint and self-pity that seems an unfortunate fact of literary life. "We poets love to parade as victims; we love the romance of alienation and insult," he wrote. Yet there is also a "lovable and sweet" reason for the poet's self-deprecation. "Some of us love poetry so dearly that its absence from everybody's life seems an outrage." The essay ran in* Harper's *under the heading "Death to the Death of Poetry."*

Donald Hall wrote: Sixty years after Edmund Wilson told us that verse was dying, Joseph Epstein in *Commentary* reveals that it was murdered. Of course, Epstein's golden age—Stevens, Frost, Williams—is Wilson's time of "demoralized weakness." Everything changes and everything stays the same. Poetry was always in good shape twenty or thirty years ago; *now* it has always gone to hell. I have heard this lamentation for forty years, not only from distinguished critics and essayists, but from professors and journalists who enjoy viewing our culture with alarm. Repetition of a formula, under changed circumstances with different particulars, does not make a formulaic complaint invalid; it suggests that the formula represents something besides its surface. In asking "Who Killed Poetry," Joseph Epstein begins by insisting that he does *not* dislike it: "I was taught that poetry was itself an exalted thing." He admits his "quasi-religious language" and asserts that "it was during the 1950s that poetry last had this religious aura." Did Mr. Epstein go to school "during the 1950s"? If he attended poetry readings in 1989 with unblinkered eyes, he would watch twenty-year-olds undergoing quasi-religious emotions—one of whom, almost certainly, will write an essay in the 2020s telling the world that poetry is mouldering in its grave.

Worship is not love. People who at the age of fifty deplore the death of poetry are the same people who in their twenties were "taught to exalt it." The middle-aged poetry detractor is the student who hyperventilated at poetry readings thirty years earlier—during Wilson's "Pound-Sandburg era," or Epstein's aura-era of "T. S. Eliot and Wallace Stevens, Robert Frost and William Carlos Williams." After college many people stop reading contemporary poetry. Why not? They become involved in journalism or scholarship, essay writing or editing, brokering or solid waste; they backslide from the undergraduate Church of Poetry. Years later, glancing belatedly at the poetic scene, they tell us that poetry is dead. They left poetry; therefore they blame poetry for leaving them. Really they lament their own aging. Don't we all? But some of us do not blame the poets.

Jorie Graham, who teaches at the University of Iowa's prestigious Writers' Work-shop, put together an eclectic and far-ranging anthology that belies the notion that graduate writing programs lead to a blinkered provincialism. "We've replaced a sense of aesthetic movements with certain enclaves where the necessary cross-pollination takes place under a university's auspices," she said during one of our phone conversations. "At their best, they are incredible salons—monasticlike places where people can enforce their commitment to an art form and take that with them when they return to the Diaspora." Our conversations were frequently interrupted. "Working here," Jorie mused, "you have to be available all the time. It's like being an obstetrician."

Jorie Graham wrote: The poetry that fails the genius of its medium today is the poetry of mere self. It embarrasses all of us. The voice in it not large but inflated. A voice that expands not to the size of a soul (capable of being both personal and communal, both private and historical) but to the size of an ego. What I find most consistently moving about the act of a true poem is the way it puts the self at genuine risk. The kind of risk Robert Frost refers to when he describes the "ideals of form" as "where all our ingenuity is lavished on getting into danger legitimately so that we may be genuinely rescued."

To place oneself at genuine risk, that the salvation effected be genuine (i.e., of use to us), the poet must move to encounter an other, not more versions of the self. An other: God, nature, a beloved, an Idea, Abstract form, Language itself as a field, Chance, Death, Consciousness, what exists in the silence. Something not invented by the writer. Something the writer risks being defeated—or silenced—by. A poem is true if it can effect that encounter. All matters of style, form, and technique refer to that end.

That is why precision is so crucial: on it depends the nature of the encounter; on it depends whether the poet achieves or fails at the discovery. That is what Pound means, I believe, by his famous formula describing technique as a measure of the poet's sincerity. How sincere are we about wanting to go where the act of a poem might take us? Do we not often, instead, take the poem merely where *we* want to go—protecting ourselves. . . . In the end how sincere we truly are, how desperate and committed we are, is revealed by how hard we are on ourselves, how sharp we are willing to make our instruments.

Mark Strand's introduction to the 1991 edition begins with Strand's recollection of the day he broke the news to his parents that he was a poet. To illustrate the magic of poetry he began reading aloud Wallace Stevens's "The Idea of Order at Key West." His mother promptly fell asleep. "Had my father lived longer, he might have become a reader of poetry," the piece concludes. "He might have found a need for it—not just a need for my poetry, but for the language of poetry, the special ways in which it makes sense. And now, even though it is years later, I sometimes think, when I am writing well, that my father would be pleased, and I think, too, that could she hear those lines, my mother would be awakened from her brief nap and would give me her approval."

Mark Strand wrote: The reading of nonfiction is no greater help than the reading of fiction in preparing one for poetry. Both my parents were avid readers of nonfiction, pursuing information not just for enlightenment but to feel in control of a world they had little say in. Their need for certainty was proportional to their sense of doubt. If one had facts—or what passed for facts—at one's fingertips, one could not only banish uncertainty but also entertain the illusion that one lived in a fixed and static universe, in a world that was passive and predictable and from which mystery was exiled. No wonder poetry was not something my parents found themselves reading for pleasure. It was the enemy. It would only remystify the world for them, cloud certainties with ambiguity, challenge their appetite for the sort of security that knowledge brings. For readers like my parents, poetry's flirtations with erasure, contingency, even nonsense, are tough to take. And what may be still tougher to take is that poetry, in its figurativeness, its rhythms, endorses a state of verbal suspension. Poetry is language performing at its most beguiling and seductive while being, at the same time, elusive, even seeming to mock one's desire for reduction, for plain and available order. It is not just that various meanings are preferable to a single dominant meaning; it may be that something beyond "meaning" is being communicated, something that originated not with the poet but in the first dim light of language, in some period of "beforeness." It may be, therefore, that reading poetry is often a search for the unknown, something that lies at the heart of experience but cannot be pointed out or described without being altered or diminished—something that nevertheless can be contained so that it is not so terrifying. It is not knowledge, at least not as I conceive knowledge, but rather some occasion for belief, some reason for assent, some avowal of being. It is not knowledge because it is never revealed. It is mysterious or opaque, and even as it invites the reader, it wards him off. This unknown can make him uncomfortable, force him to do things that would make it seem less strange; and this usually means inventing a context in which to set it, something that counteracts the disembodiedness of the poem. As I have suggested, it may have to do with the origin of the poem—out of what dark habitation it emerged. The contexts we construct in our own defense may shed some light, may even explain parts or features of the poem, but they will never replace it in the wholeness of its utterance. Despite its power to enchant, the poem will always resist all but partial meanings.

When I visited Charles Simic in New Hampshire, Charlie, a jazz aficionado, played records and tapes of Coleman Hawkins, John Coltrane, Miles Davis, and such 1920s singers as Gertrude Lawrence, Ruth Etting, and Fanny Brice. On the way to the airport, I began humming "Chattanooga Choo-Choo," good traveling music. Charlie, who grew up in Yugoslavia, said he still knew the lyrics by heart from having heard the song so often as a boy during World War II. He proceeded to sing it in Serbo-Croatian.

Charles Simic wrote: Just when everything else seems to be going to hell in America, poetry is doing fine. The predictions of its demise, about which we read often, are plain wrong, just as most of the intellectual prophecies in our century have been wrong. Poetry proves again and again that any single overall theory of anything doesn't work. Poetry is always the cat concert under the window of the room in which the official version of reality is being written. The academic critics write, for instance, that poetry is the instrument of the ideology of the ruling class and that everything is political. The tormentors of Anna Akhmatova are their patron saints. But what if poets are not crazy? What if they convey the feel of a historical period better than anybody else? Obviously, poetry engages something essential and overlooked in human beings and it is this ineffable quality that has always ensured its longevity. "To glimpse the essential . . . stay flat on your back all day, and moan," says E. M. Cioran. There's more than that to poetry, of course, but that's a beginning.

Lyric poets perpetuate the oldest values on earth. They assert the individual's experience against that of the tribe. Emerson claimed that to be a genius meant "to believe your own thought, to believe that what is true for you in your private heart is true for all men." Lyric poetry since the Greeks has always assumed something like that, but American poetry since Whitman and Emerson has made it its main conviction. Everything in the world, profane or sacred, needs to be reexamined repeatedly in the light of one's own experience.

Here, now, I, amazed to find myself living my life. . . . The American poet is a modern citizen of a democracy who lacks any clear historical, religious or philosophical foundation. Sneering Marxists used to characterize such statements as "typical bourgeois individualism." "They adore the smell of their own shit," a fellow I used to know said about poets. He was a Maoist, and the idea of each human being finding his or her own truth was incomprehensible to him. Still, this is what Robert Frost, Charles Olson, and even Elizabeth Bishop had in mind. They were realists who had not yet decided what reality is. Their poetry defends the sanctity of that pursuit in which reality and identity are forever being rediscovered.

While Louise Glück and I were hashing out the final details of The Best American Poetry 1993, *we agreed to a wager on the outcome of a competition then in the news. The winner would receive a new poem dedicated to him. Louise wrote: "Ah, David, so / the better man / wins—I envy / you your belief / in justice, your / belief in the / human need of / beauty to be / recognized—that / such demands are / met in this world! / Surely this speaks / of the power / of vision, with- / out which beauty / might elude us, / being unnamed, / therefore unseen." The poem is entitled "The Wager."*

Louise Glück wrote: I took on this project for three reasons. First, I was impressed by David Lehman's willingness to let me say a few words against it. Second, I thought it would be wholesome to actually read, for a year, everything published in American magazines; conceivably, information would check my tendency to generalization and wild hypothesis. Last, I recognized, in my habitual refusal of this sort of assignment, a kind of preening. I preferred the cleanliness of powerlessness, but the refusal of power differs from lack of power; it places one among that elect to whom a choice is given. This particular mode, this life on the sidelines, preferably the very front of the sidelines, with the best view of the errors of others, promotes feelings of deeply satisfying moral rectitude combined with an invigorating sense of injustice: the particular limitations and insufficiencies and blindnesses of one's own preferences are never exposed because those preferences are never enacted. I liked not participating in the tyranny of taste making; I liked using words like "tyranny" and "taste making" to describe enacted preference, while guarding for myself words like "purity." What disrupts this is whatever offer finally makes clear the conditions on which refusal is based. I continue to feel aversion to overt authority, but a moment arrived in which I could no longer persuade myself that avoidance and lack were the same: they differ as willed and unwilled differ, as Marie Antoinette differs from the real milkmaid; continuous refusal to exert public influence on behalf of what I valued, like continuous refusal to expose my judgment to public scrutiny, seemed vanity and self-protection.

Meanwhile, unease lingers, in part a response to terminology. I dislike the idea that a single mind, or even a collective bound together by a common theory, should determine what is called best. As critics have observed, the poets themselves decide this, over time; the great ones are those to whom the poets repeatedly return. The point here is the diversity of that plural noun. And the fact of time, which purges these judgments of all trace of personality and allows, as well, for the disruption of one conservatism by another. If we are not necessarily the best readers of what is written in our own time, how can we assume that excellence always finds its way into print? Finally, I think poets are not served by the existence of another mechanism of ranking, however sweet recognition may seem. Hierarchy dissolves passionate fellowship into bitter watchfulness—those who aren't vulnerable are usually those who are regularly honored. What is essential is that we sustain our readiness to learn from each other, a readiness that, by definition, requires from each of us the best work possible. We must, I think, fear whatever erodes the generosity on which exacting criticism depends.

A. R. Ammons wrote and discarded several introductory essays before composing the one printed in The Best American Poetry 1994. *This is from a discarded essay: "Our wish in recent decades, our dress, our mode has tended so strongly toward democratization and egalitarianism that we cannot bear to be dressed up with clever writing, with formal, high-sounding verse, because we do not want to appear elitist—so much so that we write sloppily to prove to those we want to impress that we can write stuff as bad as (or worse than) theirs. Or else, in some few cases, we slum in very expensive rags. Excellence calls attention to its separation. The excellent comes at the end of a competitive struggle. The excellent poet, rejoicing in his or her practice, must live with embarrassment and distance among friends."*

A. R. Ammons wrote: Value is represented in poems. Poems exemplify ways to behave. We can write poems that disintegrate before the reader's eyes, and by that we can mean that we refuse to respect the values of our day. The poem can be accessible or distraught, harsh or melodic, abstract or graphic, and from these traits we can form our own models and traits.

The question I ask of a poem is: What way of life does this poem seem to be representing? Is it light, witty, lugubrious, generous, mean-spirited? How does it behave? Should I behave that way? If poems are still capable of so strong a communication, however impressionistically derived, am I to think that poetry has become decentered "texts" first of all? Am I to suppose that a sloppy artist is not perhaps advocating sloppiness as a way of life, and isn't it possible that the meticulous poem can be the more beautifully finished the more disgusting? Hasn't behavior perceived early on as bad become the very image of a later good?

Poetry's actions are like other actions. They are at once action themselves and symbolic actions, representative models of behavior. As long as I have the feeling that poems are capable of evidencing matters of such crucial importance, I will not think that much has changed: poems come from where they always came from; they dance in themselves as they always have; they sing to us as they always will, and we will not need to be told what we feel or which way our inclinations lean, or what there is new and lean to find in them. We will dance and sing. Sometime later we will *talk about* singing and dancing, and in that effort, we will need all the help we can get from the critics or anyone else.

Richard Howard did not want the 1995 anthology to be dominated by familiar names, so he adopted the ad hoc rule that none of the eight guest editors to date, counting himself, could be included. He excluded, moreover, any poet who had already appeared three or more times in the series. By these means he ensured that the aim of the enterprise would be "not an anthology of confirmation but an anthology of surprise, even astonishment."

Richard Howard wrote: American poetry these days strikes me as very much *for the nonce,* a provisional stating of the case. Since our poetry (best or not: a culture is no better than its verse) is the myth by which we live and love and have our seeing, such temporizing is not unfamiliar, even if the poems are. Contemporary myth, Roland Barthes has observed, is discontinuous. It is no longer stated in extended, constituted narratives, but only in "discourse." It is phraseology.

Here then are a lot of poems by which (in which) seventy-five poets, those representative beings, phrased our existence in 1994, a year in which many other things were done and undone. I am sometimes shocked by them, shaken certainly, even, once or twice, shamed; chiefly, I think, I am shown what it is like to be alive. Were we to be asked, as by some exalted tribunal from our own religious history or by some extraterrestrial inquiry, what our life on earth had to say for itself, the ensuing volume is, I believe, a fair response—fair and rising. Such an inquiry, such a tribunal is, of course, always and only a projection of our own hopes and fears ("this thing of darkness I acknowledge mine"), as I readily concede in the case of what my repudiation of competition in poetry identifies, nonetheless, as the Best Poetry for 1995, or the way we live now.

Among the poems that Adrienne Rich wanted to include in The Best American Poetry 1996 *were several whose authors we could not track down. She named them in her introduction, and eventually we heard from them. "A poem often becomes a kind of commodity in the competitive literary world of curriculum vitae, though I deplore the fact," Rich wrote to a disappointed poet. "I would be very sorry if either this mischance, or your numerous recognitions, were to get between you and the life of poetry, which is an art, not a competition, an art demanding self-discipline and apprenticeship, often through very unencouraging circumstances, for stakes which have nothing to do with the market. I hope you will consider this, unfashionable idea though it is."*

Adrienne Rich wrote: I was looking for poetry that could rouse me from fatigue, stir me from grief, poetry that was redemptive in the sense of offering a kind of deliverance or rescue of the imagination, and poetry that awoke delight—lip-to-lip, spark-to-spark, pleasure in recognition, pleasure in strangeness.

I wanted poems from 1995 that were more durable and daring than ever—not drawn from the headlines but able to resist the headlines and the shattering of morale behind them. I was looking for poems that could participate in this historical emergency, had that kind of tensility and beauty. I wasn't looking for up-to-the-minute "socially conscious" verse; I was interested in any poet's acknowledgment of the social and political loomings of this time-space—that history goes on and we are in it. How any poet might take that to heart I could not, would not, attempt to predict. (I also wanted poems good enough to eat, to crunch between the teeth, to feel their juices bursting under the tongue, unmicrowaveable poems.)

I was constantly struck by how many poems published in magazines today are personal to the point of suffocation. The columnar, anecdotal, domestic poem, often with a three-stress line, can be narrow in more than a formal sense.

I found—no surprise—that the great majority of poets published in literary magazines are white, yet relationships of race and power exist in their poems most often as silence or muffled subtext if not as cliché. Given the extreme racialization of our social and imaginative life, it's a peculiar kind of alienation that presumes race and racism (always linked to power) will haunt poets of "color" only. Like riches and poverty, like anti-Semitism, whiteness and color have a mythic life that uncontrollably infiltrates poetic language even when unnamed—a legacy of poetic images drawn on racial fantasies, "frozen metaphors" as the critic Aldon Nielsen calls them. The assumptions behind "white" identity in a violently racialized society have their repercussions on poetry, on metaphor, on the civil life in which, for better or worse, oppositionally or imitatively, all art is rooted. For this racialization is more than a set of mythic ideas: it is a system of social and demographic power relations and racially inflected economic policies, and the de facto apartheid of our institutionalized literary culture reflects that system.

"What's the verdict, Jim? Shall I place that poem in the 'yes' pile?" "I guess so," James Tate said. "But remember, everything is tentative." He paused. "Everything I do in my life is tentative." He paused again. "Well, that's not entirely true. Every now and then there's a fabulous decisive gesture." Pause. "But this is not one of those times."

James Tate wrote: Writing a poem is like traversing an obstacle course or negotiating a maze. Or downhill skiing. We tell ourselves, for the sake of excitement, to up the ante, that the choices we make could prove fatal. Anything to help us get where we must go, wherever the hell that is. When poets are actually working, theorizing is the last thing they have time for.

Once the poem is heated up and seems to be going someplace exciting, there is very little the poet would not do to insure its arrival. And of course it is always supposed to appear easy and natural. (About as natural as baking a live yak pie.)

Some fine poems are written in one sitting; others take a year or more. That doesn't seem to matter. Just as it doesn't matter if they are written with lipstick on the back end of a pig. It doesn't matter if they are written about a mite or the end of the world. One of the things that matters is the relationship of all the parts and elements of the poem to each other. Is everything working toward the same goal? Is there anything extraneous? Or if there is some kind of surface disunity, can that be justified by some larger purpose?

Why is it that you can't just take some well-written prose, divide it into lines, and call it poetry? (Thank you for asking that question, you jerk.) While most prose is a kind of continuous chatter, describing, naming, explaining, poetry speaks against an essential backdrop of silence. It is almost reluctant to speak at all, knowing that it can never fully name what is at the heart of its intention. There is a prayerful, haunted silence between words, between phrases, between images, ideas and lines. This is one reason why good poems can be read over and over. The reader, perhaps without knowing it, instinctively desires to peer between the cracks into the other world where the unspoken rests in darkness.

I had completed the foreword to the 1997 edition but had trouble writing an appropriate final paragraph. I thought perhaps a poem in the form of an abecedarium would do the trick. This is what I came up with.

Articles about the dismal state of poetry
Bemoan the absence of form and meter or,
Conversely, the products of "forms workshop":
Dream sonnets, sestinas based on childhood photographs,
Eclogues set in Third Avenue bars,
Forms contrived to suit an emergent occasion.
God knows it's easy enough to mock our enterprise,
Hard, though, to succeed at it, since
It sometimes seems predicated on failure.
Just when the vision appears, an importunate
Knock on the door banishes it, and you
Lethe-wards have sunk, or when a sweet
Melancholic fit should transport you to a
North Pole of absolute concentration,
Obligations intrude, putting an end to the day's
Poem. Poetry like luck is the residue of
Quirky design, and it
Refreshes like a soft drink full of bubbles
Sipped in a stadium on a lazy August afternoon
That was supposed to be spent at a boring job.
Ultimately poetry is
Virtue if it is our lot to choose, err, regret and
Wonder why in speech that would melt the stars.
X marks the spot of
Your latest attempt. Point at a map, blindfolded:
Zanzibar. Shall we go there, you and I?

ACKNOWLEDGMENTS

The series editor wishes to thank his assistant, Mark Bibbins. Thanks are due as well to Glen Hartley and Lynn Chu of Writers' Representatives and to Gillian Blake, Nan Graham, and Giulia Melucci of Scribner.

Jonathan Aaron: "Dance Mania" appeared in *The Paris Review*. Reprinted by permission of the poet.

A. R. Ammons: "Anxiety's Prosody" first appeared in *Poetry,* October 1988. Copyright © 1988 by the Modern Poetry Association. Reprinted by permission of the poet and the editor of *Poetry.*

A. R. Ammons: "Garbage" appeared in *American Poetry Review*. Reprinted by permission of the poet.

A. R. Ammons: "Strip" appeared in *The Paris Review.* Reprinted by permission of the poet.

John Ashbery: "Baked Alaska" from *Hotel Lautréamont* by John Ashbery (Knopf, 1992). Copyright © 1992 by John Ashbery. Reprinted by permission. The poem appeared in *The New Yorker,* June 29, 1992.

John Ashbery: "Myrtle" from *And the Stars Were Shining* by John Ashbery. Copyright © 1994 by John Ashbery. Reprinted by permission of the poet and of Farrar, Straus & Giroux. The poem initially appeared in *The New Yorker,* March 15, 1993.

John Ashbery: "The Problem of Anxiety" from *Can You Hear, Bird* by John Ashbery. Copyright © 1995 by John Ashbery. Reprinted by permission of Farrar, Straus & Giroux, Inc. Appeared originally in *Arshile.*

Elizabeth Bishop: "It Is Marvellous . . ." was first published in *American Poetry Review,* vol. 17, #1. Copyright © 1988 by Alice Helen Methfessel. Reprinted by permission of Farrar, Straus & Giroux, Inc. Lorrie Goldensohn's comments appeared in *American Poetry Review.* Reprinted by permission.

George Bradley: "The Fire Fetched Down" appeared in *The Paris Review.* Reprinted by permission of the poet.

Lucie Brock-Broido: "Inevitably, She Declined" appeared in *Michigan Quarterly Review.* Reprinted by permission of the poet.

Anne Carson: "The Life of Towns" was published first in *Grand Street.* Reprinted by permission of the poet and the editor of *Grand Street.*

Amy Clampitt: "My Cousin Muriel" appeared originally in *The New Yorker,* February 20, 1989. Reprinted by permission; copyright © 1989 Amy Clampitt.

Douglas Crase: "True Solar Holiday" appeared originally in *The Yale Review.* Reprinted by permission of the poet.

Carolyn Creedon: "litany" appeared in *American Poetry Review.* Reprinted by permission of the poet.

The following are the annual listings in alphabetical order of poets and poems reprinted in the first ten editions of The Best American Poetry.

1988
Edited and Introduced by John Ashbery

1989
Edited and Introduced by Donald Hall

1990
Edited and Introduced by Jorie Graham

1991

Edited and Introduced by Mark Strand

1992

Edited and Introduced by Charles Simic

1993
Edited and Introduced by Louise Glück

1994
Edited and Introduced by A. R. Ammons

1995
Edited and Introduced by Richard Howard

1996
Edited and Introduced by Adrienne Rich

1997

Edited and Introduced by James Tate